100% chocolate

This edition published in 2002 by

TODTRI Book Publishers

254 West 31st Street

New York, NY 10001-2813

Fax: (212) 695-6984

E-mail: info@todtri.com

Visit us on the web!

www.todtri.com

English trans   on produced by Translate-A-Book, Oxford, UK

Typesetting by Organ Graphic, Abingdon, UK

Printed and bound in Italy

ISBN 1-57717-307-4

Katherine Khodorowsky
Dr Hervé Robert

recipe photography
Jean-François Rivière

design
Marie Leteuré

100% chocolate
the saga of chocolate, with 40 gourmet recipes

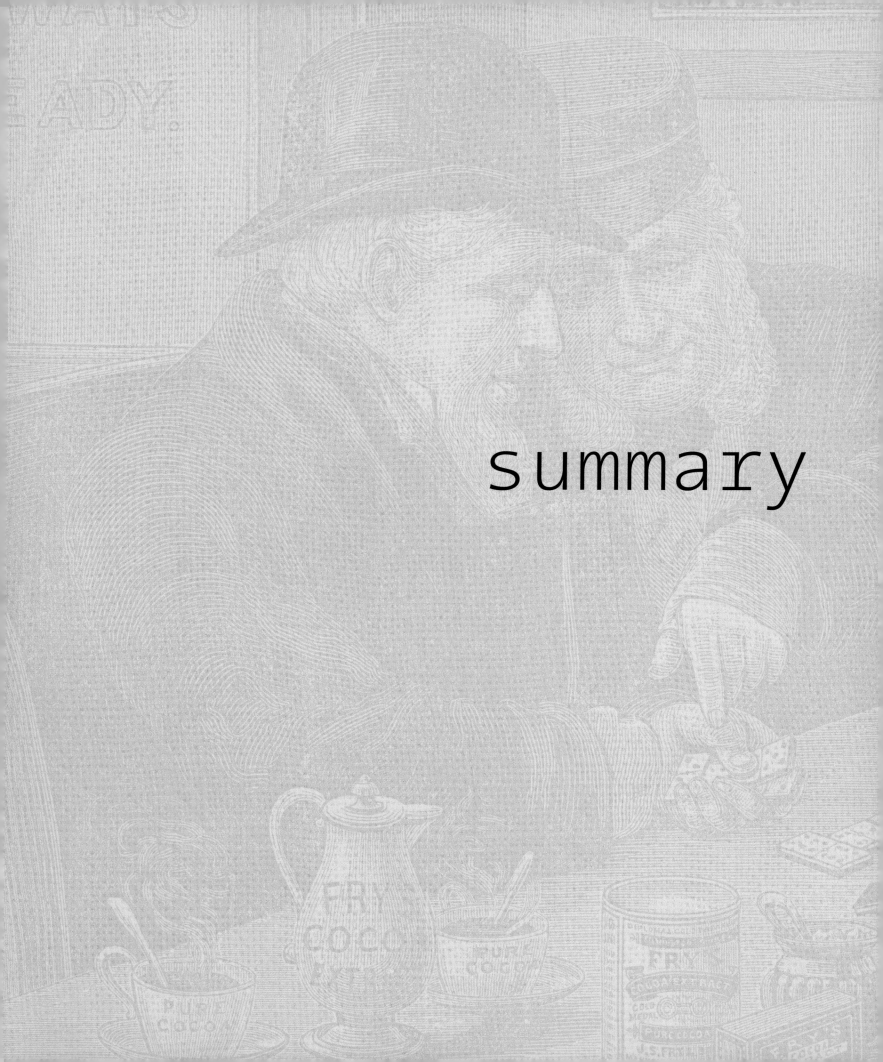

summary

1 the saga of chocolate 6

2 the cacao: nature's gift 38

3 chocolate every which way 48

4 world taste in chocolate 66

5 chocolate, from fashionable to universal 84

6 a pleasure that does us good 106

7 classic chocolate recipes 114

8 for true lovers of chocolate 172

index 184

index of recipes 186

table of recipes 187

contents 188

photographic credits 190

acknowledgments 192

1
the saga
of chocolate

ong before the word "chocolate" came to denote something sweet and delicious to eat, it was already used to refer exclusively to a hot beverage. Produced by many subtle processes from the seeds found in the fruit of the cacao tree, chocolate has been regarded since the days of the conquistadors as a very special food.

Pre-Columbian America

The birthplace of the cacao tree was probably the region located between the Upper Orinoco and the Amazon Basin, on the borders of Guyana. A number of animals, such as monkeys, rodents, and parrots, were partial to the slightly acid pulp around the cocoa bean and gradually spread the seeds of the cacao tree until it grew as far away as Mexico.

For a long time the cacao tree grew wild but is then said to have been cultivated by the Olmec, who were probably the first consumers of cocoa. No doubt it was their observations of animals that gave them the idea of using these seeds for food, after heating and crushing them as they did with grain. From that time on a real mythology grew up around the cacao, and it was this mixture of true facts and legends that was to give the tree its special aura.

THE MAYA CIVILIZATION

As early as their classical period (third to tenth centuries A.D.), the Mayas in the Yucatán region made the tree an integral part of their sacred world. Ek Chuah, the god of merchants and cocoa, is shown in sculptures, paintings on funeral vases, and illustrations in the ritual pre-Hispanic books known as Codices.

The Mayas consumed chocolate in the form of a cold drink called *xocoatl*. The methods they used to cultivate the cacao involved a number of very strict rituals. At the time of planting, sacrificing a dog whose coat had cocoa-colored patches honored the

tree. Before the sowing period, the best seeds were exposed to the moon's rays for four nights, during which the sowers had to remain chaste; on the fifth day, which was when the seeds were planted, the sowers were allowed to return to their wives. The beans were used as a unit of weight and were among the gifts presented to mark the most significant passages in life, such as the choice of a first name for a newborn baby, the onset of puberty, or a proposal of marriage.

In the ninth century, classical Maya civilization began to decline, seemingly as a result of drought and a shortage of arable land. The great Maya cities were then abandoned to the forest.

THE LEGEND OF FEATHERED SERPENT

From the tenth to the twelfth centuries A.D., the Toltecs dominated Mexico. Their capital, Tula, (located a few miles to the north of modern-day Mexico) was ruled around 980 A.D. by the king-priest Quetzalcóatl, the "feathered serpent," who was venerated as a god. According to legend this guardian of the Garden of the Sons of the Sun stole a cocoa bean and offered it to men in order to "console them for having to live on earth." He showed them how to cultivate the cacao tree, harvest its fruit, and extract a drink from it. In his eagerness to achieve immortality, he turned to the sorcerer Tezcatlipoca, who, because he was jealous of the king's great fortune, gave him a potion to drink that drove men insane. Quetzalcóatl fled to the shore and boarded a raft made of interlocking serpents. Before setting off towards the east, he promised to return in a year that was under the sign of the Reed, when he would reestablish his authority.

THE AZTECS

At the end of the twelfth century A.D., the Chichimeca tribes came down from the north and invaded the center of Mexico, thus bringing the rule of the Toltecs to an end. One of these tribes was the Aztecs, who gradually took control of most of

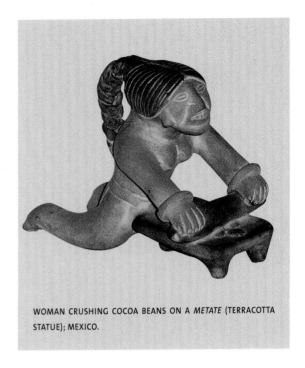

WOMAN CRUSHING COCOA BEANS ON A *METATE* (TERRACOTTA STATUE); MEXICO.

RABBITS AND PROSTITUTES

In the Aztec world, the official monetary system used the kernel of the cacao fruit as its unit. It was broken down as follows:

1 zontli = 400 kernels
1 canasta = 1,600 kernels
1 xiquipilli = 8,000 kernels
1 carga = 24,000 kernels
1 tribute = 64,000 kernels
1 tertio = 72,000 kernels

Francisco Oviedo Valdès relates that at the beginning of the sixteenth century A.D. a rabbit was worth ten kernels and the services of a prostitute from eight to ten kernels, while a slave cost one hundred beans.

Mexico and in the second half of the fifteenth century began to invade the Maya region in the Yucatán.

The Aztecs retained the use of cocoa beans both as currency and as a means of paying taxes to the king. It was their language that gave us the word "cacao," which is derived from *cacahuatl*, pronounced "kakawa."

They also greatly appreciated chocolate as a nutritious, fortifying drink. It was also reputed to have aphrodisiac qualities, and they drank it cold, lukewarm, or hot.

The seeds of the cacao tree were dried in the sun and then roasted in an earthenware pot or a container pierced with holes. The beans were then shelled and crushed on a heated stone, the *metate*, using a stone roller, the *metlapilli*. This produced a paste, which the common people would then mix with a grain pulp called *atolle*. Those who were better off would add, according to their means, some capsicum, spices, and vanilla or sometimes some agave sugar. The king, on the other hand, just added some water to the cocoa paste and heated it up before drinking it. The cocoa butter that rose to the surface when the mixture was beaten was skimmed off and then reincorporated. This created a froth that the Aztecs believed brought them closer to the gods. In 1550, the Spanish Franciscan Bernardino de Sahagún wrote: "If there is only a small quantity of water, no foam can be produced. For this drink to be well made, it has to be sieved

"THE WAY IN WHICH THE INHABITANTS OF NEW SPAIN PREPARE COCOA FOR CHOCOLATE," ENGRAVING FROM THE *AGREEABLE GALLERY OF THE WORLD* BY PIERRE VAN DER AA (C. 1710).

and then poured down from a height so that it forms a foam as it falls." At that time, chocolate was reputed to combat fatigue, cure digestive problems, and protect against snakebites. The cocoa fat that was brought to the surface by cooking was used to prepare ointments to treat wounds, burns, and hemorrhoids. It was also one of the ingredients that went into making beauty products.

The fruits and beans were also used in religious rituals. To create a potion symbolizing blood, the beans were dried and ground up and then mixed with water to which some achiote seeds (*Bixa orellana*) had been added to give the liquid a brick red-color when it was boiled. The cacao fruit itself was used in rituals to represent the human heart, which was torn out in the course of sacrifices.

The conquistadors and chocolate

CHRISTOPHER COLUMBUS: A MISSED OPPORTUNITY

Contrary to popular belief, it was not Christopher Columbus who introduced chocolate to the Europeans. In 1502, this shrewd Genoese, who had already shown his ability in three expeditions, obtained permission from Isabella of Castile to set off on the oceans once again. It was on this fourth voyage that he discovered cocoa beans, on July 30, 1502, near the island of Guanaja (off the coast of modern-day Honduras).

His natural son, Fernando Columbus, who was with him at the time, later told the story: the Spanish

MEXICAN CHOCOLATE POT, WITH FOAMER; REPRODUCTION OF AN AZTEC POT.

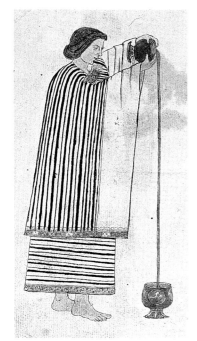

INDIAN WOMAN DECANTING CHOCOLATE FROM ONE POT TO ANOTHER TO MAKE IT FOAM (CODEX TULEDA; C. 1553).

Chocolate throughout the day

When they got up in the morning the Aztecs did not have breakfast. In the middle of the morning they took a break and ate a corn porridge seasoned with capsicum and sweetened with honey. At the end of the meal, the wealthier members of society treated themselves to some chocolate, served in a decorated gourd or a tortoise's shell. The midday meal, which was eaten during the hours of the greatest heat, consisted of corn pancakes, beans, sometimes meat (game, poultry), and water.

Before going to honor their womenfolk, the notables and the king ended this meal with one or several cups of chocolate, which remained a luxury product. In the evening, people of modest means made do with a porridge made of corn, amaranth, or sage. Dignitaries and merchants, on the other hand, dined or feasted all night. The cocoa that brought these banquets to a close was served just before the tobacco pipes were brought out.

fleet (four caravels, each of five hundred men) saw a canoe approaching rowed by twenty-five oarsmen, "as long as a galley and eight feet wide, carved out of a single tree-trunk [...]. By way of provisions they were carrying some of the roots and seeds that are eaten in Hispaniola, and a sort of wine based on grain that is similar to English beer, and a large number of those kernels that are used in New Spain as money. These seeds must have great value in their eyes because when they were taken on board with the foodstuffs, I observed that each time one of them fell, everyone rushed to pick it up."

Christopher Columbus did mention cocoa in a letter to King Charles V, but it seems that he did not like the taste of the chocolate that the natives gave him to try and so paid no attention to it.

THE GOOD FORTUNE OF CORTEZ

On April 21, 1519, Hernando Cortez landed on the coast of what is now the state of Tabasco, to the west of the Yucatán peninsula, with eleven ships, sixteen horses, five hundred men, and about ten cannon.

The year 1519 was under the sign of the Reed; a comet appeared, and there was an earthquake. It had been predicted that Quetzalcóatl would return on the ninth day of the month of the Wind in a year of the Reed, and April 21, 1519 was exactly that. It appears that the Aztec king, Moctezuma II, was convinced that Cortez was indeed the god Quetzalcóatl, who had now come home as the legend had foretold. He therefore welcomed the conquistador in November 1519 by declaring: "You will have everything here that you and your followers need, since you are now at home in your native land." The Spaniard took great care not to let Moctezuma know he was mistaken. And so it was that with a handful of men he was able to make himself master of the Aztec Empire, despite the fact that it was a very well-organized regime with eleven million inhabitants. Cortez allowed himself to be showered with gifts, notably a twenty thousand square-foot cacao plantation, whose value he quickly realized.

THE SECRET OF CHOCOLATE

Even so the Spaniards who settled in these "West Indies," also known as New Spain, did not form a liking for chocolate right away. Benzoni even went as far as to say: "This mixture is more like pig slop than a drink meant for humans." Some nuns in Oaxaca improved the taste of the chocolate,

MOCTEZUMA RECEIVES HERNANDO CORTEZ, BY MIGUEL GONZALES (1698; MUSEO DE AMERICA, MADRID).

however, by adding sugarcane, musk, and orange-blossom water, while at the same time decreasing the amount of spices. After that the liquid chocolate became a drink that was highly prized by the conquistadors and their wives, rising to heights of popularity that exceeded all expectations. At the same time, Spanish nuns and monks in Mexico were beginning to produce "solid" chocolate in the form of pastilles.

The craze for chocolate spread rapidly, not least because it could be drunk without breaking a fast. The conquistadors were now anxious to gain control of cacao growing and tried to do so by reducing the Aztecs who had survived the massacres to slavery. In 1537, however, Pope Paul III published a bill in which he threatened any Christian using natives as slaves with excommunication. The Aztecs were only made to do "hard labor."

The Spanish in the West Indies started to send chocolate back to the motherland in 1527. For a long time they transported it as a finished product in order to keep their know-how a secret. It is very difficult, however, to keep chocolate for over two months in boats without it spoiling, and as a result they had to resign themselves to sending beans—and their precious recipe. Around 1585, the first official shipment of beans was sent from Veracruz to Seville, and it was not long before chocolate jmakers began to set up in Spain. Chocolate was regarded first and foremost as a medicine, but it quickly became a popular drink that could be drunk at any time of day.

The spread of chocolate throughout Europe

The court of Spain was, of course, the first to adopt chocolate at the end of the sixteenth century. Thanks to travelers and merchants, the "drink of the gods" then spread slowly throughout war-torn Europe. At that time the hub of trade in spices and exotic products was Flanders and the Netherlands, and it is very likely that cocoa first arrived in their ports at the very beginning of the seventeenth century. In 1635, there was mention of chocolate being served as a beverage at the abbey in Baudeloo, near Ghent. In 1685, Philippe Sylvestre Dufour's book, *De l'usage du café, du thé et du chocolat* (*On the Use of Coffee, Tea and Chocolate*) (published in 1671), was being read throughout the country.

Chocolate is said to have been introduced to Italy by a Florentine merchant, Francesco Carletti, who apparently acquired a taste for it during a voyage to New Spain and brought it back to the court of Holy Roman Emperor Ferdinand I in 1606. At that time, however, part of what is now Italy belonged to the Duchy of Savoy. It may have been the duke, Emmanuel Philibert, who first brought chocolate to the duchy's capital, Turin, as early as 1562.

Before long, chocolate had spread throughout Italy, thanks no doubt to the Jesuits, who carried on a very lucrative trade in cocoa. The Tuscans discovered "a way of introducing as ingredients fresh lemon zest and the very sweet flavor of jasmine, which, along with cinnamon, amber, musk, and vanilla, has a prodigious effect on those who have the pleasure of drinking chocolate" (Francesco Redi, *Bacchus in Tuscany*, 1666).

Chocolate featured in a large number of recipes. In 1786, a cookbook gave one for a lasagna sauce consisting of almonds, anchovies, nuts, and chocolate. Another book published in 1794 gave a recipe for cocoa sorbet.

Italian monks brought chocolate to Vienna around 1640, but it did not arouse any particular interest until Charles VI came back from Spain. He had developed a taste for it there, and when he returned to Austria in 1711 and became Holy Roman Emperor, he played a large role in establishing the delectable drink in the court of Vienna.

IN THIS STILL LIFE BY ANTONIO DE PEREDA Y SALGADO (1652; THE HERMITAGE, ST. PETERSBURG), THE COPPER CHOCOLATE POT AND ITS FOAMER SIT IMPOSINGLY ON THE LEFT, WHILE THE *CHURROS* WAIT IN THE FOREGROUND TO BE DIPPED IN THE HOT CHOCOLATE.

EIGHTEENTH-CENTURY POPES AND CHOCOLATE

In 1740, the conclave that assembled in Rome to elect the new pope dragged on interminably. Every day, 35 pounds of chocolate were delivered to the Sistine Chapel to refresh the cardinals. It took six months before Benedict XIV was elected.

Pope Clement XIV was a great lover of chocolate. He died in 1774, probably from poison, as Sir Horace Mann relates in his correspondence: "It is clear that the Pope has been assassinated. At the Vatican, where he was taking part in the ceremonies for Holy Thursday, his own servant unwittingly administered a slow poison to him, which was concealed in his chocolate. I am surprised that this man, who from the beginning of his pontificate had taken every precaution to avoid what he had always feared, continued to drink his chocolate when he had indicated from the first few sips that it had a bad taste."

OLD POSTCARD SHOWING A REPRODUCTION OF *THE BEAUTIFUL CHOCOLATE MAKER* PASTEL BY JEAN-ÉTIENNE LIOTARD (C. 1745; STAATLICHES MUSEUM, DRESDEN). NANDL BALDAUF, A VIENNESE MAID, SERVES HOT CHOCOLATE IN A "TREMBLING CUP."

At the same time, chocolate made its appearance in Prussia in 1641, thanks to Johann Georg Volckamer, who had discovered it in Naples. After being regarded for several decades as a medicinal beverage, cocoa found an ardent defender in Cornelius Bontekoe, who wrote a treatise on it in 1685. Chocolate then became so successful that Frederick I imposed a heavy tax on it in order to limit the amount of it being imported. This did not prevent his grandson, Frederick the Great, from being a connoisseur of hot chocolate, a passion that he was to share with his friend Voltaire. Prince William of Schaumburg-Lippe founded the first German chocolate-making firm in Steinhude in 1756.

In 1579, chocolate was not yet known in England, with the result that some British privateers who attacked a Spanish ship threw its cargo of cocoa beans overboard in the belief that they were "mere garbage." It was not until 1633 that the English first heard of cocoa through John Gerard and only in 1648 that they learned of chocolate from John Gage in the first edition of his accounts of his travels.

AN INCOMPARABLE WAR GAIN

In 1655, the British took control of the island of Jamaica, a major producer of cocoa that until then had been under Spanish rule. From then on the island sent beans to England, where chocolate was beginning to be consumed, mainly as an early morning drink.

In 1657, a Frenchman opened a shop in London, at Queen's Head Alley in Bishopsgate Street, and here the English came to discover the exotic drink. From 1674, another shop, The Coffee Mill and Tobacco Roll, sold solid chocolate, ready to eat in the form of "Spanish rolls" and "pastilles."

Things were different here from the rest of Europe in that chocolate was not only consumed at home but also in public "chocolate houses," where people came to meet and enjoy it as a beverage prepared with milk and, if desired, with an added egg yolk and a drop of Madeira. The best known of these establishments was White's, which was opened in 1697 by an Italian and quickly became a "temple" of gambling. A year later, Martin Lister expressed his opinion of coffee, tea, and chocolate, saying that although great things were said about these drinks according to the mood and whim of the drinker, he believed that divine providence had allowed them to exist in order to reduce the human population by shortening life. The year 1764 saw the foundation of the Cocoa Tree, which was frequented mainly by Tory politicians. A number of these establishments became a central focus of the political and cultural life of the nobility and the wealthy middle class, and over the years some of them were turned into private clubs from which women were excluded.

Strange though it may seem, it is likely that North America (and in particular Virginia) discovered chocolate thanks to British colonial officials rather than to imports from Jamaica.

Although Switzerland was to become one of the major "homelands" of chocolate, the product was, in fact, introduced there as late as 1697 through the Bürgermeister of Zürich, Henri Escher, who had tasted it on the Grand-Place in Brussels.

At that time, chocolate was not at all popular in Turkey. The Italian merchant Gemelli Carreri found this out the hard way in 1693: "The Agha of Seyde came to see me. I served him a chocolate, but the brute had never drunk any before, or else he was drunk, or perhaps was affected by the tobacco smoke. He lost his temper and told me that I had made him drink a liquid that was intended to disturb him and rob him of his judgment. In short, if his anger had lasted, things would certainly have turned out badly for me, and that has taught me to offer chocolate to such a boor."

Later on, the colonization of Africa and Asia by various European powers contributed to the spread of cacao plantations to different parts of the world. This meant that the supply of cocoa to the countries that were opening up to the industrial production of chocolate was ensured ...

Chocolate in France

"There was once an angel who guided a mysterious sailing ship with cocoa all along its sides to the port of Bayonne. He offered the beans to the inhabitants and even taught them the art of making good chocolate." So the legend goes, lending certain poetry to the arrival of chocolate in France. The reality is more prosaic and less agreeable. Jewish chocolate makers fled from Spain to escape the pogroms and took refuge in Portugal, where they were subjected to further persecution. They then went to France and settled in Bayonne, probably from 1609 on. There is no mention of chocolate makers in the city's archives until 1687, however,

since they were not authorized to open shop, and instead went directly to the homes of private individuals to prepare their chocolate.

A ROYAL DRINK

In fact, Anne of Austria, the daughter of King Philip III of Spain, officially introduced chocolate to France in 1615 when she married Louis XIII. She was a great drinker of hot chocolate and made herself the product's ambassador at the French court. Gradually this rare, very costly beverage became part of the everyday life of the wealthy. They drank it at breakfast, at supper, and in alcoves as a prelude to love games. In 1660, Louis XIV married Marie-Thérèse of Austria, the daughter of Philip IV of Spain. The infanta adored chocolate, but this passion was not shared by her royal husband, who was of the opinion that "this staves off hunger but does not fill the stomach" and preferred hearty meals accompanied by plenty of Burgundy wine. Even so, the queen went on drinking chocolate in secret ...

At that time, every chocolate firm required a royal permit. In 1659, David Chaliou obtained a patent from Louis XIV to sell chocolate: "To us, Louis, our dear and well-beloved David Chaliou has very humbly demonstrated that after various journeys to Spain, during which, having applied himself to the search for secrets which could be useful to the human body, he has among other things gained knowledge of a certain combination of ingredients known as chocolate which, its use being very healthy, he would like to make known to the public. He will be able to make it and sell it here and in other cities and other places in this kingdom as he sees fit, whether as a liquor or in pastille form, in boxes or in whatever other manner it pleases him." Nonetheless cocoa remained a rare product, a luxury foodstuff, and only the king's entourage and the nobles at court had access to the "drink of the gods."

In 1681, the state took control of the cocoa trade and gave itself the monopoly of it. Chocolate, although forbidden at the time by a number of doctors, became more widely used, but in 1692, Louis XIV taxed it heavily to finance his war against the German states. A year later, the king founded a corporation of café owners, and after a few initial problems it was they who then became the leaders of the chocolate business.

In this period there were many different recipes for hot chocolate. Monsieur Saint-Disdier gave the following in 1692: 2 pounds of prepared cocoa,

CHROMOLITHOGRAPH SHOWING QUEEN ANNE OF AUSTRIA, GIVEN AWAY TO CHILDREN AT THE END OF THE 19TH CENTURY BY POULAIN CHOCOLATE.

Sévigné de qui les attraits
Me servirent de modèles
Pour que les boîtes fussent belles
Et dignes de ses portraits,
········· La Marquise de Sévigné à Paris

1 pound of fine sugar, 3 drachmas (1 tsp) of cinnamon, 1 scruple ($^{1}/_{4}$ tsp) of powdered clove, 1 scruple ($^{1}/_{4}$ tsp) of powdered capsicum, and $1^{1}/_{4}$ ounces of vanilla. Some people added musk or ambergris. Spices, musk, and amber were reputed to be aphrodisiacs, and so hot chocolate was very much associated with lovemaking. It prepared lovers for wild embraces or restored their strength after a night of passion.

A VERY SLOW DEMOCRATIZATION

Chocolate was also drunk first thing in the morning, however, as can be seen from the habits of Philippe of Orléans, who was regent during the minority of Louis XV: "After the Regent's *levée*, the usher of the chamber opened the hidden staircase, and his Royal Highness went to take his chocolate in a room where people came to pay court to him. It was an honor to be admitted to the chocolate of his Royal Highness."

Some chose to take chocolate as an aperitif before meals, as Martin Lister noted in 1722: "The advocates of chocolate will tell you that it gives them an appetite if they take it two hours before dinner. Very good! Who can doubt it? You say that you are much more hungry after your chocolate than if you had taken nothing, that is to say that your stomach is weak, in need, it feels hollow, and empty. I suspect that things that pass so quickly through the stomach have arrived there the wrong way and that nature is in haste to get rid of them."

Louis XV only took chocolate on fast days, but the queen, Marie Leszcynska, was very fond of it and drank it regularly. Madame de Pompadour, the king's favorite, although considered by him to be "a very cold fish," had a triple vanilla and amber chocolate for lunch, along with a handful of truffles, and some celery soup—all no doubt to stimulate her amorous appetites!

It is not known whether Louis XVI liked chocolate, but Marie-Antoinette certainly did. She created the post of "queen's chocolate maker," which was first occupied by the Chevalier de Saint-Louis, then by Debauve in 1780. Chocolate bars had already made their appearance; they are mentioned in the *Journal des affiches-annonces* of January 19, 1774, in which there is high praise for the products of Sieur Delondres on the rue des Lombards.

Chocolate remained a costly commodity, consumed by a minority of aristocrats and wealthy bourgeois. The common people had to make do with dreaming about it or surreptitiously dipping their lips into it, as Despina the maid does in *Cosi fan tutte*, Mozart's opera set to a libretto by Lorenzo Da Ponte:

I've been stirring for half an hour now;
The chocolate is finished, and there's nothing left for me
But the smell and an empty mouth.
Isn't my mouth like yours?
Oh, ladies,
You have the drink, and I have the smell!
Oh Lord, I want to taste it too!
It's so delicious!

THE MORNING CHOCOLATE BY PIETRO LONGHI (C. 1778; CORRER MUSEUM, VENICE)

Once the French Revolution started, any progress towards the popularization of chocolate ground to a halt, and the cocoa business collapsed, not recovering until the Empire had restored some stability to the country. At that point the cultivation of cocoa and the growing demand for sugar did a great deal to perpetuate black slavery, which at the same time was meeting with ever increasing opposition from philosophers and liberal economists.

Napoleon Bonaparte himself was a great lover of chocolate, to which he attributed numerous virtues. Bourienne tells us that in order to stay awake on the field of battle, the Emperor liked to drink several cups, served by his faithful butler, Colin. But although Napoleon drew a great deal of attention to chocolate, it was his nephew Napoleon III who brought it into more modest homes. "Chocolate is not a luxury commodity or a delicacy. Its health-giving properties are indisputable and undisputed, and because it has an aroma and a flavor which delight the palate, it is to be categorized as one of the foodstuffs for general consumption which I proclaim exempt from tax. It

PORTRAIT OF MADAME DU BARRY, ENGRAVING BY JACQUES-FABIEN GAUTIER-DAGOTY (1710–1781), AFTER A PAINTING BY JEAN-BAPTISTE GREUZE (STAATLICHES MUSEUM, BERLIN).

Danzig chocolate

After the capture of Danzig in 1807, Napoleon Bonaparte gave Maréchal Lefebvre the title of Duke and a box of chocolates. When Lefebvre opened the box, he found that it contained 300,000 francs, a colossal sum for the time! From then on, soldiers referred to their pay as "Danzig chocolate."

THE FIRST FAKES
According to Pomet, chocolates from Spain, Portugal, Italy, and Saint-Malo, which until then had had a very good reputation, began to be less highly regarded than those made in Paris. Shoddy fakes began to appear in the capital, however, as Savary noted in 1740: "It must be admitted that there is no place where worse chocolate is being made than in Paris, since there is nothing so common there as to be offended by this commodity, when in order to procure it more cheaply one buys it from hawkers who churn it out in houses and sell as chocolate wretched pastes made of ordinary almonds mixed with a few scraps of cocoa, vanilla, and mere brown sugar."

THE JESUITS' GOLD

Saint-Simon relates that in 1701, eight large cases were unloaded in Cadiz, addressed to "The Very Reverend Father General of the Company of Jesus." Intrigued by the fact that they weighed so much, the porters opened them and found heavy lumps of chocolate, which when they were pressed burst open to reveal little balls of gold. The Jesuits cautiously refrained from laying claim to this somewhat compromising shipment of chocolate, preferring to lose it rather than let their trafficking be discovered. The chocolate was shared among the porters—and the gold was given to King Philip V.

is physically and morally beneficial," he declared on January 5, 1860. No doubt he still recalled the day of the Battle of Solferino, when he had nothing to eat but a bar of chocolate that he had found in a pocket of his saddle. Even so, this exemption from tax did not place chocolate within the means of everyone. That would not happen until the industrial era, when it became possible to make quality chocolate available at a low price.

Chocolate and the church

It is impossible to tell the story of chocolate without mentioning the controversy that it triggered in the religious world, starting in the second half of the sixteenth century. The church's influence was omnipresent in daily life, including matters of food. There were feast days and fast days, and the notion of the sin of greed was very much alive.

FOOD OR DRINK?

In 1523, Pope Clement VII received a report entitled *O felicem monetam*, in which its author, Father Petrus Martyre de Angleria, stated that "not only is chocolate a useful and delicious drink, but the cocoa beans that are used as money do not allow for avarice since they cannot be kept for a long time." In addition to that, the beverage was not intoxicating, and so it looked as if it had all the necessary qualities to win the blessing of the authorities.

The use of chocolate spread rapidly in the convents and monasteries of Spain, where it was appreciated both for its taste and for its ability to satisfy hunger. Starting in 1569, however, certain theologians began to react to this fad by thinking that chocolate was so nourishing that it must be a food rather than a drink and that as a result those who consumed it were breaking their fast. Pope Pius V based his ruling on the subject of Saint Thomas Aquinas's doctrine, *"Liquidum non frangit jejunum"* ("A liquid does not break the fast") and decided that since despite its nutritional value chocolate was still a drink, it could be consumed on fast days. After his death in 1572, scrupulous men of the church began asking questions again about the nature of chocolate: was it a drink or a food? The controversy raged.

Franciscus Rausch declared in 1624 that chocolate not only broke the fast but also was also responsible for the excesses being committed in monasteries; he therefore took the view that "this drink should be forbidden to monks." In 1636, Leon Pinelo, in *The moral question of whether chocolate breaks the ecclesiastical fast*, produced scholarly evidence to prove that Rausch was wrong. Gaspar Caldera de Heredia argued the opposing case in 1638, on the basis that chocolate was clearly very nutritious. In 1645, the theologian Thomas Hurtado added his view that chocolate did not break the fast if it was taken as a medicine and prepared with water, not milk, eggs, and spices. Cardinal Francesco Maria Brancaccio closed the debate in 1664 in a way that was believed at the time to be final: chocolate, like wine or beer, was quite definitely a drink, which despite its nutritious qualities could not be compared to a foodstuff and did not break the fast in any way.

WHEN THE DOCTORS GET INVOLVED ...

Curiously, doctors revived the debate half a century later. In 1710, Hecquet, who was then Dean of the Faculty of Medicine in Paris, wrote his *Treatise on exemptions from fasting*, in which he claimed that chocolate was more of a spiritual than a temporal support and could therefore be consumed on fast days. In the same year, his colleague Nicolas Andry expressed the opposite view, accusing chocolate of "weakening the faith," since it was, he declared, primarily inhaled for the voluptuous pleasure of its aromas, which was contrary to the spirit of penitence.

After two centuries of prevarication, the church finally abandoned its grievances against chocolate. In 1740, the sovereign pontiff even took up the habit of offering chocolate during canonization ceremonies to the officers of his guard in varying quantities according to their rank.

Today the sin of greed is still one of the seven deadly sins, even if it is the one that is most easily forgiven. The tendency to regard it as a venial sin to which it is human to succumb has even made it an argument used by advertisers to sell chocolate.

Chocolate and the medical profession

As we have seen, churchmen were not the only ones to debate the subject of chocolate. From a very early stage, doctors were called upon to give their opinion of this exotic drink, full of medicinal and aphrodisiac virtues and reserved at that time for the most influential members of society.

One of these was Alphonse Louis du Plessis, Prelate of Lyons and brother of Cardinal de Richelieu, who at the beginning of the seventeenth century was no doubt one of the first people in France to taste chocolate. He is said to have been given it by Spanish monks for medicinal purposes and used it "to calm his spleen and control his rage and his bad character," according to Bonaventure d'Argonne. It is certainly true that foodstuffs were regarded at that time as potential remedies.

It was believed then that the body was characterized by four humors: blood, phlegm, yellow bile, and black bile (otherwise known as atrabiliar or melancholy) and that diseases were due to an imbalance between these different substances. All treatment was therefore based on the principle of combating the ill with its opposite;

a cold substance was prescribed for bilious and sanguine ailments, whereas phlegmatic and melancholic ones called for a hot substance. Thus a fever needed to be fought with drugs or foods that were refreshing, while any kind of "chill" had to be treated with something "warming."

THE HOT AND THE COLD

Given this view of things, it was essential that every remedy or food be classified according to whether it was of a hot or cold nature. But in that case, how was chocolate to be categorized? Was it a hot substance, a warm substance, or a cold substance? To answer this question, the men of science of the age were asked to give their opinions. Some doctors started from the principle that cocoa is cold; if adding spices, which were considered hot, combated that tendency the mixture would be moderately warm. Others opposed this idea, arguing that the fat contained in cocoa made it a hot substance, since oily matter is required to make fire. Between 1605 and 1772, the doctors stubbornly took sides on the issue, on the basis of

---

CHOCOLATE IS JUST AS IMPORTANT AS MASS

The relations between the church and chocolate were illustrated by a regrettable affair that was reported by Thomas Gage, a Dominican who traveled to New Spain in 1625. The Spanish women who lived in Mexico loved their chocolate and liked to drink it every two hours without fail. They had their servants bring it to them wherever they were, even during divine offices—especially when these were particularly long and drawn-out. The comings and goings of the vivacious ladies' maids caused considerable disruption during the religious services, so much so that Don Bernard de Salazar, the bishop of the town of San Cristobal de la Cazas in what is now the state of Chiapas, took a stand against this practice and threatened anyone who consumed chocolate during the offices with excommunication. The ladies continued to sip their favorite drink nonetheless, and gentlemen were even seen drawing their swords openly in church against canons who had the audacity to jostle the bearers of chocolate. Since the prelate refused to relax his position, the women decided to attend services in monasteries, where the monks were more tolerant; the bishop then extended his ban to the monasteries. He died shortly afterwards, probably from poison that had been poured into his chocolate ...

ALL THE VIRTUES IN THE WORLD

Chocolate, however it is taken, is a good restorative, capable of reviving failing strength and renewing vigor; it resists the malignancy of the humors; it fortifies the stomach, the brain, and the other vital parts; it soothes the excessively acrid ferocities that pass down from the brain to the chest; it stimulates the digestion; it does away with the vapors of wine.
NICOLAS LEMERY, 1698

arguments that were more theoretical than scientific. Most of the works published on chocolate at this time were written by doctors, who among other things discussed the best way of preparing it and detailed the benefits that it offered or the risks associated with drinking it. Here again the debates were of epic proportions, with some doctors claiming that chocolate did incalculable damage, while others saw it as the mother and father of every virtue!

THE APOTHECARIES

In 1720, the medicinal properties of chocolate, along with those of the substances that were often added to it (pepper, vanilla, cinnamon, cloves, aniseed, hazelnuts, almonds, musk, logwood pods, etc.), gave an apothecary called de Caylus the idea of creating "medicinal chocolates." He suggested that it was possible to mask the unpleasant taste of certain remedies by incorporating them into chocolate. It was not until the beginning of the nineteenth century, nearly one hundred years later, that the idea was actually put into practice.

Many pharmacists then began to produce medicinal pastilles flavored with chocolate. Some, such as Debauve and Menier, quickly abandoned their first profession to become full-time chocolate makers. In pharmacies a multitude of chocolate-based preparations were on sale without prescription to treat fatigue, anemia, constipation, coughing, worms, and even syphilis. At the beginning of the nineteenth century, the Debauve and Gallais catalog offered chocolates flavored with ambergris (as tonics), arrowroot (for stomach complaints), orange blossom (for ladies' nervous systems suffering from shock), almond oil (for convalescence), Persian salep (for fatigue), and Icelandic lichen (to soothe chest diseases).

In 1866, chocolate received the supreme, if belated, honor of being registered in the pharmacopoeia of France. This was its official recognition as a medicine.

An apology for chocolate

Let any man who has drunk a few sips too many from the cup of pleasure; any man who has worked for a notable portion of the time when that should be spent sleeping; any man of intelligence who finds that he is temporarily becoming stupid; any man who finds the air humid, the time long, and the atmosphere difficult to bear; any man who is tormented by an obsession that prevents him from being free to think; let him in every case, we say, administer to himself a good half liter of chocolate flavored with amber, adding seventy-two grains of amber per half-kilogram, and he will find that it works wonders. In my way of expressing things, I call amber-flavored chocolate the "chocolate of the afflicted."

ANTHELME BRILLAT-SAVARIN, 1826

 o ensure that chocolate was served with the proper decorum, it became surrounded over the centuries by various implements, from the simplest to the most refined. Whether made of wood, gold, or porcelain, they all had only one purpose: to glorify the taste of the beverage.

Implements used for chocolate

The earliest implements associated with chocolate were those used by the Aztecs, who drank their chocolate-flavored pulp, *atolle*, from coconut shells (*tecomate*) or dried half-gourds (*xicalli*) after the women had crushed the cocoa beans and grains of corn on a curved stone called a *metate*. King Moctezuma II, on the other hand, drank his *tchocolatl* out of a fine gold cup, into which it was poured after being beaten with a finely worked wooden instrument with a fluted base. When Hernando Cortez landed in Mexico, he drank the sacred beverage of the Aztecs out of tortoise shells decorated with gold arabesques.

THE FIRST CHOCOLATE POTS

In the seventeenth century, the Carmelites of Oaxaca in Mexico used a sort of earthenware vase with a rounded belly, which was the precursor of the chocolate pot. Owing to the craze among the Spanish nobility for hot chocolate, this receptacle gradually became more elegant and more practical; silver and china were used as materials, and it now had a right-angled handle. Empress Marie-Therèse of Austria, who had been brought up at the Spanish court, could not live without this refined piece of equipment.

The chocolate pot first came on the scene in France in the second half of the seventeenth century. This new item became known as a "conversational convenience" because it presided over every aristocratic gathering, and we can tell how important it

rapidly became from the letter that Madame de Sévigné wrote to her daughter on February 11, 1671: "But you have no chocolate pot, I have thought about it a thousand times: how will you manage?"

In 1686, the ambassador of Siam presented Louis XIV with a silver chocolate pot, which became an inspiration to the best silversmiths and the greatest workshops in France.

PORCELAIN TREMBLING CUP MADE IN
PARIS (C. 1830)

SÈVRES PORCELAIN TREMBLING CUPS (19TH CENTURY)

From the cup to the saucer

In 1709, the formula for hard porcelain (known only in China before then) was discovered in Meissen, Germany. This opened the way to European production, but chocolate pots continued for a long time afterwards to be decorated with Asian motifs.

THE USE OF THE FOAMER

In 1722, the missionary priest Jean-Baptiste Labat gave the earliest description of the foamer in his travel notebooks: "a stick which is about ten inches taller than the chocolate pot, so that it can be freely moved about between two open hands." This foamer was used by the servants to mix the cocoa into the water or milk, after which they served the frothy chocolate in a pot that was brought to the table with the lid closed. Anne of Austria went so far as to give the nickname Molina to a maid who was particularly expert in the art of "milling" chocolate. The chocolate pot and its foamer are described in Diderot's *Encyclopedia* as follows: "Chocolate pots are made from silver, plated copper, tinplate, and earthenware. The latter are of no value because once they have been heated, they keep the liquid boiling vigorously for a long time, which is liable to remove all that is most exquisite in the chocolate. Silver and copper pots often have the defect of a bulge near the bottom, which means that a considerable part of the contents escapes the action of the foamer. The form of a truncated cone is that best suited to the vessel in which the dish is prepared. The lid of a chocolate pot is pierced in the middle so that the handle of the foamer can be inserted. Today this foamer is normally made up from several pieces of boxwood or some other hardwood, formed more or less in an S-shape and with

a protruding section on the end which is divided into several levels and interspersed with cavities."

THE QUEEN CUP

In 1761, the Sèvres workshop produced its first "coffee pot designed for chocolate," then the first "cup and deep saucer" in 1762. The Marquise de Pompadour, under whose aegis the Vincennes workshop came under royal patronage before establishing itself at Sèvres, commissioned these pieces. The "queen cup" was shaped like a flattened cone and usually had a lid. It had one or two handles and was used for drinking milk or hot chocolate. The large "trembling cup," sometimes accompanied by a flat-bottomed saucer, was at that time called a "mancerinas," after the Marquis of Mancera, who was viceroy of New Spain from 1664 to 1673. In some cases it was very concave or had a credenza, thus preventing the ladies who attended the Marquis' parties from spilling on their dresses, although rumor was at the time that the Marquis suffered from the shakes and had devised this cup so that he

could drink his chocolate in bed. In *The Cup of Chocolate*, painted in 1768 by Jean-Baptiste Charpentier the Elder and showing the Duke of Penthièvre surrounded by his family, and *Woman Drinking Chocolate*, an eighteenth-century lithograph by Louis-Martin Bonnel, we see the practice that was customary during this period of pouring one's scalding chocolate into the saucer in order to cool it down and then drinking it directly from the saucer.

Until the beginning of the nineteenth century, the chocolate pot always had three feet that were tall enough to enable a small burner to be slipped underneath it. The need for this was removed when Van Houten invented powdered cocoa in 1828; there was now no need to keep the chocolate hot with a flame, since it no longer formed a fatty deposit. As a result, completely new models of chocolate pots appeared, either with a low pedestal or a flat bottom. These items have continued to provide inspiration for silversmiths and porcelain makers, and some contemporary craftsmen are still producing very beautiful pieces.

SILVER AND IVORY CHOCOLATE POT CREATED BY
L. BONVALLET FOR CARDEILHAC (MUSÉE
CRISTOFLE, SAINT-DENIS)

TERRACOTTA CHOCOLATE POT
DESIGNED BY FRANÇOIS
BELLIARD (1997)

SILVER CHOCOLATE POT
(19TH CENTURY)

SILVER ART DECO CHOCOLATE POT
IN THE SHAPE OF A COCOA FRUIT
(20TH CENTURY)

SÈVRES PORCELAIN CHOCOLATE POT
(19TH CENTURY)

LIMOGES PORCELAIN CHOCOLATE
POT (19TH CENTURY)

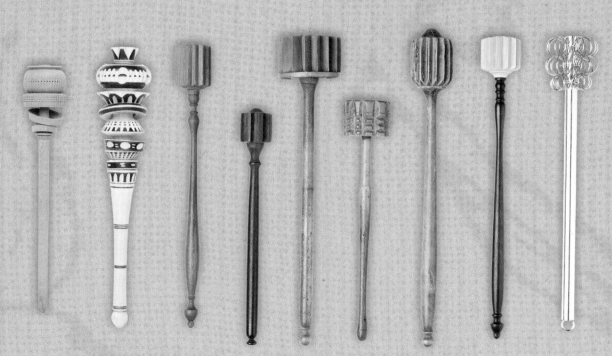

COLLECTION OF FOAMERS (AZTEC, MEXICAN, 19TH-CENTURY, AND CONTEMPORARY)

COPPER CHOCOLATE POT
(18TH CENTURY)

COPPER CHOCOLATE POT
(18TH CENTURY)

SILVER CHOCOLATE POT WITH
RAISED FEET (18TH CENTURY)

SILVER CHOCOLATE POT
(19TH CENTURY)

SÈVRES PORCELAIN CHOCOLATE
POT WITH PEDESTAL
(19TH CENTURY)

MOUTIERS EARTHENWARE
CHOCOLATE POT
(20TH CENTURY)

100% chocolate

THE COLONIAL COMPANY CHOCOLATE
FACTORY IN PARIS (19TH CENTURY)

The birth of the chocolate industry

"WORKER PREPARING CHOCOLATE ON A
HORIZONTAL HEATED TABLE," PLATE FROM
THE DIDEROT AND D'ALEMBERT *ENCYCLO-
PÉDIE OU DICTIONNAIRE RAISONNÉ DES
ARTS, DES SCIENCES ET DES MÉTIERS* (1753).

The eighteenth century was marked in every sphere by the rise of technology and in particular by the invention, then perfection, of the steam engine. Like everything else, chocolate reaped the benefit of progress and so the chocolate industry came into being.

TOWARDS MECHANIZATION
In 1728, the first chocolate factory run by hydraulic power was founded by Walter Churchman in Bristol, England. From then on what had previously been a craft industry steadily advanced towards mechanization throughout Europe. Factories would initially set up business on a river site where they could use hydraulic power and then subsequently move on to use steam engines.

The *Encyclopédie ou Dictionnaire raisonné des sciences, des arts et des métiers* (*Encyclopedia of Sciences, Arts, and Occupations*), compiled under the direction of Diderot, gave precise descriptions of the crafts and techniques of the period. The illustration (left) of the preparation of chocolate shows a worker standing at a horizontal, heated table, invented in 1732 by du Buisson. Previously, workers had done their job on their knees, like the

Aztecs using their *metate*. The first industrial chocolate maker in France was the Compagnie des chocolats et thés (Chocolate and Tea Company), known as Pelletier and Co. when it was founded in 1770, and later to become Schaal in 1871. Ten years later, the chocolate makers of Bayonne were using steam engines, and the city became home to the first mechanized chocolate factory. It was a Frenchman, Poincelet, who in 1811 perfected a mixer for cocoa beans.

THE VAN HOUTEN REVOLUTION
Important though these changes undoubtedly were, it was the discovery made by Coenraad Johannes Van Houten that would literally revolutionize the small world of the chocolate industry. This Dutch pharmacist set up business in Amsterdam in 1815 and in 1828 perfected the production of cocoa powder. In his search for a means of extracting the cocoa butter in some other way than by skimming the foam off boiling chocolate, he created a hydraulic press that produced "cakes" of dry cocoa, which could then simply be powdered. To make it dissolve in water more easily, the powder was then treated with

alkaline salts (sodium and potassium carbonate), a process known as "dutching," which also helped to give it a sweeter aroma and a darker color. Van Houten is said to have gotten the idea for this technique by reading some travelers' accounts of Indians mixing ashes with chocolate to make it more digestible. With the production of pure, fat-free cocoa powder, the familiar thick, frothy drink gradually disappeared, and chocolate pots and foamers were used less and less.

The industrial manufacture of chocolate, in solid or liquid form, was now able to develop fully. The English firm of J.S. Fry and Sons was quick to exploit the Dutch pharmacist's discovery. This Quaker family had already broken new ground in 1789 by crushing cocoa beans, using energy from a Watt steam engine. In 1847, cocoa butter extracted by the Van Houten method was added to the paste, which made it more malleable and thus capable of being poured into moulds. This was the beginning of the molded chocolate bar, which bore the French name (French being the language in vogue for all things culinary) of *"chocolat délicieux à manger"* (delicious chocolate to eat). It should be noted that the chocolate bars sold prior to this had been simply pressed, not molded.

With the exception of conching, which was invented by Rodolphe Lindt in 1879 (*see p. 73*), the main techniques involved in large-scale chocolate manufacture were all operational by the middle of the nineteenth century. By moving from a hot drink to a solid bar, chocolate diversified its presentation and multiplied its modes of consumption.

The great names of chocolate

In the nineteenth century, chocolate firms came into being whose names are still known today and to which the modern chocolate industry owes its vast economic scale and its pedigree. Just some of the names worthy of mention are: Menier and Poulain in France; Suchard, Kohler, Sprüngli, Klaus, Nestlé, Tobler, and Lindt in Switzerland; and Cadbury and Barry in England.

THE SWISS PIONEERS
The ingenuity of the Swiss chocolate makers was to contribute decisively to the technology of chocolate and to enable Switzerland for many long years to retain its supremacy in the field. The facts speak for

themselves: as early as 1826, Philippe Suchard installed several cocoa-crushing machines at Serrières, near Neuchâtel; in 1830, Charles Amédée Kohler perfected the manufacture of hazelnut chocolate; in 1845, 1865, 1868, and 1879 respectively, David Sprüngli, Jacques Klaus, Jean Tobler, and Rodolphe Lindt each founded their own chocolate factory.

However important these pioneers' discoveries were, it is to another chocolate maker, Daniel Peter, that Switzerland owes its place in legend. From his business in Veney he followed with great interest the work of Henri Nestlé, whose lengthy research led in 1875 to the discovery of a process that reduced milk to powder. Daniel Peter immediately used this technique to produce the first block of milk chocolate. Shortly afterward the invention of conching by Rodolphe Lindt in 1879 finally elevated Switzerland to the rank of premier chocolate-making nation.

THE ENGLISH QUAKERS
Meanwhile in England the Frys, who belonged to a Quaker community, made a breakthrough by launching the chocolate cream bar. They were not the only representatives of their religion to play a role in the British chocolate industry, however. The Quakers regarded chocolate as a temperance product that should be promoted as widely as possible, and the competition between them encouraged creativity. When George Cadbury, the Quaker son of the dynasty's founder, John Cadbury, launched a brand of powdered cocoa called Cocoa Essence in 1866, it was hugely successful. About thirty years later the town of Bournville near Birmingham was built specially for the workers at the Cadbury's factory. The social paternalism that drove the enterprise was in keeping with the Fourier-inspired ideas of the time (*see p. 25*).

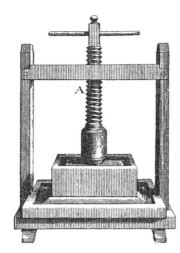

"PRESS USED TO REMOVE FAT FROM COCOA," ENGRAVING FROM NICOLAS DE BLÉGNY'S WORK OF 1687.

wo illustrious dynasties whose names are of major importance in the history of chocolate came into being in France at the beginning of the nineteenth century: Menier and Poulain.

The French dynasties

MENIER: THE VISIONARY INDUSTRIALIST

Jean Antoine Brutus Menier came from a family of pharmacists and surgeons, and was aged twenty-one when he opened a drugstore in Paris. Like some other makers of pharmaceutical products, he used chocolate to mask the bitterness of certain medicines. Three years later he rented a mill at Noisiel on the River Marne, where at first he used waterpower simply to drive the grinders that produced his medicinal powders. He then invented a system of millstones for pulverizing vegetable and mineral drugs, which he applied to the treatment of cocoa, made a pendulum grinder and stamping system, and mastered the art of cooling. In 1836, the first packs of chocolate emerged from his establishment in Paris, each made up of six semi-cylindrical bars wrapped in yellow paper. After that, the quantities of chocolate produced increased rapidly, but even so, Menier's main activity still remained the manufacture of "pectoral and medicinal products."

In 1851, Louis Napoleon Bonaparte, then President of the Republic, showed his gratitude toward this enterprising man who had always supported him by visiting the workshops in the rue Sainte-Croix-de-la-Bretonnerie. The President congratulated Menier on "the order prevailing there and his good and paternal management." The chocolate maker's spectacular rise to fame and Bonapartist connections aroused jealousy among his fellows, and Menier, worn down by the persecution and attacks they inflicted on him, fell seriously ill and died in 1853.

The business was taken over by his son Emile Justin, a real visionary who was then aged twenty-seven, and with the support of wealthy in-laws was destined to build up the Menier empire. He was a pragmatist who quickly understood that in order to manufacture chocolate he needed cacao fruits, milk, and sugar. He purchased the mill at Noisiel and then extended the firm's agricultural estate by over 3,700 acres and bought a herd of cows that

THE FIRST FRENCH CHOCOLATE BAR WAS PRESENTED BY J.A.B. MENIER, AS SHOWN IN THE FORM OF SIX SEMI-CYLINDRICAL SECTIONS, IN ORDER, HE SAID, TO "MAKE THE PRODUCTS OF HIS FACTORY COMPLETELY DISTINCT, WITH A WRAPPING AND A LABEL WHICH WAS A FACSIMILE OF MEDALS HITHERTO UNKNOWN TO COMMERCE."

PAINTING SHOWING THE MILL AT NOISIEL IN 1825.

would grow to as many as two thousand. In 1862 (only nine years after his father's death), he bought a Nicaraguan cacao plantation of almost twenty thousand acres, which is still known today as Valle Menier. He acquired yet more plantations, created his own fleet to facilitate the transportation of cocoa, and chartered other ships, including the famous three-master, *Belem*. Finally, to produce his own sugar he grew sugar beets, and in 1869, he had a model refinery built in the Somme.

In 1860, this outstanding entrepreneur commissioned the architect Jules Saulnier to build a factory on his land at Noisiel. It took twelve years to construct the buildings, which were organized to suit the production process, with each one being given over to one stage of manufacture. As for the new mill, it was probably one of the first examples in the world of a building with a metal load-bearing frame.

Emile Justin Menier patented several inventions, including the first machine for packaging chocolate bars. He encouraged innovation by employing chemists such as Marcelin Berthelot, who was the first to carry out the synthesis of alcohol, and Jean-Paul Rigollot, who invented the mustard poultice in 1866.

As well as being an industrial genius, Menier was also interested in politics (representing Seine-et-Marne in parliament) and the press.

In the 1870s, the workforce at the Noisiel factory rose to 1,700, including seven hundred women. Emile Justin Menier's concern for the social welfare of his employees led him to built a town where they

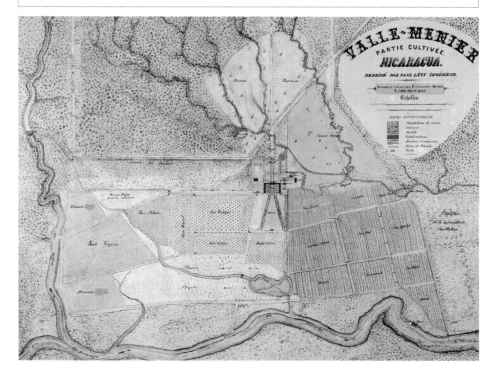

OIL ON CANVAS SHOWING PART OF THE VALLE MENIER PLANTATIONS. TO AVOID ANY BREAK IN THE SUPPLY OF RAW MATERIALS, EMILE JUSTIN MENIER ACQUIRED NEARLY 20,000 ACRES OF CACAO TREES IN NICARAGUA.

chocolate factory, The Cathedral, between 1906 and 1908. They also continued to use the services of the most renowned scientists and technicians.

Until 1914, Noisiel remained famous throughout the world as a center of technical, scientific, and architectural progress.

POULAIN: ON THE LOOKOUT FOR INNOVATION

The history of the Poulain brand is also part of the industrial heritage of France. Victor Auguste Poulain was born in 1825 at Pontlevoy in the Loir-et-Cher region. He was apprenticed from the age of ten and then became an assistant in a Parisian grocery store, where he learned how to prepare chocolate. Once he had accumulated some savings, he decided to set up business independently and moved to the Grande Rue in Blois to make his own brand of chocolate. In 1850, he bought a Hermann grinder to increase his output and put out his first advertisement. Always on the lookout for innovations, he used a five-horsepower steam engine to drive his grinder. He registered his brand in 1852 and decided to imprint his name on his chocolate bars as a safeguard against counterfeits. In 1864, he built a factory and then, three years later, first published the slogan "Goûtez et comparez" ("Taste and compare") on posters with a three-color background. In the 1880s he entered into partnership with his son Albert, marking the beginning of his progressive withdrawal from the business.

The creation in 1884 of Petit Déjeuner à la crème vanillée (Vanilla Cream Breakfast Chocolate) played a decisive part in the democratization of the product. Albert Poulain also showed that he was truly ahead of his time by developing the vogue for chromolithographs that had been started by Aristide Boucicault for the department store Au Bon Marché in Paris. With his chocolate bars he included small cards showing colored, educational pictures as free gifts to be collected by children. The Blois factory printed up to 350,000 of these per day. In 1896, Firmin Bouisset created posters for the famous brand showing his son as a schoolboy and then as a Pierrot. Later, in 1905, Leonetto Capiello designed the little foal, which was to become the Poulain emblem. At this time the chocolate was wrapped in tinfoil, but tin was a rare and costly metal, and so in 1907, aluminum foil was introduced instead. By buying ever more advanced machinery, Poulain was able to launch new products at prices that were affordable to everyone, such as cocoa powder and soluble

could live and that would be copied by other industrialists in the world of chocolate (see framed insert on preceding page). When he died in 1881, all the workers were present to bid farewell to him at the start of the funeral procession, and a ten-mile cortège led by Jules Ferry and Louis Blanc accompanied the coffin to the Père-Lachaise Cemetery.

His two sons, Henri and Gaston, carried on their father's work with the construction of a new

CHROMOLITHOGRAPH PICTURE OFFERED AS A FREE GIFT BY POULAIN CHOCOLATE.

powdered cocoa in 1909. During the First World War, the Blois factory produced twenty tons of chocolate a day despite the difficulties of supply; in October 1914, Joffre ordered fifty tons of chocolate for the army after the first victory in the Marne.

The company was sold in 1915, and in 1918, the Beauséjour factory in Blois was completely destroyed by fire. A few days later Victor Auguste Poulain died in despair after seeing his life's work go up in smoke.

LITHOGRAPHED TIN OF POULAIN POWDERED COCOA (1904)

SCHOOLBOY SITTING ON A STOOL (1896), POSTER BY FIRMIN BOUISSET WITH THE FAMOUS SLOGAN "TASTE AND COMPARE."

1920   1930   1934   1935

From Banania to chocolate bars

Chocolate continued to evolve in the twentieth century with the arrival of chocolate powder, which found its way into every home as a hot drink at breakfast time or in the afternoon.

PROMOTIONAL POSTCARD SHOWING A SOLDIER IN THE FIRST WORLD WAR DRINKING BANANIA IN THE TRENCHES. THE PICTURE WAS DRAWN BY MAURICE LELOIR AT THE END OF 1914.

On a journey to Nicaragua in 1909, Pierre Lardet tasted a drink, dating back to the ancient Mayas, which was based on cocoa, sugar, crushed cereals, and powdered banana. He returned to his workshop in Courbevoie, altered the recipe slightly, and in 1912 created Banania, a chocolate powder whose publicity promised the consumer "energy, vigor, health, and strength." It was sold in metal tins showing a picture of a Caribbean woman surrounded by bananas under the inscription "Whole food." This was the label that Lardet registered in 1915. Shortly afterwards, however, a wounded Senegalese infantryman who was convalescing came to stay with him. The man was always smiling, and Lardet had the inspired idea of making him the emblem of his brand and adding the slogan "Y'a bon Banania" ("Banania be good"), which would quickly become famous.

The First World War seemed to have ruined Lardet's commercial prospects, but he then had the idea of giving his product away free to the soldiers in the trenches. This gesture was greatly appreciated, so much so that Leven and Lemonier, the authors of a cartoon strip that appeared in 1916, even claimed that the distribution of Banania to the troops would help lead the army to victory. As a result, the Pierre Lardet brand shot to fame, and after the war he was able to build up a loyal, grateful clientele.

The success of Banania was based on the colonial ideology that prevailed at the time; the black man produces and the white man consumes. The Caribbean woman and the Senegalese infantryman with his smiling face and accompanying slogan were early signs of the association that

1947

1959

1990s

would very soon be made between chocolate and the black man. In the 1930s, the infantryman's head was stylized and shown against a yellow (banana-colored) background. To attract young consumers in the politically correct 1990s, it was replaced by a little blond boy, but the subsequent mode for authenticity resulted in the return of the Senegalese infantryman on Banania tins now marked "historic recipe."

TINS AS COLLECTIBLES

Many cocoa and chocolate brands began to sell their products in attractively lithographed tins. Banania went further; it was the first brand to print the words "flour," "sugar," or "pasta" on the famous blue tins so that housewives could keep them later as useful, decorative kitchen containers. At the same time, solid chocolate continued to evolve, until it finally became accessible to everyone. In Switzerland, Jules Séchaud launched the first filled chocolate in 1913, marketing it as a luxurious delicacy. In 1905, Cadburys invented Dairy Milk, a caramel-flavored milk chocolate of the type that is still popular in Britain today, then a dark, crunchy chocolate called Bournville Plain. By now the famous Cadbury brand also specialized in making chocolate cookies and, in 1921, they created the first fruit and nut chocolate bar.

The United States had also acquired a taste for chocolate. In 1907, Milton Snavely Hershey built the model town of Hersheyville around his factory. His Hershey's Kisses, unsweetened chocolate, and cocoa powder quickly became everyday consumer goods.

**Y'A PAS DU TOUT BON ...
(THERE ISN'T GOOD AT ALL ...)**

The slogan "Y'a bon Banania" comes directly from the conception that many people in France had of native colonial speech. On April 9, 1916, the newspaper les Annales *gave an explanation of the famous slogan's origin: " ... one phrase, always the same, forms the basis for [their] singular idiom: 'Y'a' ('There is') or 'Y'a pas' ('There isn't'). When they want to express their satisfaction, the Moroccans or Senegalese add an epithet to these words: 'Y'a bon!' For them, things are divided into two distinct categories: those in which there is good and those in which there isn't good."*

Stand BANANIA — Exposition Coloniale

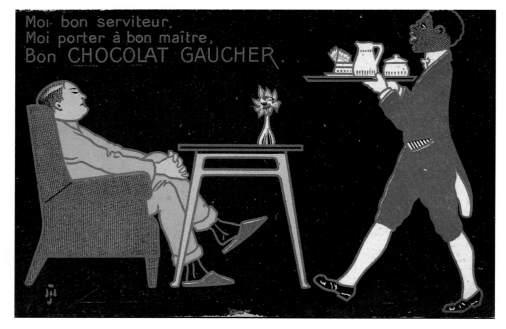

 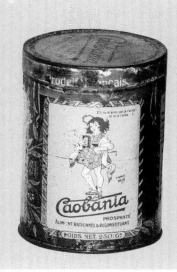 

TO COMPETE WITH THE REMARKABLE FAME OF BANANIA, MANY MANUFACTURERS LAUNCHED SIMILAR PRODUCTS. AT THE END OF THE 1920S, FOR EXAMPLE, FELIX POTIN MARKETED BANIKA, "A BREAKFAST DRINK BASED ON COCOA AND BANANA POWDER, WITH ADDED NUTRITIOUS, VITAMIN-RICH INGREDIENTS."

It was when he saw his wife dipping a doughnut into malted milk that the Chicago chocolate producer Franck Mars had the idea for a chocolate-coated bar with a filling, which he called Milky Way and marketed in 1920. With the invention of the Mars Bar in 1932 by Franck Mars' son, Forrest Mars Junior, the evolution of chocolate into a snack for nibbling was complete. Very soon millions of these bars were being sold every day, and they even became part of the soldier's ration after they were given to GIs in the Second World War. For the American units that were sent to the Pacific, the Pennsylvania Manufactury Confectioners' Association created a four-ounce bar called Field Ration D. Five hundred thousand of these per day were produced from 1941 to 1945. Apart from being enriched with Vitamin C, this bar had the advantage of not melting at any temperature below one hundred degrees Fahrenheit, and because of this it was also used in the subsequent conflicts in Vietnam and Iraq.

Chocolate and advertising

At the end of the seventeenth century, chocolate was still a little-known product and accessible to only a very small section of the French population. To bring it to the public's attention and fight off the competition that soon began to rage, grocers and craftsman chocolate makers vied with each other to produce the most imaginative publicity and thus promoted the development of the "advertisement." One example was Sieur Renaud, who around 1695 was the first skilled chocolate maker to open a store in Paris. He distributed a little poem in praise of his chocolate to all his customers:

> [...] Go and buy at Renaud's
> You'll be amazed at what you find.
> Only the best real chocolate
> Is sold in his boutique.
> You want it really delicate?
> This merchant is unique!

It was a Paris grocer, Sieur Roussel, however, who in 1776 was the first to think of marking his name on his chocolate, a fact that he publicized far and wide in the press at the time.

The *Illustration* was founded in 1843 and rapidly became France's top weekly paper for advertising. Interestingly, it encouraged its advertisers to be creative by refusing to let them use the same advertisement twice.

In the nineteenth century, when Europe was entering the industrial era, chocolate makers made

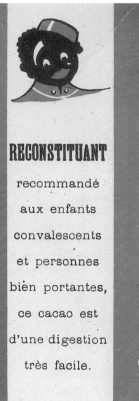
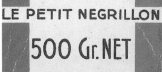

TO SYMBOLIZE ITS EXOTIC COLONIAL ORIGINS, COCOA WAS ASSOCIATED FOR MANY YEARS WITH THE IMAGE OF THE BLACK MAN.

ABOVE, PROMOTIONAL POSTCARD FOR LOMBART CHOCOLATE, FOUNDED IN 1760. THE TWO SCHOOLBOY BROTHERS ARE REMINISCENT OF ANDRE AND JULIEN, THE LITTLE HEROES OF *TWO CHILDREN ON A TOUR OF FRANCE*, A BOOK FOR SCHOOLS BY G. BRUNO, WHICH APPEARED IN 1877 AND WAS REPUBLISHED IN MANY FURTHER EDITIONS.

RIGHT, POSTER BY E. BRUN (1894), USING A BABY IN AN ADVERTISEMENT FOR THE FIRST TIME (THE FAMOUS "CADUM BABY" DID NOT APPEAR UNTIL 1912).

full use of advertising to promote their products. Chocolate still had a "medicinal" image, and so the first theme to be developed was health; chocolate gave children energy and helped convalescents to recover their strength.

In the fight against adulterated and counterfeit chocolate, Victor Auguste Poulain coined the slogan "Goûtez et comparez" ("Taste and compare") in 1867, and this became the first publicity campaign to spread throughout the whole of France. His son Albert then thought of adding a metal figurine and a chromolithograph picture to every tin of Petit Déjeuner à la crème vanillée (Vanilla Cream Breakfast Chocolate) in the hope that these free gifts would win the loyalty of young consumers.

Jean Antoine Menier sold his chocolate in the form of blocks consisting of six semi-cylindrical bars. He wrapped each block in his famous yellow paper, thus giving birth to the concept of the trademark. The late nineteenth century was a time when the idea of universal schooling was very popular, and as a result, children became the special targets of advertising; every image and every object had to have some pedagogical significance. One example was the "little girl with pigtails," designed by Firmin Bossuet for the first national publicity campaign, who at Menier's request was shown on her way to school.

Teachers were sent educational "pictures for schools," which demonstrated and explained all the stages that cocoa beans from the colonies went through, right up to the molding of the chocolate bars.

ADVERTISEMENT FOR THE WIDOW ROUSSEL, 18TH-CENTURY CHOCOLATE MAKER.

From Menier chocolate to la Mère Denis

After being invited to think of a theme for a poster for Menier, the painter Firmin Bouisset (1859–1925) was taking a walk around the Noisiel property when he noticed the warden's granddaughter, who was six or seven and named Louise Hedeline, standing with her face to a wall. This immediately gave him the idea for the little girl using a piece of charcoal to write the words "Beware of counterfeits" on a wall in her childish handwriting. Her typical model schoolgirl's garments, natural posture, basket of goodies, and protective umbrella made her so representative of life at that time that every family could identify with the image. Firmin Bouisset often used his children in his illustrations; his son Jacques was the schoolboy for Lu petit-beurre cookies and the chimney sweep for Job cigarette papers, and his daughter Yvonne, who was also used to promote Maggi products, remained the symbol of the Menier brand for forty years.

In the years that followed, other illustrators developed the theme of the little girl with pigtails , but no poster ever had the same success as Bouisset's, which even today still symbolizes childhood, the afternoon goûter (when French children traditionally eat chocolate), and nostalgia for a bygone era. The idea of a character turning away to write a message was taken up and used in advertisements by other brands, including Vedette. In 1979, la Mère Denis (Mother Denis)—a figure who at that time was representative of the famous make of household appliances—was filmed writing on a wall: "It's true, you know." The way she was standing with her feet turned inward, her umbrella, and her basket were borrowed directly from Firmin Bouisset's poster.

FIRMIN BOUISSET WITH HIS TWO CHILDREN, WHO WERE THE MODELS FOR HIS POSTERS (1894).

POSTER OF THE LITTLE MENIER GIRL, DESIGNED BY FIRMIN BOUISSET, AN ARAB VERSION FOR SHOP COUNTERS IN NORTH AFRICA (1910)

POSTER OF THE LITTLE GIRL IN THE ART DECO "URCHIN" STYLE (1928).

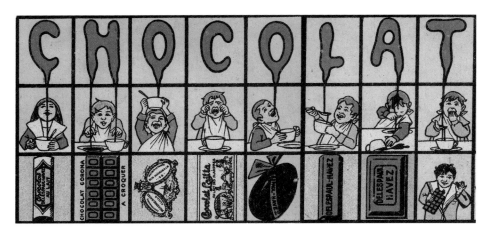

THE FAMOUS POSTERS

1895: Henri Gerbault drew a mother with her baby next to a black cat lapping its cup of Carpentier chocolate.

1905: For Auguste Poulain, Leonetto Capiello depicted a group of children playing with a frisky young horse. This image, although more stylized, is still the brand's emblem today.

1925: A worker at the Delespaul factory designed a poster on which the letters of the word "chocolate" are melting down the wall to the delight of the children at the table.

During this early part of the twentieth century, even Alfons Mucha provided illustrations for chocolate with The Ideal Chocolate, *a poster for the Compagnie française des chocolats et des thès (French Chocolate and Tea Company), and* Mexican Chocolate, *a poster for the Masson company.*

Children collected the pictures from their blocks of chocolate and stuck them into albums, which became real museum catalogs of a child's imagination. Poulain distributed twenty-five thousand different pictures between 1880 and 1904 and even set up a printing press in its own factory to run them off. The advertising of this period produced some genuine little masterpieces, such as the vending machines in the form of a *colonne Morris* (a pillar used in French streets as a billboard), which sat on grocers' counters and gave out small bars of chocolate.

In the mid-nineteenth century, companies began to produce advertising boards and give them to shopkeepers. These were made of cardboard and ranged from small objects to complete billboards, with every kind of display shelf and stand in between. Grocers were delighted with these since they enabled them to decorate the front of their stores without effort or expense. From 1885 on, they were gradually replaced by enamel plates. These gave an enormous impetus to advertising, not just because they were very widely distributed but also because enamel was so durable (guaranteed for forty years), glossy, and brilliantly colored.

SCHOOLCHILDREN WERE THE SPECIAL TARGET OF ADVERTISING.

Chocolate collections

Few collections arouse as much passion as those having to do with chocolate, and there is no doubt that the promotion of this product has generated the creation of many magnificent objects. There are several types of collections.

Collections of point-of-sale advertising. Few cardboard display shelves have survived, but there are still imitation metal chocolate bars, enamel plaques, and vending machines shaped like Morris columns (billboard pillars).

Collections of objects of the same make.
With brands such as Félix Potin, Menier, Poulain, and La Marquise de Sévigné, it is possible to pick up collector's items, for example chromos, blotters, tins, catalogs, posters, lunch boxes, etc.

Collections of implements for chocolate, such as chocolate pots, chocolate cups, and trembling cups.

Collections of lithographed tins from Poulain, Banania, and other makes of chocolate powder by Van Houten, Caffarel, etc.

Collections of promotional objects, for example albums, pictures and toys for children, blotters, pencils, school exercise-book covers, posters, newspaper advertisements, clocks, mirrors, keyrings, lapel pins, etc.

Collections of postage stamps concerning cacao growing in the countries that produce it (including the former colonies of European countries) and the methods by which cocoa is processed.

2
the cacao:
nature's gift

a tree of life to the Mayas, born of a princess's blood according to the Toltecs and a divine gift in Aztec eyes, the cacao tree is full of symbolism.

The cacao tree

Originally labeled *Amygdala pecunaria*, the "money bean," the cacao was subsequently given the more solemn name of *Theobroma*, from the Greek *theos*, "god," and *broma*, "food" ("the food of the gods"), by Carolus Linnaeus in 1737. In the first edition (1753) of his *Species plantarum*, the famous naturalist added the term *cacao* to create the present botanical name, *Theobroma cacao*.

The cacao tree, which most probably originated in Latin America's upper Amazon, is a member of the Sterculiaceae family. It grows only in the hot, humid climates of equatorial countries.

Hybrid cacao trees (those created by crossing two species) produce pods, known in French as *cabosses*, from their second year of life, while the Criollo variety produces pods from their fifth year. The trees then continue to produce for a further twenty to fifty years depending on soil quality.

Left to develop fully, an adult tree will reach thirty-three feet in height, but the planters normally prune them so as not to exceed thirteen to twenty-three feet. The straight, slender trunk, no more than one foot in diameter, finishes in a crest or "crown" of five branches. The oblong, pointed leaves average eight inches in length and three inches in width. When mature, they are dark green and generally last for about one year before falling. The flowers are white or a rose-tinted pale yellow, one-third of an inch in size and scentless. One cacao tree bears approximately six thousand flowers but produces only about sixty pods five or six months later. The pods are joined directly to the trunk by a short peduncle and are shaped like a small rugby ball.

As the tropical climates in which the trees grow do not have clearly defined seasons, the flowers, young fruits (or *cherelles*) and *cabosses* (the mature pods) are all found together on the same tree throughout the year.

The mature pod is four to fourteen inches long, weighs between seven and thirty-five ounces, and contains about forty seeds covered in a whitish, mucilaginous pulp. The seeds are between three-fourths to one and one-fourth inches long and weigh between one-half to three-fourths ounces each. After fermentation and drying they become what are known as "cocoa beans."

Cacao cultivation

The cacao tree has particular ecosystem requirements: a maximum temperature of 86 to 90 degrees Fahrenheit with a minimum of 65 to 70 degrees; annual rainfall between sixty to eighty inches. The atmosphere therefore has to be very damp (i.e., eighty to one hundred percent humidity), and the cacao is vulnerable to drying winds. Planting is to a density of three hundred trees for each two and one-half acres. The shade—or rather semi-shade—that the tree requires is provided by other trees: the erythrinas, bananas, or

ORIGIN OF THE WORD "CABOSSE"

The word "cabosse" comes from the Spanish cabeza, or "head". It was given to the fruit of the cacao tree by the conquistadors since it recalled the shape of the heads of the Mayas. The Mayas used to tie flat stones on the heads of their young infants before the fontanel closed so as to give the skull a more elongated form, considered more aesthetically pleasing.

39

ON THE CACAO TREE THE FLOWERS, FRUITS, AND PODS GROW STRAIGHT OFF THE TRUNK.

coconut palms, which the natives of Latin America call the *madre del cacao*, "mother to the cacao." Planting has to be at an altitude below 2,300 feet, in soil that is well drained yet relatively damp. Cacao plantations are often destroyed by predators (rats, squirrels, monkeys) or insects (mirids, caterpillars mining the pods, etc.). They are also highly susceptible to fungus attacks (brown rot on the pods, "witches' broom," moniliosis) and viruses (swollen shoot). These diseases and parasites cause considerable damage and tend to spread rapidly, while phytosanitary measures are cumbersome, rather ineffective, and seldom practiced.

Losses due to predators are reckoned to average at twenty-five percent of the anticipated harvest and those attributable to disease at twenty-one percent. In order to minimize such losses of production, scientists are currently endeavoring to develop more resistant cacao varieties.

THE CACAO IN THE CARIBBEAN

The cacao tree is part of the natural vegetation of the islands of the Caribbean, where the climate is ideal for its development. Martinique introduced it in 1660, and by the end of the seventeenth century it had become France's main supplier of cocoa. Cacao tree cultivation then assumed prime importance in the Caribbean through the late nineteenth century, when it became much rarer owing to competition from African plantations, natural catastrophes (earthquakes and hurricanes, etc.), and competition from the development of other crops, namely coffee, bananas, and sugarcane.

The ICCO lists the Dominican Republic, Grenada, Jamaica, Santa Lucia, Saint Vincent, and the Grenadines, as well as Trinidad and Tobago, in the so-called "Caribbean arc," a zone characterized by the exclusive production of high-class cocoa. In this zone annual production runs to seventy thousand metric tons.

At long last, after a break of nearly forty years, Martinique is returning to the cocoa industry. Without opening new plantations, the industrial plant run by Agrocacao is milling top-of-the-range beans drawn from the islands of the Caribbean, Venezuela, and the island of Trinidad.

Differing types of cacao

CRIOLLO, FORASTERO, AND TRINITARIO

There are three distinct groups of cacao tree: the Criollo, the Forastero, and the Trinitario, the third of these being a hybrid of the first two. The *Nacional* subgroup, believed by some to be an independent group, continues to be classified among the Forastero.

The Criollo group (*criollo* means "creole" in Spanish, i.e., "of the locality") is sometimes nicknamed "caraque." Originating in Mexico, Central America, and Venezuela, it was the only group of cacao trees cultivated in the seventeenth century. One of the best known of the Criollos is the Porcelana from Maracaibo in Venezuela. Green or red before the mature stage, Criollo pods suddenly turn an orangey red when they ripen. The group is losing popularity owing to its fragility and susceptibility to disease; moreover, it is of limited productivity. At present only one percent of world cocoa production comes from the Criollo group, cultivated essentially in Mexico, Colombia, Venezuela, Madagascar, and the Comores. Criollo beans, however, yield a high-class, powerfully aromatic cocoa with a very sought after, subtle taste. As production costs are very high, they tend to be blended with beans from other varieties of cacao.

The Forastero group (*forastero* means "foreign" in Spanish) originated in the Amazon. This group, which has justly earned the nickname the "robusta" variety of cacao, accounts for about seventy-nine percent of the world production of cocoa beans. Its success is due to its homogeneity and great adaptability to differing terrains. Green in their unripe state, Forastero pods ripen to a yellow color. The resultant beans supply everyday grades of cocoa that are fairly bitter, strong tasting, and not especially subtle. Nevertheless, there are several subgroups of Forastero cacao trees that do yield a more aromatic cocoa, such as the Amelonado of the lower Amazon region; this is also grown in Africa.

Traditionally grown in Ecuador, the *Nacional* subgroup produces a high-class cocoa. In fact, Ecuadorian cocoa enjoys a solid reputation for quality. However, the *Nacional* variety is highly susceptible to "witches' broom" and therefore increasingly less widely grown, its place being taken by Trinitario trees.

The Trinitario group is a hybrid resulting from crossing the Criollo and Forastero groups. This extremely heterogeneous group has inherited characteristics from both of its source groups. Trinitario was first identified in Trinidad in 1727, hence its name. The trees are often extremely vigorous and very productive when young. Cocoa made from Trinitario beans accounts for about twenty percent of current world production. Trinitario cacao trees are currently found in all the countries where Criollo used to be grown (Mexico, Central America, the Caribbean, Colombia, and Venezuela), as well as on the plantations of Cameroon, Southeast Asia, and Oceania. Some Trinitario trees yield high-class cocoas with subtle aromas.

ORDINARY VERSUS HIGH-CLASS COCOAS

The market distinguishes between ordinary cocoas, representing around ninety-five percent of production, and aromatic or high-class cocoas. The ordinary cocoas come mainly from trees of the Forastero group. Although the term "aromatic cocoas" does not have the same meaning to researchers, consumers, and chocolate makers, they all come from Criollo cacao trees or certain trees of the *Nacional* subgroup or Trinitario group. It is noteworthy that Western consumers now like to know where their chosen products come from, what their features are, and so on. Cocoa is not exempt from this tendency. This no doubt explains why high-class "single origin" cocoas, like that produced by the small village of Chuao in Venezuela, are so successful.

The cocoa-producing countries

The production of cocoa has grown strongly since the beginning of the twentieth century, from 115,000 metric tons in 1900 to 2,673,000 metric tons in 1999.

Traditionally, Latin America was the world's foremost cocoa-producing region, but lost its supremacy to Africa in the 1920s. Africa now supplies over sixty percent of the world's cocoa crop. Similarly, the production of Asian countries is also on the increase.

Currently, more than twenty million people in the world live directly off cocoa production, and almost ninety percent of production comes from small holdings of less than twelve acres, where generally extensive cultivation is the rule.

COCOA POWDER TIN DEPICTING A HARVESTING SCENE (EARLY 20TH CENTURY).

They had cocoa in their souls...

The gum from the green cacao stuck to the plantation workers' feet, where it formed a thick skin that no water could ever dissolve away.

And all of them, workers, jagunços, colonels, lawyers, doctors, merchants, and exporters had cacao gum in their soul, in the deepest reaches of their heart [...]. No amount of education, culture, or feeling could wash them clean of it. The cacao was power and money; it was their entire life; it was in their very soul, not merely planted in the rich, black earth. It grew in each one of them, casting its baleful shadow over their hearts and blotting out their good sentiments.

Jorge Amado, Les Terres du bout du monde, *1946*

From harvest to transformation

HARVESTING AND DEPODDING

It takes roughly six months for a flower to turn into a mature pod; the cacao tree therefore generally provides two crops per year. The fruit has to be harvested when it is "just right": too ripe and the seeds will have begun to germinate; not ripe enough and the seeds will be lacking in flavor after fermentation. Harvesting is done by hand, with a machete or a pruning hook on the end of a pole. Particular care is required, as the harvester has to avoid damaging flowers and unripened fruits still on the tree.

The best and simplest method of opening the pods is to burst them with a wooden club where they are harvested. This method of depodding means that the seeds can be harvested without damaging them. A trained agricultural worker can collect or depod approximately fifteen hundred fruits in one day.

FERMENTATION

The seeds are placed for fermentation in wicker baskets or wooden boxes that can contain as much as eleven thousand pounds. The seeds are sometimes merely heaped up on banana leaves. Yeast cells spontaneously culture the white pulp surrounding the seeds. During this fermentation, which takes place without oxygen, the temperature rises to around 120 degrees Fahrenheit, which enables the pulp to be transformed into alcohol. The seeds are then stirred to allow the air to circulate, and the oxidation changes the alcohol into acetic acid (from which, in some countries, cocoa vinegar is made). The procedure renders the cell walls of the seeds permeable, and therefore encourages chemical exchanges between the different constituents. Enzymes acting on the proteins and sugars create precursors to the aromas. During oxidation, the polyphenols give the cacao the characteristic cocoa-brown color, and the seeds' bitterness is diminished.

The fermentation of Criollo seeds lasts for two or three days, while Forastero and Trinitario seeds take five to seven days. If the fermentation is allowed to go on too long, there will be a foul taste owing to the beginnings of putrefaction.

It is worth clarifying that the seeds as such contain neither aroma nor flavor. Fermentation is what produces the aromatic precursors, and these do not develop fully until torrefaction (roasting) has taken place.

DRYING

Drying may be effected naturally (by the sun) or artificially. Natural drying consists in laying out the beans for ten to twenty days on sheets, mats, or, in case of rain, on grids with corrugated roof coverings running on rails (a "bus dryer"). In the case of artificial drying, the beans are placed in contact with a heated partition or put under a hot draft. They then have to be monitored to avoid taking up any unpleasant, smoky flavors. Well-regulated drying both stops the fermentation and prevents the onset of mold.

The drying process reduces the moisture content of the beans from sixty percent to less than eight percent, thereby enabling them to be stocked and transported in good storage conditions. A bean's quality is assessed by cutting its cotyledons (cut test). Defective beans may be moldy, slate-gray (aborted fermentation), or insect-damaged. When the delicate operations of fermentation or drying are badly handled, the resulting chocolate will have a bitter, burnt, or smoky taste.

Quality beans are sorted, cleaned, put in sacks, and then stocked in strictly hygienic conditions to prevent attacks by rodents, insects, or mold. In this "trade" form, the cocoa is shipped to the consumer countries or else processed locally into cocoa mass, for the big chocolate makers are now tending to develop local processing industries.

The cocoa dance

Drying the beans is sometimes a pretext for festivities. In Ecuador, the Indians practice the "cocoa dance". This means that they walk all over the drying areas, singing and using their feet to stir the beans drying in the sun. In Venezuela, on the feast of Corpus Christi, men dress up as devils, lie down in a recently emptied drying area, and are stepped over by a priest bearing the Eucharist.

IN AFRICA

The growing of the cacao tree is relatively recent in Africa, as it was introduced only at the end of the nineteenth century. From then on, the growing world production has been chiefly sustained by extension of peasant cultivation in Ghana, Cameroon, the Ivory Coast, and Nigeria. With sixty-five percent of produced volume—forty-three percent in the Ivory Coast—Africa today dominates the cocoa trade.

THE IVORY COAST

Although introduced in colonial times, cacao tree cultivation really got underway only in 1960 after independence, encouraged by President Houphouët-Boigny, whose parents were planters. With 1,127,000 metric tons representing the 1999–2000 harvest, the Ivory Coast has been the largest single producer of cocoa in the world for some twenty years. One-fifth of this production is converted into half-finished products (oil cake, cocoa butter) in factories belonging to large milling groups (ADM, Barry-Callebaut, or Cémoi, among others), and these are making a significant contribution to the country's economic development. The vast majority of the plantations are family concerns; those over twenty-five acres generally hire paid workers, often immigrants. The cacaos grown are hybrid varieties of Forastero. Geared to the mass market, they are suppliers to the main industrial groups in the world.

The political instability of the Ivory Coast since the coup of December 1999, its ethnic rivalries, and the disengagement of the state nevertheless weigh heavily on the future of cacao cultivation here. In addition, brown rot is currently threatening entry to the country and consequent cacao pod disease (phytophthora). Finally, the adoption of the European directive on chocolate, permitting industrialists to add up to five percent vegetable oil other than cocoa butter in the manufacture of chocolate, is giving rise to fears of lowered demand and a consequent fall in prices.

GHANA (FORMERLY THE GOLD COAST)

In 1869, a Ghanaian worker returned from Fernando Poo (now Bioko) in Equatorial Guinea with some cocoa pods. These tentative beginnings, augmented in 1886 by other introductions from São Tomé, resulted in the famous West African *Amelonado* cacao trees; these belong to the Forastero group and grow in an area extending across the entire forest zone of West Africa. In general, the majority of the varieties grown are of the Forastero type.

Ghanaian cocoa production was the largest in the world in the 1960s but has been declining since the 1970s owing to the aging of the tree stock and the poor remuneration of the planters. From 566,000 metric tons in 1964–1965, it has fallen to 370,000 in 1999. In 2000, Ghana fell back to third place, behind the Ivory Coast and Indonesia.

CAMEROON

The history of cacao growing in Cameroon goes back to the very late nineteenth century in Limbé, where there was a settlement of German planters. In 1999, Cameroon was the world's sixth-largest producer of cocoa, but the tree stock (mainly Trinitario) is old and susceptible to brown rot, and there is no prospect of production increasing at present.

NIGERIA
Cultivation was introduced in the late nineteenth century. Currently, the Nigerian cacao crop has fallen from 300,000 metric tons in 1970–1971 to 190,000 metric tons in 1999, representing a decline from second to fourth position in the world. The drop in production is due to the aging of the plantations and the exodus from the countryside linked to the petroleum boom. Nigerian cacaos are of the Trinitario group, together with Forastero hybrids.

MADAGASCAR
Introduced only in the late twentieth century, cacao cultivation here produced only 2,500 metric tons in 1999, but the trees, of the Criollo type, yield very high-quality cocoa.

SÃO TOMÉ AND PRINCIPE
The earliest cacao saplings here came from Brazil and were planted on Principe in 1822 and then several years later on São Tomé and Fernando Poo (Bioko). Cocoa production has fallen from seventeen thousand metric tons in 1900 (when São Tomé and Principe were the world's third-largest producer) to 4,500 metric tons in 1999, a figure that relegates this island state to the twenty-second

place in world production. Cocoa nevertheless remains the country's foremost cultivated crop, and all types of cacao trees are represented, apart from the Criollo.

IN SOUTH AMERICA
At the start of the twentieth century, Latin American cocoa represented eighty percent of the world market. Today it retains only seventeen percent of the market. The decline has been due, first, to the introduction of the cacao into Africa in the late nineteenth century and, more recently, to the strong advance of Asian production from the 1970s on.

BRAZIL
The cacao tree is native to this region but was apparently not in cultivation before the eighteenth century. From eighteen thousand metric tons in 1900 (Brazil then being the world's second-largest producer), Brazilian production reached 350,000 metric tons in the 1980s, only to fall back to 170,000 metric tons in 1999. This recession, which began in 1990, was caused by "witches' broom," a fungus endemic to the entire region of Bahia, the most important basin of cultivation in the country.

TOWARDS FAIR TRADE
For producing countries— often these are also developing countries—a high level of exports is vital, being the only guarantee of a decent life for the planters, hence the essential need to maintain a fair price level for cocoa. After coffee, which has led the way, certain brands of chocolate have undertaken to respect fair trade conditions, whose principles are as follows:
- *fair prices;*
- *regular purchases;*
- *good working conditions;*
- *respect for human rights;*
- *respect for the environment.*

The first "fair trade" chocolate appeared in Europe in 1991 under the name Mascao.

THE TOP PRODUCING COUNTRIES
(percentage of world production of cocoa in 1999)

Ivory Coast: 43%
Ghana: 15%
Indonesia: 14%
Nigeria: 7%
Brazil: 4%
Cameroon: 4%
Malaysia: 3%
Ecuador: 3%

ACCRA. ~ La Plage un jour de Chargement de Cacao

Collection C. O. A. - N· 34

HISTORIC POSTCARD SHOWING LOADING OF SACKS OF COCOA BEANS, PORT OF ACCRA, GOLD COAST (MODERN GHANA).

Le Cacaoyer

Dans les Grandes Cultures

Séchage des fèves de cacao au Vénézuéla

Brazil is the only cocoa-producing country where domestic consumption exceeds national production. Although it is no longer a cocoa-exporting country, in spite of being the world's fifth-largest producer, Brazil is the leading exporter of half-finished cocoa goods (powder, cocoa butter, oil cake, etc.). The cacao trees in cultivation essentially belong to the Forastero type, the group that produces the stock cocoas used in the chocolate industry.

ECUADOR

Native to Ecuador, the cacao has been cultivated here since the eighteenth century. From being the world's largest producer in 1900, with 23,000 metric tons, the country in 1999 ranked only eighth (with seventy thousand metric tons), but its cocoas are among the best in the world. Around ninety percent of these are high-class cocoas with no bitterness, and one percent of current production offers the floral *arriba* flavor.

Nacional cocoa is much sought after by chocolate makers for its flavor, but the cacao trees from which

it comes are so prone to "witches' broom" disease that they are gradually being replaced in the plantations by Trinitario trees. Given the age of the tree stock and its composition by less productive varieties, it is not possible to envisage any increase in production in the foreseeable future.

VENEZUELA

Having originated in this region, the cacao tree has been in cultivation here since the eighteenth century. With around fifteen thousand metric tons in 1999, the country currently stands ninth in terms of world production. Despite its modest production, Venezuela is an important supplier to the world market owing to the reputation of its Criollos: *chuao*, reckoned to be one of the world's finest cocoas, is the best known. Trinitario and Forastero trees are also cultivated in Venezuela.

TRINIDAD

Although the cacao tree was introduced to Trinidad in the seventeenth century, cacao cultivation produced only twelve hundred metric tons of cocoa in 1999. On the other hand, the varieties grown here are among the best in the world. The Trinitario group, a hybrid between the Criollo and Forastero groups, was first identified on Trinidad.

IN ASIA

Asian production was insignificant until the beginning of the 1970s but has rapidly increased to represent eighteen percent of the world crop in 1999. Peasant cultivation developed in Indonesia after 1970, and large-scale plantations were established in Malaysia. However, their production fell abruptly at the end of the 1980s.

INDONESIA

Cacao cultivation was introduced to Indonesia in the sixteenth century, and the Criolla entered Java in 1670. Indonesia ranked third in the world in 1999, with production of 355,000 metric tons; in 2000, it outstripped Ghana to take second place. With the exception of the Javanese Criollos, Indonesian cocoa beans are of middling quality and used above all for the extraction of cocoa butter. Indonesian cacao cultivation can draw on many advantages, including abundant labor and the paucity of diseases affecting the trees. These explain the extent of its upsurge.

THE MARKETPLACE IN COCOA

Among agricultural commodities exchanged in international markets, cocoa ranks third, after sugar and coffee. The 2.6 million metric tons produced in the world represent a turnover of $4 billion.

Cocoa is subject to the law of supply (the harvest) and demand (consumers), and it is priced on the commodity markets in Paris, New York, and, above all, London. The very large fluctuations in price reflect the tensions between the producing and processing countries. Their regular decline is capable of inducing planters to burn a portion of their crop, and certain countries are ready to move out of cocoa in favor of other, more profitable crops (spices, opium poppies, coca, etc.) In this respect, Peru is the only country to be replacing coca (the crop from which cocaine comes) with cacao trees. Here the government has put in place an aggressive anti-drugs campaign, and forty percent of the cocas have been destroyed with the support of American chocolate-making industries such as Hershey and Mars.

State organizations have long intervened to manage the channels through which the cocoa market functions. Over the last decade or so, plans of structural adjustment have been pushing these organizations to limit their interventions to matters of agricultural policy, though the situation still varies greatly from one country to another. In Africa, market liberalization in the producing countries is effecting a profound and rapid evolution in the socio-economic environment of the cocoa market. The consequences of this evolution are the emergence of organizations of producers and the establishment of manufacturing facilities to convert the beans into half-finished products in the very places where they have been grown.

THE EVOLUTION OF COCOA PRODUCTION

Over the next ten to fifteen years, various problems threaten possible stagnation, if not even a significant contraction, of cocoa production.

First, there are insufficient forest zones to continue extensive cultivation practices. The classic development of cacao cultivation has depended on fallow forestland with its very high fertility.

Noteworthy, too, is an appreciable disengagement on the part of planters, deterred by low prices, political problems in some countries, and market liberalization.

Phytosanitary problems are equally important. These affect all the producing countries, though the various zones of cultivation each have their own specific parasite profile. Production levels are always going to be subordinate to particular countries' capacity to contain the advance of parasites.

Lastly, plantations are getting older, and as they become less fertile, they will produce less. Of course, research is going on to render the cacao tree more resistant to disease and parasites, but this is unlikely to be enough to fully offset the drop in production that is already on the horizon.

chocolate every which way

for centuries, people have shown great ingenuity in transforming the cocoa bean. From the *tchocolatl* of the Aztecs to the refined chocolate of today, this marvel of a product has evolved through various forms, colors, and presentations for the greater pleasure of gourmets.

Chocolate alchemy

The beans arrive in sacks at the chocolate maker's. They then undergo multiple transformations before turning into the chocolate that will be the craftsman's material.

WIDE-AWAKE SENSES

In this business, you need lots of sensitivity. A sensitive nose, a sensitive palate ... but also a sensitive ear, to hear the beans begin to sing when they are fully roasted.
Maurice Bernachon, 1995

This delicate alchemy invariably goes through the following stages

Cleaning eliminates all the impurities that may have gotten mixed up with the beans during harvesting and depodding, i.e., stones, scraps of pod, metallic debris, and a variety of foreign bodies.

The beans are then torrefied (roasted) for ten to thirty minutes in huge turning spheres at a temperature of 250 to 185 degrees Fahrenheit. The length and intensity of roasting depends on the beans' origin and the nature of the final product. Throughout the roasting process it is important to see that they do not scorch (which would make for an unpleasant burnt taste) and that the heat actually bursts the bean shells. The roasting process gives the beans their characteristic brown color and enables the aromas to develop.

The next stage is crushing, i.e., the reduction of the cocoa beans to smaller and smaller pieces, having first separated them from their shells by means of extremely powerful fans. The broken pieces thus obtained are known as "nibs."

STÉPHANE BONNAT STILL USES THIS LATE 19TH-CENTURY WINNOWER TO SORT AND CLEAN THE COCOA BEANS BY FAN.

The crushing process goes on to transform the nibs into a liquid paste known as cocoa mass. This is then refined by a process in which the grains of cocoa are reduced still further until they are very fine. The liquid cocoa is then mixed with sugar, cocoa butter, and vanilla: this is the process of malaxation, or kneading. At this stage it is possible, if desired, to add powdered milk and/or filberts (also known as hazelnuts).

A second round of crushing, or lamination, is effected in a cylinder crusher. This reduces still further the size of the grains (to a diameter less than 30 microns) and very closely blends the fatty and non-fatty elements together, which gives the chocolate greater smoothness.

The mixture thus obtained turns for some hours, or even days, at a constant temperature between 140 and 180 degrees Fahrenheit in huge pans called *conches*. This phase contains two stages. Stage one comprises a dry "conching," in which the friction between the cocoa particles and the sugar facilitates the smoothing off of sharp angles, while stage two, the liquid conching, involves the addition of cocoa butter. This essential operation allows all the basic ingredients to be mixed to perfection, to evaporate remaining excess water, and, above all, to round off the remaining particles in order to allow the chocolate to become fully smooth and unctuous. At this stage, one-half percent lecithin is added to improve the liquidity and homogeneity of the mixture. The chocolate is then pumped into tankers and transported to other chocolate plants for further processing.

The chocolate mass thus obtained is then tempered by being subjected to a precise temperature regime in order to attain regular breaking quality, a shiny appearance, and good storage quality.

The last stage is the molding. The chocolate is poured into plastic molds set into a vibrating surface, which ensures that the paste is evenly distributed and that air-bubbles are removed. The molds then pass through a cold tunnel, where the chocolate contracts and crystallizes. It can then be cleanly removed from the molds in blocks of ten pounds or in slabs ready for packaging.

THE ORIGIN OF THE WORD "CONCH"
Years ago, the vats were shaped like seashells (concha in Spanish), hence the word "conch."

LES GRANDS CRUS
DU CACAO

THE GRANDS CRUS DE CACAO LINE
DEVELOPED BY THE CHOCOLATE MAKERS
BONNAT, VOIRON (FRANCE).

Dark chocolate

Chocolate is legally defined in terms of dark or black (*noir*) chocolate. It is necessarily derived from cocoa beans, cocoa paste, cocoa powder, and sugar, with or without the addition of cocoa butter. In Europe, until application of the European Union Directive adopted in June 2000, the only added vegetable fat permitted was cocoa butter.

Dark-chocolate lovers have begun to look to the wine world for their rites and vocabulary. They therefore now speak of *crus* (growths), *terroirs* (defined growing zones), and associations of *terroirs*. The creativity of chocolate craftsmen and the push of industrialists for quality, driven by the ever more refined and exacting demands of gourmet consumers, have led to insistence on pure, single-origin cocoas. In France, the first craftsman to offer a line of Grands Crus de Cacao was Raymond Bonnat in 1984, marking the hundredth anniversary of the foundation of his chocolate factory. Valrhona, meanwhile, was the first supplier to professionals (and private customers) to orient its marketing toward cocoa *crus*. From 1985 on, the firm used terms normally reserved for the world of wine tasting when encouraging its customers to consider their sensory responses to the product. Nowadays, there are many craftsmen who label their ganaches and chocolate bars according to the specific origins of the cocoa used in their manufacture. The use of such subtleties of vocabulary has slowly educated chocolate lovers. Industrialists have realized this and have quickly followed the lead given by chocolate craftsmen by marketing "pure origin" chocolate bars and placing them in all the supermarkets.

DARKER AND DARKER

A study of dark chocolate bars reveals how the product has evolved. Less popular in terms of volume than milk chocolate, it is decked in colors indicating luxury (black and gold or black and red). The fashion for the "darker and darker," which often confuses the percentage of cocoa with indicators of quality, is responsible for new products that rely upon their numerical rating (70% to 99% cocoa) more than on the chocolate itself. The names of these bars all suggest the same intensely dark character: Noir Dégustation, Folie Noire, Noir de Noir, Noir Extra-Amer, etc.

PUR CRU (SINGLE GROWTH)

Where French craftsmen led, the industrialists followed. Because knowledge of the exact *terrroir* of origin endows confidence, single-growth chocolate (derived from cocoa beans all grown together in one place) are filling supermarket shelves and sending the consumer on exotic travels. These brands now promote themselves in language drawn from the world of the gourmet, with a sprinkling of sensuous adjectives.

PURE PLANTATION (SINGLE ESTATE)

With their single-estate chocolate bars, Valrhona and Michel Cluizel sell themselves as chocolate specialists: every bar speaks of a plantation and its last harvest. As you eat the dark chocolate, you become a cocoa *gringo*: you go traveling.

THE FIRST YEAR-DATED CHOCOLATE
Valrhona launched the first year-dated chocolate in 1999. Restricted to the 1998 crop, the best beans from a single plantation, Gran Couva in Trinidad, were selected for a product of not more than six tons. In 1999, the fine cocoa-bean harvest of the village of Chuao, in the Arragua valley in northern Venezuela, was also used to create a year-dated product.

A few definitions

Cru (or growth): *A product developed in a particular region and special to it. Like the grape varieties in the wine world, so cocoa has its three varieties: the Criollo, the Forastero, and the Trinidad.*

Terroir: *Again, as with wine, where the cocoa is grown will closely affect the quality of the finished product. The type of soil, the aspect, the atmosphere, not forgetting the strictness of the grower's methods—these all make a difference.*

Year: *The year of the cocoa crop used in a particular chocolate.*

Milk chocolate

Milk chocolate is the type most eaten throughout the world. Even in France, where dark chocolate has received its highest accolades, milk chocolate remains the favorite of children, who love it for its soft consistency and sweet taste. It provides the coating of the majority of bars and candies aimed at young consumers.

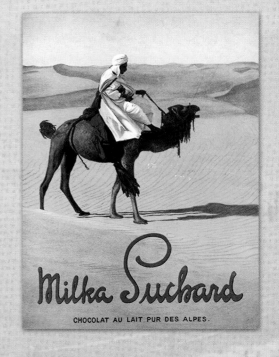

COCOA IN THE SWISS ALPS

First marketed in 1905, the earliest bars of milk chocolate launched the perennial image of Swiss chocolate: a herd of cows with a herdsman against a Swiss mountain background. Ever since, milk chocolate has been a source of Swiss national pride, not on account of its cocoa content, which is not mentioned on the bars, but for its milk, the quintessential local product, whose reputation is linked with the mountains and the cows that feed on its lush, green grass. Swiss milk chocolate is all about the taste of Alpine pastures and has nothing to do with equatorial plantations. You might even think the cacao tree grew in the Alps ...

Meanwhile the edelweiss, that other strong symbol of Helvetic cultivation, has often been used on chocolate bars. As it is a rare, protected plant that grows only at high altitudes, the implication is that milk likewise is a precious gift that comes to us from nature.

COWS OF MANY COLORS

The cows shown on French bars are full of color: children's drawings, cutouts, or patchworks of squares of chocolate, for example. In a similar vein, Lanvin has drawn inspiration from Salvador Dali with a somewhat surrealist cow. It is true that, in an advertisement that is still famous, the genial artist said he was "Crrrrrrazy about Lanvin chocolate." As for the Swiss, they experienced a warm, hair-ruffling breeze blowing over their cherished mountains when Suchard put a mauve cow on their Milka chocolate in 1972.

GRAND CRU MILK CHOCOLATE

Valhrona were the first to launch a milk chocolate bar (Jivara) showing a map of South America with a text stating the percentage of cocoa in the chocolate. With the wrapper for its Lait Arriba bar created in 2000, Nestlé achieved the impossible in enabling the Swiss to forget their Alpine pastures and sacred Swiss cows. On the outside label an Aztec mask pointed to the origins of the *"pur cru fruité"* (literally, "fruity single origin"). For a Swiss milk chocolate bar to invoke an *arriba* cocoa bean means that a revolution in taste is well underway.

FOR A LONG TIME, THE MOST IMPORTANT INGREDIENT IN MILK CHOCOLATE WAS, WELL, MILK. BUT THE CURRENT CRAZE FOR DARK CHOCOLATE IS EQUALLY CHANGING MILK CHOCOLATE, NOW ENJOYING ITS SECOND YOUTH. RELIEVED OF ITS EXCESSES OF SUGAR AND FAT, IT IS ENTERING THE WORLD OF GASTRONOMES, TRUMPETING ITS BEANS' ORIGINS AND ITS PERCENTAGE OF COCOA. TODAY, HAVING RECONQUERED THE HEARTS OF ADULTS AND COCOA-BEAN PURISTS, MILK CHOCOLATE TAKES PRIDE IN ITS COCOA-NESS.

MARBLED CHOCOLATE

Yves Thuriès is the first to have launched slabs of marbled chocolate, made either of a mix of chocolates of differing colors—dark chocolate marbled with milk or white chocolate marbled with dark—or a mixture of flavors, i.e., marbling with mint, vanilla, or mocha.

White chocolate

From a legal point of view, white chocolate has to contain at least 20% cocoa butter, 14% dry matter of lactic origin, and 55% sugar. The cocoa butter extracted from the pod is the only ingredient that makes it legitimate to be indetified as chocolate, while 25% cocoa is actually needed to merit the term. Thus white chocolate is a usurper. It is not chocolate proper but a mix of fat and sugar, which is pleasing above all to children. It is, however, used in patisserie, often to offset other flavors. The Belgians use it to coat some of their pralines.

Filled chocolate bars

The chocolate contained in the filled bar must be at least one fourth of the total weight of the product. The filling may be fruit, marzipan, nougat, various flavored creams, etc.

This category also includes bars enriched with filberts (hazelnuts), puffed rice, raisins, honey, or nougat. The most interesting innovation of recent years is unquestionably the use of cocoa nibs. It was the great Paris chocolate maker Michel Chaudun who in 1993 had the idea of adding cocoa nibs to the chocolate. It was something of a taste revolution: the splinters of the roasted, crushed beans give the chocolate an unaccustomed internal contrast, as their light crunchiness and subtle bitterness develop a long toasted finish in the mouth. Michel Chaudun exploited his innovation for a year and then sold it to the chocolate manufacturers Weiss. Today the best chocolate makers and principal manufacturers have taken up the idea ...

Chocolate candies

BOUCHÉES, BÛCHÊTTES, AND OTHER MARVELS

The shapes and names of chocolate candies vary from country to country and region to region. In general, they are called simply *chocolats* in France, *bouchées* (literally, "mouthfuls") in Switzerland, and *pralines* in Belgium. Certain specialties have acquired special names in France.

As its name indicates, a **bouchée** is supposed to need no more than to be put in the mouth (this one is for gluttons). It weighs anywhere between three-fourths and two ounces and is often praline-filled.

Crottes en chocolat (literally, "chocolate droppings") are traditionally given to well-behaved children on Saint Nicholas' Day. According to legend, the shape of these small, dense chocolate drops recall the droppings left by the saint's donkey ...

Orangettes are chocolate-coated pieces of crystallized orange peel.

The **palet d'or** (literally, "golden quoit") is the only regional specialty that has become a generic term in chocolate. Bernard Sérardy, a chocolate crafts-man at Moulins in the Allier department, created the recipe in 1898. Flat and irregular in shape, it is chocolate filled with a coffee ganache; the fine, bitter coating is decorated with a fragment of real gold leaf. Since 1977, Evelyne and Jean Jarrigues have continued to use the original recipe in Bernard Sérardy's former store, now a listed building.

The **truffe** (or "truffle") is named after the famous Périgord fungus whose rough and earthy appearance it mimics. This ball of ganache rolled in bitter cocoa powder is supposed to have been created by Louis Dufour, a patisserie maker at Chambéry, in 1895.

Bûchettes ("little logs"), **rochers** ("rocks"), **roseaux** ("reeds"), **paillettes** ("flakes"), and **bâtons** ("sticks") all take their names from the natural world. **Sarments** ("vine shoots"), **bouchons** ("stoppers"), **escargots** ("snails"), and **menhirs** (the Celtic monoliths of Brittany) all allude to French regional heritage.

Ideally, the filling in chocolates runs to 75% of the total weight. The coating (the covering chocolate) needs to be made carefully: too thick and it will mask the flavors in the filling; too thin and it will not fulfill its protective role, especially if the filling is cream-based. Finally, the coating needs to harmonize with what is inside, since an overly bitter flavor will mask the subtlety of the filling, while excessive sugar will upstage it and disappoint the gourmet.

Filling options

CARAMEL

Caramel is made from sugar, glucose syrup, milk, and aromatic products such as dried fruits and nuts, chocolate, or coffee. Milk, butter, or cream, if cited on the label, have to constitute at least five percent of the finished product. Caramel ought not to be so hard that it solidifies with the coating: it should remain unctuous. On the other hand, it will not keep well if it is too soft. The flavoring (vanilla, coffee, chocolate) should be a natural product and sufficiently strong to avoid developing a sweetish taste that could become sickly.

CHERRIES IN BRANDY

It is necessary to choose round, fleshy, light-colored cherries of a sort whose substance will not harden during the period of conservation in alcohol. Before being coated in chocolate, they are carefully pitted and then soaked in melted sugar flavored with good-quality kirsch. The sugar then hardens over the fruit. These candies need to be kept for a certain period before eating so that the alcohol in the cherries can dissolve the sugar coating.

CREAM
Cream is the filling needing the most careful handling. It has to be heated with care during cooking to retain its smooth character.

FEUILETTÉ
This generally consists of alternating layers of cooked sugar and praline.

FONDANT
Sugar is cooked and beaten to make a butter-cream; it is essential to use only natural flavorings.

FRUITS AND NUTS
Dried and crystallized fruits are often used in chocolate candies. The roasting of almonds and filberts (hazelnuts) is a particularly important stage, requiring considerable attention in order to obtain maximum taste yet avoid bitterness. Citrus peel and pineapple need to spend time in syrup prior to being chocolate-coated.

GANACHE
Ganache is a delicate cream made by the hot mixing of dairy cream and chocolate. The resulting flavor marries the richness of cream with the flavor of chocolate. It may be used as it is or with uncomplicated flavorings added. Storage is problematic and of limited duration.

GIANDUJA
This is a milk chocolate praline, where the taste of finely crushed filbert (hazelnut) predominates.

LIQUEURS
Craft manufacture of liqueur chocolate candies is so delicate that it requires highly specialized labor, which explains why the process was quickly industrialized. The chocolate coating needs to be neither too fragile nor too thick because otherwise the sugar would crystallize.
The industrial process consists in filling previously molded chocolate cavities with liqueur and then capping them. Only high-class liqueurs produce good quality candies.

HONEY
Honey is sweeter than sucrose and is chiefly used as a flavoring.

NOUGAT
The nougat paste used to fill chocolates contains sugar, egg white, honey, almonds, and sometimes pistachios.

Playing at being grown up

Chocolate cigarettes are presented in packs that look like real ones, the tobacco manufacturers having permitted the candy makers to reproduce their trade name or logo ... American pediatricians are pleading for these delights to be banned, a study having shown that the children who eat them face two times more risk than others of becoming smokers. Chocolate cigarettes are banned in Canada, the United Kingdom, Finland, Norway, and Australia but are still on sale in France and the United States. Numerous trade names also manufacture chocolate cigars aimed at adults ...

Chocolate coins and other medal forms are also very popular. Perhaps this custom has come down to us from the Aztecs, who used cocoa beans as money. It is worth noting that, with the launch of the euro, chocolate euro coins have appeared on the market ...

NOUGATINE

Nougat is a mixture of caramelized sugar and nuts, mainly almonds or filberts (hazelnuts). The nuts should represent at least 30% of the total.

ALMOND PASTE

Almond paste is made of cooked sugar and blanched almonds. Careful storage is required as it easily ferments.

PRALINE

This is a fifty-fifty composition of sugar and almonds (or of sugar and hazelnuts). The nuts have to be roasted on a low heat, while the sugar lightly caramelizes. This delicate operation is what gives the praline its final taste.

Chocolate Coatings

Chocolate coatings are used by chocolate and candy makers, cookie makers, and makers of patisserie in order to put a chocolate finish on the merchandise. The marriage of the chocolate finish with the other ingredients draws on the intelligence and taste of the craftsman. Some chocolate makers make their own coatings, while others buy them from manufacturers.
In France, the main suppliers of chocolate coatings are Barry-Callebaut, Valrhona, and La Chocolaterie de l'Opéra.

Barry-Callebaut is the world's leading converter of cocoa beans. Owned by the Swiss concern Klaus J. Jacobs, the group was formed by the amalgamation in 1996 of Cacao Barry, a French firm, with Callebaut, a Swiss company (originally Belgian). It converts eleven percent of the world crop and retains thirty-five percent of the market in products supplied for professional use. Barry-Callebaut is responsible for over six hundred chocolate coatings (forty percent of the European market), as well as half-finished products such as cocoa powder and cocoa butter.

Valrhona was established in 1922 under the name La Chocolaterie du Vivarais by a patissier in Tournon. Today the company employs 250 people and makes 3,900 tons of chocolate a year. Valrhona mainly makes chocolate coatings for chocolate makers and makers of patisserie. It is supplied by a multitude of small plantations from the Caribbean

to Indonesia. These can only supply limited quantities; their crop receives intensive attention, and the cocoa quality is extremely high, permitting the production of coatings endowed with remarkable flavor and finesse. This firm was the first to supply professionals with Grand Cru coatings. Since then, makers of chocolate coatings in France have tended to sell pure or single-origin products (i.e., coming from one defined regional source), while everywhere else in the world chocolate coatings continue to be made from blending cocoa from a variety of sources.

Founded in 1994 by Olivier de Loisy, a descendant of the founders of Valrhona, *La Chocolaterie de l'Opéra* immediately specialized in single-origin coatings. As the founder says, "Chocolate coaters look for aromatic content in the chocolate they use and want the manufacturing process to preserve it."

La *Chocolaterie du Pecq* (founded in 1937), the firm of *Weiss* (founded in 1882), and *DGF* (founded in 1986) also make chocolate coatings and laboratory products aimed at professional users.

DRIVEN BY DEVELOPING CONSUMER TASTE, INDUSTRIALISTS HAVE EVOLVED "SINGLE-ORIGIN" COATINGS.

BASTIONS OF TRADITION

In France, four craftsmen prepare their chocolate directly from cocoa beans.

• In Lyon, Jean-Jacques Bernachon has opted to master all the stages of making chocolate, like his father, Maurice Bernachon.

• In Voiron, Stéphane Bonnat continues the tradition inaugurated by Félix Bonnat, the founder of this famous chocolate maker—France's first—for its Grands Crus cocoas.

• In Roanne, François Pralus took over from his father, Auguste Pralus, in 1988.

• In Saint-Étienne, the firm of Weiss has continued the work begun in 1882 by Eugène Weiss, who was joined in 1907 by his father-in-law, Albert Margainne.

STÉPHANE BONNAT, WHO REPRESENTS THE FOURTH GENERATION OF CHOCOLATE MAKERS IN THE FAMOUS FAMILY, CONTINUES TO MAKE HIS CHOCOLATE FROM COCOA BEANS.

CAGED EGGS WITH OVERFLYING BIRD; DESIGN
BY CHRISTIAN CONSTANT.

Surprise, surprise ...

In Italy, it is traditional to slip a surprise into Easter eggs. So when Ferraro launched their Kinder Surprise line in 1976, it was not altogether an innovation. Their small chocolate egg opens to reveal a construction toy designed to delight children.

Ferraro thus encouraged parents to purchase chocolate eggs all year round.

The biggest egg

From the days of Charlemagne to those of Louis XVI, a big, red bow was tied as decoration on the largest egg laid in France during Holy Week before it was given to the king.

Molded chocolate shapes

Today Easter is the period in the year when the most chocolate shapes are sold. Clocks, hens, fish, and rabbits decorated with shiny ribbons then invade the store windows. These miniature subjects go on to charm the palates of small and large candy lovers alike.

The molding of chocolate subjects became possible in 1830, when crushers and tempering techniques appeared. Tempering involves melting the chocolate coating material at 110 degrees Fahrenheit and then letting it cool to below its crystallization threshold before reheating it to 90 degrees. The prepared material is then used to coat the internal walls of a mold maintained at 30 degrees. After cooling, the chocolate slips easily out of the mold to reveal a shiny figurine. Though rarely used except in bars, white chocolate is a precious facility for shape makers: it can be used to whiten the beard of a Santa Claus or Saint Nicholas and to create contrasts on an otherwise uniform surface, etc.

The Easter tradition comes from a number of sources. From the fifteenth century on, people would do penance by going without eggs during the forty days of Lent. The eggs laid during that period would be kept, decorated, and hidden in the bushes for children to find on Easter morning. An eighth-century legend tells how the church bells went off to Rome during Holy Week. They came back on Easter Day and, with a mighty ringing, released eggs into fields and gardens to announce their return. In Alsace and Eastern Europe, the legend was that rabbits laid Easter eggs. In subsequent centuries, as Lent became less and less strictly observed, the eggs became simply a treat.

Today's calendar offers a thousand and one opportunities to create chocolate shapes, for instance hearts for Mother's Day or Saint Valentine's Day.

Yet chocolate makers and patissiers are not always as poetic as that. Black and white chocolate soccer balls mark the soccer World Cup, and the cellular phone is another of today's icons ... no doubt to tickle the appetite of chocolate-loving chatterboxes.

CACAO
SOLUBILISÉ
CACAO
"KWATTA"
SOLUBILISÉ
FABRIQUÉ SUIVANT PROCÉDÉ ORIGINAL HOLLANDAIS
A. WILQUIN
KWATTA
RD. 677_10.080. 1-27

HOT CHOCOLATE, PREPARED FROM CHOCOLATE CHIPS, OFFERS SMOOTHNESS AND A ROBUST TASTE. MANY CRAFT CHOCOLATE MAKERS, INCLUDING HENRIET OF BIARRITZ, HAVE MADE A SUCCESS OF IT.

Hot chocolate

Symbolic of childhood, hot chocolate is charged with emotions. Adults often stay loyal to the brand name that brightened up their breakfasts as children. When they themselves become parents, they carry on the tradition by giving their own children the very hot chocolate they loved in their youth. Hot chocolate is drunk at breakfast in eighty-three percent of homes with children, which explains the large number of products on the market. Let's look at some of them here.

Nesquik (a contraction of the trade name Nestlé and "quick") is the most popular chocolate drink in the world. It is also the leading brand aimed directly at children (from six to twelve years old); its recipe, which adds a touch of cinnamon to just twenty percent cocoa, is truly instant.

For adolescents, those great lovers of chocolate bars, Nestlé in 1996 created their Lion Powder. Adopting the name and recipe of the bar marketed by Mars, the hot drink offers a special taste of caramel and cereals.

Poulain has held onto the reputation it acquired in 1904 with the launch of the famous orange tin containing its powdered *pulverisé*. Today its Grand Arûme (Big Taste) chocolate contains the highest proportion (thirty-two percent) of cocoa present in all breakfast hot chocolates.

Chocolate-flavored starchy drinks only contain a tiny proportion of cocoa; they may contain extracts of malt or banana, sugar, honey, eggs, or powdered milk. With their *chocolat à l'ancienne* (old-fashioned chocolate) Banania has revived its traditional cooking recipe for modern tastes. As the brand's marketing manager says, "At a time when newness is everywhere, you need to find a way of standing out from the crowd. Insisting on your roots and history is a powerful tool." Another example is Ovomaltine (Ovaltine): invented by a Swiss doctor in 1897, with its malt extracts, it remains a force to be reckoned with.

Van Houten is still the predominant brand name for bitter powdered cocoa, whether one wants a hot drink or an ingredient for a tasty recipe.

Chocolate bars and candies

Chocolate bars tend to weigh between three-fourths and two ounces; they constitute the biggest proportion of chocolate confectionery sold throughout the world. The first chocolate bar appeared on the market in 1920 (Milky Way). Others quickly followed, with a base of caramel, nougat, coconut, filberts (hazelnuts), cereals, or cookies coated in dark or milk chocolate.

First marketed in France in 1962, the Mars Bar transformed the way in which chocolate was consumed by usurping the privileged place of the chocolate slab. French memories still echo to the sound of its slogan: "*Un coup de barre, Mars, et à repart*" ("One hit with a Mars Bar, and we're off again"). The Mars group, a world leader in its sector, has been responsible for numerous bars of confectionery, including Bounty in 1960. Nestlé's first bar on the world stage, Kit-Kat, appeared in France in 1970 with three "fingers" and then acquired a fourth in 1982.

What the French colloquially call *turbiné* (pill-like candies) are also popular with children. Smarties were created in 1950, and M&Ms replaced Treets in 1987.

Chocolate desserts

MOUSSES, CREAMS, AND PATISSERIES

The first chocolate cookie recipe dates from 1691. But it was only in the nineteenth century that chocolate found its way into middle-class kitchens. It was then that chocolate *marquises*, soufflés, creams, and bavaroises all appeared.

Where food for the family is concerned, chocolate mousse remains the favorite dessert of young and old alike. *Quatre-quarts* (Victoria sponge), fondants, and cookies, all made with chocolate, have been children's snacktime favorites for decades. Chocolate tart owes its success to the contrast between the slightly sweet, crumbly pastry and the

THE ANGLO-AMERICAN WORLD IS A VAST CONSUMER OF CHOCOLATE BARS. QUICKLY BOUGHT AND NO LESS QUICKLY EATEN, THEY ARE THE SIGN OF A HURRIED WORLD THAT DOESN'T EAT WELL. CHILDREN AND ADOLESCENTS EASILY FALL PREY TO ADVERTISEMENTS FOR THIS KIND OF NIBBLING.

LA CHOCOLATERIE DE BEUSSENT LACHELLE CREATED ITS SHOE-WAX SURPRISE IN 2000. IT IS A HIGH-QUALITY CHOCOLATE SPREAD CONTAINING 52% ALMONDS AND HAZELNUTS.

Patisserie innovators

Gaston Lenôtre greatly honored chocolate patisserie by innovatively associating it with different textures and flavors. Since then, chocolate has gone on to inspire the most creative cake makers.

• The Gâteau du Président, *an imposing génoise with praline chocolate and hazelnuts, bristling with crystallized cherries and topped with chocolate chips, was designed by Maurice Bernachon to celebrate the occasion when the President of France Valéry Giscard d'Estaing gave Paul Bocuse the Legion of Honor award.*

• La Cerise sur le Gâteau *(The Cherry on the Cake), created in 1993 by Pierre Hermé, helped to revalue milk chocolate. Yan D. Pennor designed the shape of this cake, with its cherry on top.*

• *Pascal Morabito, a Parisian jeweler, had the idea of celebrating the millennium by designing a piece of jewelry. It was presented on a cake shaped like a jewel case, designed by Jean Daudignac and created by Yannick Lefort. Thus the Sésame was born, its shape inspired by the ziggurat, offering a crescendo of chocolate flavors.*

CREATED BY PIERRE HERMÉ, *LA CERISE SUR LE GÂTEAU* EXPRESSES ALL THE FINESSE OF MILKY CHOCOLATE WITH NOTES OF CARAMEL AND VANILLA.

• Croquettes de Chocolat *(Chocolate Croquettes) are always on the menu in the restaurants of the talented patissier Philippe Conticini. They are balls of chocolate, crumb-coated and fried in oil. "Pick them up and burst them between your tongue and palate," he counsels. "I love their extreme sensuality, the feelings of desire, as they roll around on the tongue, the sweetness as they urge their way towards the back of the throat. They explode in the mouth; the semiliquid, grainy chocolate flows out over the taste buds like a torrent of lava. It is a dessert that women find very pleasing."*

• *Sébastien Godard, the head patissier at Fauchon, has created the Gâteau Auguste, made of interlocking pieces whose five different chocolate flavors offer a multitude of combinations. The first cake toy.*

YANNICK LEFORT, WHOSE MACAROONS ENJOY A WORLDWIDE REPUTATION, CREATED THIS JEWEL OF A CAKE.

• *In October 2000, chefs from fifteen countries elected as their "Dessert de l'Union" ("European Union Dessert"), a chocolate and peach cake, l'Européen (The European), created by Julien Kientzler, a young French patissier from the Dalloyau school.*

bitter, unctuous ganache filling; it is today one of the favorite desserts of all chocolate devotees.

Every country and region invents its own chocolate cake. In France, the Périgord region adds walnuts, while in Nancy they add almonds. The Ardèche uses chestnuts, and the people of Alsace, like the Germans, like to add a Morello cherry filling. Brownies, imported from the United States, are a fairly dense mix of dark chocolate, pounded walnuts, and flour. The *Bûche de Noël*, or Chocolate Yule Log, is a late-nineteenth-century Parisian invention. Black Forest gâteau, German in origin, is a chocolate cookie filled with whipped dairy cream and crystallized cherries. Sacher torte, created in Vienna in 1832, was the first cake to combine chocolate with jam.

The éclair, meaning literally a "lightning flash"—because it can be eaten in a flash—remains one of France's most popular bought cakes. The chocolate sauce that is poured over the *Religieuse*—a delicious cake invented by Frascati in 1856 and supposed to resemble a nun, as the French name suggests—is enlivened by a white band of cream upon which the head sits. As this is the part of the cake most generally eaten first, you could say that they are most often decapitated ... The *Opéra*, created in Paris by Dalloyau in 1955, is a coffee and chocolate symphony of very fine layers of cookie and buttercream. The ganache-filled chocolate macaroon is one of the most delicate of cakes to achieve.

CHOCOLATE ICE CREAMS

Chocolate and vanilla ice creams are the most widely sold. But what lovers of bitter chocolate like the best is the chocolate sorbet: made with water, cocoa, and sugar, the taste is not buffered by a dairy element and is therefore on the robust side.

Ice-cream desserts are often set off with a chocolate sauce, which may be hot or cold. Profiteroles were invented in Italy in 1875, being hollow *choux* pastry balls filled with vanilla ice cream and coated with hot chocolate sauce. *Dame Blanche* (white lady) is a vanilla ice cream topped with hot chocolate.

The *Liégeoise*, which originated, as its name suggests, in the Belgian town of Liège, is made of chocolate ice cream covered with a hot chocolate sauce and topped with whipped cream. *Poire Belle-Hélène*, or Pear Hélène, owes its name to the title of Offenbach's famous operetta and consists of a pear stewed in light syrup, placed on vanilla ice cream, and topped with hot chocolate sauce.

Quelques délicieuses recettes
d'Entremets et Patisseries
au CHOCOLAT

4

world taste
in chocolate

When it comes to chocolate, the world is divided into two parts: there are the richer countries of the north that consume the chocolate and the producing countries of the equatorial zone, which have neither the means to eat it nor a climate in which it may be kept.

World consumption of cocoa has steadily increased over the past century, especially in the last fifteen years. The emergence of new markets in Eastern Europe and Asia presage an explosion in consumption over the coming decade.

In France

In twenty years French chocolate has acquired a high reputation, and consumer taste has changed. Quality dark chocolate is now considered a high-class foodstuff, which is prized for its flavor. There are ganaches galore, offering myriad savors. Three men were behind this change: Jean-Paul Aron, Maurice Bernachon, and Robert Linxe.

With his degree in philosophy and the post of director of studies at the École Pratique des Hautes Études in Paris, *Jean-Paul Aron* (1927–1988) labored to build bridges between the history of science proper on the one hand and social and cultural history on the other. Nutrition, "a pivotal area between the history of civilizations and that of the living," interested him greatly. The afternoon snacks of his childhood, comprised of a piece of bread and a small slab of chocolate, gave rise to his enthusiasm for chocolate. He was the first gourmet to use aesthetic language to praise dark chocolate and ganaches, which he described as "the most sophisticated manifestations of the art of chocolate." Part of this forerunner's contribution to the evolution in taste was that he helped to build the reputations of Maurice Bernachon and Robert Linxe.

Maurice Bernachon (1919–1999) is the chocolate maker who encouraged the French to appreciate the cocoa bean and the ganache. Son of a signalman on French Railways, he used to say that the only sins he had to confess when he was a child were sins of overfondness for food. An eschewer of fashion, he always made his own chocolate and rejected all extravagance: "Chocolate is simplicity itself. If you have beans from a good source, that's all you require. Nothing else is needed. Would you seek to modify the taste of fine clarets like Pétrus or Château-Yquem?" In the food lovers' paradise he doubtless serves his ganaches and truffles to the delight of Jean-Paul Aron, who used to say of him: "He's a man of the old days, whose zeal is rooted in love."

The chocolate maker *Robert Linxe* was dubbed the "Ganache Wizard" by Jean-Paul Aron. Born in the Basque country, the original homeland of French chocolate, Linxe is a trainer of chefs. He teaches classes on chocolate at the famous international chocolate school in Basel, Switzerland (COBA), and in 1978 he founded La Maison du Chocolat in Paris. He has also invented unsweetened chocolate, exemplified by some fifty different ganaches.

CHOCOLATE CONSUMPTION IN DIFFERENT COUNTRIES IN 1998 (IN POUNDS PER INHABITANT)

Switzerland: 22.5
Germany: 21.7
Belgium: 21.4
Denmark: 19.7
United Kingdom: 19.2
Norway: 19
Iceland: 18.3
France: 15.4
Australia: 13.3
United States: 12.2
Sweden: 11
Netherlands: 10.4
Finland: 8.8
Spain: 7.5
Italy: 3.3
Greece: 6.2
Brazil: 4.4
Japan: 4.4
(Source: Caobisco)

The Oldest French chocolate makers

DEBAUVE AND GALLAIS (1800)

WEISS (1882)

FOUQUET (1852)

THE BONNAT STORE IN 1884

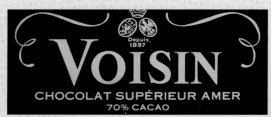

VOISIN (1897)

SIGNBOARDS OF THE HISTORIC STORE LES PALETS D'OR, ESTABLISHED AT MOULINS IN 1898.

LA MARQUISE DE SÉVIGNÉ (1898)

The chocolate hall of fame

If Aron and his two protégés have rehabilitated chocolate by giving it new prestige, many preceded them to make it what it is today.

SULPICE DEBAUVE (1759–1837)

Sulpice Debauve was a Saint-Germain-en-Laye pharmacist who studied the properties of "salep de Perse" (a starchy foodstuff derived from orchid bulbs) and cocoa. In 1800 he opened his first store in the Boulevard Saint-Germain under the sign reading "A la renommé des chocolats de France" ("The famous chocolates of France"). As an expert in medicinal chocolates, he became the appointed supplier to King Louis XVIII and subsequently to Charles X and Louis-Philippe. He was celebrated throughout Europe, where he was known for his "hygienic and tonic" chocolates. His association with his nephew Antoine Gallais encouraged the firm's development. Since 1989 Paule Cuvelier has continued the tradition of the historic chocolate makers Debauve and Gallais.

ANTOINE GALLAIS

A pharmacist, he joined his uncle, Sulpice Debauve, in 1823. By royal appointment, Sulpice was chocolate maker to the kings of France. Antoine developed dietary chocolates (so-called "hygienic chocolates"), chocolates with almond milk, and pastilles flavored with vanilla or orange blossoms. In 1827 he published his *Monographie du cacao, ou manuel de líamateur du chocolat* ("Monograph On Cocoa or The Chocolate Lover's Manual').

JEAN ANTOINE BRUTUS MENIER (1797–1853)

In 1825 this maker of pharmaceutical powders leased a mill at Noisiel on the River Marne where he used waterpower for his manufacturing operations. It was the beginning of an empire, which developed over four generations. Today the name of Menier is still linked to one of the greatest successes of the French industrial revolution.

ÉMILE JUSTIN MENIER (1826–1881)

When Émile Menier took over his father's business in 1853, the Noisiel factory chiefly made medicinal chocolates. In order to turn it over definitively to chocolate making, he bought cacao plantations in Nicaragua, chartered boats, and organized his own sugar production. His total mastery of the vertical process, constant search for technical innovation, and early understanding of the value of advertising turned his company into the "World's First Chocolate Manufacturer" at the Chicago World Fair in 1893. Although the factory closed its doors in 1959, the Noisiel site, a masterpiece of nineteenth-century architecture, is the headquarters of Nestlé-France. Since 1913, the Menier family has owned the Château of Chenonceau.

Auguste Poulain (1825–1918)

At the age of twenty-two, Auguste Poulain opened a chocolate making plant in Blois. The excellent value for money his products represented brought him instant success. In 1862 he built a factory containing the most modern machines. One of the earliest to use advertising, he fought against the imitations of which he was victim by creating the slogan "Goûtez et Comparez" ("Taste and Compare").

The genius of French chocolate makers

Excited by the nature of his material, the chocolate making craftsman is a true artist; his act of creation is the combination of his own know-how, use of the best ingredients, and the spiritual input of love and generosity without which no product can become magic. Today's French chocolate makers are recognized worldwide not only for the quality of their products but also for their talent for innovation. They are inventors of new chocolates with fruits and nuts, spices, herbs, or flowers, always on the lookout for the best coating to produce a harmonious result. Through daring combinations of flavors or textures, their creations have advanced the image and taste of French chocolate to such an extent that some are now classics. Here are the names of some of the finest names in contemporary French chocolate, together with their leading specialties:

• Francis Boucher (Paris): Perle de Cacao (Chocolate Pearl—a coffee ganache);
• Jean-Claude Briet (Prévenchères): chocolates associated with produce from the Lozère region, with meadow mushrooms, including morels, cepes, truffles; with tea from the Aubrac plateau; ganache with bison grass;
• Frédéric Cassel (Fontainebleau): dark ganache with darjeeling;
• Michel Chaudun (Paris): truffle paste with pepper; ganache with nine spices; and, most notably,

chocolate incorporating splintered and crushed cocoa nibs;
• Christian Constant (Paris): chocolate with roses and currants; chocolate with ylang-ylang from the Comores;
• Louis Dubois (Brest): La Recouvrance (a trio of different pralines); Océanopolis (with an infusion of fresh seaweed);
• Bernard Dufoux (La Clayette): chocolate foie gras (a confection of chestnuts, dark chocolate, and almonds);
• Joël Durand (Saint-Rémy-de-Provence): Chocolat Numéro 13 (lavender-flavored); Chocolat Numéro 30 (with black olives); Chocolat Numéro 33 (with notes of raspberry, blue poppy, cinnamon, and lemon zest); Chocolat Numéro 36 (with foie gras);
• Christine Ferber (Niedermorschwihr): earl-gray-flavored ganache and quince jelly coated in rose-petal-encrusted chocolate;
• Rémi Henry (Colombes): water ganache; olive oil ganache; chocolate with citrus fruits;
• Jean Jarriges (Moulins): banana ganache;
• Le Roux (Quiberon): CBS (chocolate-coated, salted butter caramel), Sarrazin (ganache with a buckwheat infusion);
• Robert Linxe (La Maison du Chocolat, Paris): Garrigue (with root fennel); Maïko (with root ginger); Zagora (with mint-flavored green tea);
• Thierry Mulhaupt (Strasbourg): raspberry ganache;
• Gérard Mulot (Paris): Mélissa (milk and licorice ganache);
• Michel Richart (Paris): curry-flavored or clove-flavored chocolates; ganache with a rose- and mimosa-petal infusion;
• Maison Saunion (Bordeaux): Vendanges (grape and almond paste under a milky coating).

CHOCOLATES WITH ROSE PETALS BY JOËL DURAND

THE FRENCH MARKET IN CHOCOLATE (1999)

Consumption:
15.4 pounds per inhabitant (94% of the French population consume chocolate at least once per week)

Turnover:
1.7 billion dollars

Product shares:
Sweetened chocolate powder: 13.6%
Slabs: 28.9%
Confectionary: 44.5%
Chocolate spreads and imitation products: 13%

CHOCOLAT KOHLER LA

In Switzerland

Switzerland discovered chocolate in 1697, later than Spain and France, but it has made up for lost time by becoming *the* land of chocolate. Since it was perfected by Daniel Peter, milk chocolate has truly come to symbolize Switzerland, its Alpine pastures, and its incomparably good-tasting milk. Based on high-quality ingredients, Swiss chocolate is well-conched and very smooth. The current move toward less sweet and more bitter chocolate is not all that evident in this country, where milk is the supreme national product. The Swiss are the largest per capita consumers of chocolate in the world, though the figures do not disclose how much chocolate is bought by foreign visitors passing through. Officially, the Swiss annually eat an average of nine pounds of solid chocolate per person and four pounds of chocolate bars and slabs of filled chocolate ... all this principally in the form of milk chocolate.

The chocolate hall of fame

FRANÇOIS-LOUIS CAILLER
(1796–1852)

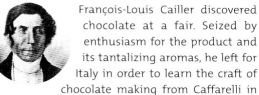

François-Louis Cailler discovered chocolate at a fair. Seized by enthusiasm for the product and its tantalizing aromas, he left for Italy in order to learn the craft of chocolate making from Caffarelli in Turin. He returned four years later to his native Switzerland, where he perfected a forerunner of the conch, a crusher that included two stone cylinders. In 1819 he opened the first Swiss chocolate factory at Corsier, near Vevey.

THE CHOCOLATE LANDSCAPE ON A SLAB OF MILK CHOCOLATE WITH RAISINS AND COINTREAU

THE FIRST GALA PETER MILK CHOCOLATE SLAB (1905)

PHILIPPE SUCHARD (1797–1884)

Philippe Suchard learned the confectionary trade from 1815 to 1824 at his brother's establishment in Berne. After a brief stay in the United States Philippe opened a confectioner's business in Neuchâtel and then in 1826 set up in Serrières. His daily production at that time amounted to some fifty-five to sixty-five pounds ... with just one worker. He was awarded gold medals at the Great Exhibitions in London (1851) and Paris (1855). In 1880 at Lörrach in Germany he opened the first foreign branch of the Swiss chocolate-making business. The famous Milka slab, still sold today worldwide, was created in 1901. A Suchard factory opened in Paris in 1903, followed by a second in Strasbourg. The Suchard firm merged with Tobler in 1974 and now is part of the Kraft-Jacobs-Suchard group.

CHARLES AMÉDÉE KOHLER (1790–1874)

Kohler was a wholesaler in colonial goods and quite naturally marketed chocolate. Beginning in 1830 he decided to make this product himself. In an effort to create his own specialties, he invented hazelnut, or filbert, chocolate. His factory later merged with that of Daniel Peter.

DANIEL PETER (1836–1919)

Peter was an apprentice to a candlemaker in Vevey when in 1863 he married the daughter of François-Louis Cailler. Becoming a chocolate maker by virtue of his marriage, he spent his evenings experimenting to find a way to combine milk with powdered cocoa. With his brother Julien, he established the name Peter, Caillier & Compagnie in 1867. Making use of the condensed milk procedure elaborated by Henri Nestlé, he invented the first milk chocolate in 1875, called it Gala-Peter, and obtained a diploma of honor at the Universal Exhibition of 1878 in Paris. In 1904 he took over the Kohler company, and the new group took the name Société Générale Suisse de Chocolats. Later the same year Peter and Kohler took direct control of the Nestlé label's milk chocolate manufacture, which at the time marketed their products, and their slabs of chocolate were finally sold under their own names in 1905. Peter, Cailler & Kohler merged in 1911 with Chocolats SA, the company then marketing Nestlé chocolates. Ever since Peter's invention, the Swiss have remained the uncontested masters of milk chocolate.

RODOLPHE LINDT (1855–1909)

Lindt was a chocolate maker in Berne who created two revolutionary manufacturing processes. First he produced the first fondant chocolate by adding cocoa butter. Second, in 1879, he perfected the process of kneading and refining the cocoa mass, namely conching. It was an innovation that put the Swiss at the forefront of European chocolate making. Rodolphe Sprüngli-Schifferli bought out the factory in 1899, but he retained the product trademark, the bust of the genial Rodolphe Lindt.

JEAN TOBLER (1830–1905)

Tobler established his chocolate-making works in 1899. Toblerone, the famous chocolate bar containing almonds and honey, dates from 1908. Tobler drew his inspiration for Toblerone from the nougat of Montélimar. The bar's triangular form, supposed to illustrate his masonic convictions, is today interpreted as no more than one of Switzerland's symbols, Mount Cervin. Millions of Toblerone bars are still eaten today throughout the world.

«Oh ! oui... une bouchée pour moi»

«Et ces trois là pour moi aussi mum...»

«Celle-là encore pour moi pour mieux savourer les amandes»

«Celles-ci pour le lait, et le miel»

«Une pour toi ? ah... trop ta

Vous avez bien droit à un petit moment d'égoïsme Toblerone.*

TOBLERONE AS ADVERTISED IN *MARIE-CLAIRE* (1972)

SWISS INDUSTRIAL GROUPS

• *Klaus J. Jacob holding company, which includes the Barry-Callebaut group, the largest cocoa-bean processor in the world.*

• *Lindt & Sprüngli: Lindt, Ghirardelli, Caffarel.*

• *Nestlé: Nestlé, Kohler, Crunch, Kit-Kat, Lion, Cailler, Quality Street, Smarties, After Eight, Nuts, Menier, Lanvin, Galak, Frigor.*

IN 1952, CHARLES TRENET HONORED
NEUHAUS CHOCOLATE IN A SONG
ENTITLED *IN THE PHARMACIES*:

In the pharmacies,
In the pharmacies,
They sell nougat
And chocolate …

In Belgium

Belgium is one of the most famous countries for chocolate. The Belgians call chocolates "pralines," and they are usually molded: chocolate is poured into small metal or plastic cavities to form a seashell that is then filled on cooling with a liquid or cream-like garnish. Finally, the chocolates travel onto a conveyor belt that takes them under a jet of liquid chocolate to close up the cavity.

Léonidas, established in 1931, is the brand with the highest sales in Belgium, but Godiva is the brand best known throughout the world. Owned since 1978 by the Campbell group, it is the brand leader in the luxury Belgian chocolate sector in the United States with over 2,500 points of sale. Godiva offers its vendors a number of collections during the year around classic themes like Saint Nicholas Day, Christmas, Saint Valentine's Day, Mother's Day, Father's Day, and so on. Though the chocolates are made in factories in Pennsylvania (for the North-American market) and in Belgium (for Europe and Asia), the firm retains a unit for handmade chocolates. The workers still use stencils to hand-produce the motif that adorns Autant chocolate

THE BELGIAN POET AND SINGER JULOS BEAUCARNE, WHOSE CONCERTS HAVE OFTEN BEEN SPONSORED BY GALLER CHOCOLATE, APPETIZINGLY DECLARES ON STAGE:

*And if poetry were chocolate
That tasting ears
Savored
Through the day and through the night
In the music of the voice
And if poetry were so good to speak
And speak again and hear and whisper low
At evening or at midnight
At midnight even sometimes
leaving in the mouth
Some chocolate to melt
With good fresh coffee
So fresh that it was green
Ah well!
If poetry were chocolate
Then I
I should call it Galler.*

and that recalls the feather in the hat that Scarlett O'Hara wore in the movie *Gone with the Wind*.

Although Belgian chocolate craftsmen all design their own pralines, certain towns have stayed loyal to historic specialties. In Antwerp, for example, you find dark, white, and milk chocolate tiny hands, recalling the legend of the Roman soldier who rid the city of a terrorizing giant. The legend tells how, after the soldier had killed the giant, he threw his hand into the river—thereby giving the town its name, in Flemish *Andwerpen*, meaning "throwing a hand."

In 1921 Kwatta created the small one- to one-and-a-half-ounce bar called a "bâton," of which the Belgians are still very fond in both filled and non-filled forms. Belgians on average eat eight pounds of these every year.

Children are enormous consumers of chocolate spreads, the most famous being Chocopasta, launched in 1960 by Côte d'Or.

The chocolate hall of fame

JEAN, FRÉDÉRIC, AND JEAN NEUHAUS

In 1857 Jean Neuhaus left his native Switzerland and settled in Brussels, where at 23 Galerie de la Reine he and his brother-in-law established a pharmaceutical confectionary. When his brother-in-law died, Jean asked his young son Frédéric, who was living in the canton of Neuchâtel in Switzerland, to come to Brussels to do his confectioner's apprenticeship. The business was then less known for its confectionary than for its pharmacy activity, but several years later Frédéric gave the firm a new direction: he gradually replaced the medicinal preparations with sugar and chocolate candies, as well as by the amalgam of almonds and burnt sugar called "praline." When he died in 1912, his son (Jean), representing the third generation, took over. He invented the first chocolate bouchées incorporating a cream filling, which he gave the name "pralines." After the First World War the store expanded. Jean's wife, Louise, who had inherited a sure artistic sense from her sculptor father, gave the establishment a highly recognizable and individual style. In 1915 she invented the "ballotin," a cardboard package that prevented the pralines from being crushed, coloring it green and gold. This is still used today, like the Napoleonic-style "N" for "Neuhaus."

The main trade names in Belgian chocolate

Côte d'Or: *This name, the French for "Gold Coast," was originated by Charles Neuhaus in 1870. The Gold Coast (today's Ghana) was the main source of the beans he used. The elephant logo has endured, as have the intense cocoa taste and particular conching style. Côte d'Or slabs are sold worldwide.*

Jacques: *Charles Delacre created his chocolate concern in Vilvoorde in 1872. The name continues and is especially recognized for its small filled bars, invented in 1930.*

Barry-Callebaut: *The Callebaut family threw itself into producing slabs and bars in 1911. Chocolate for the first time began to be transported in liquid form in tank trucks. Since 1995, when Barry was taken over, Barry-Callebaut has become the biggest supplier of chocolate to professionals in the world.*

Godiva: *Foreign sales account for seventy percent of the turnover of this firm, which has had a worldwide presence since 1929.*

Léonidas: *This brand was established in the United States in 1931 by Léonidas Kestekidès, who settled in Belgium after marrying a woman from Brussels. The firm has a worldwide reputation and markets over eighty types of pralines.*

CHOCOLATE TAGLIATELLI ARE A
VENETIAN SPECIALITY.

In Italy

In Italy hot chocolate has long had somewhat rakish associations. Casanova immortalized that velvety beverage in his writings, notably the chocolate served at the Café Florian in Venice. And indeed it is still possible to enjoy one of the best hot chocolates in the world there, in rooms whose mirrors and gilding suggest the gallant secrets of the eighteenth century. Italians have long drunk hot chocolate in their cafés. The Turin specialty, *bicerin*, is an equal mixture of coffee, chocolate, and cream. The waiter brings the three pots to the table and mixes them in a small glass (*bicerin* in Italian) according to the customer's instructions. The *bicerin pur-e-fior* mixes cream and coffee, the *pur-e-barba* coffee and chocolate, and the *po'dtut* mixes literally "a bit of each." *Bicerin* is also a paste comprising cocoa, honey, and filbert (hazelnut); it replaces sugar in coffee. *Cappuccino* (the name taken from the brown and white habit of the

Capuchin friars) is an espresso with milk and cream with cocoa scattered on top. This love of refinement around coffee is what led to the Neopolitan tradition in the luxury establishments in the Naples region of serving a small rectangle of chocolate with coffee. This custom of accompanying the "little black" spread through Europe in the early 1980s, often spurred by advertising.

Economic problems during the nineteenth century led to a scarcity of cocoa, and the need to supplement it to make up the weight lay behind the first mixture of cocoa and hazelnuts. The Gianduja and Cremino are the most typical examples.

In the twentieth century the developing Italian chocolate industry gained a reputation that went beyond its shores. Certain chocolate craftsmen, however, remain defenders of Aztec traditions, like Romanengo at Genoa, who still use *metate* to crush the chocolate.

The Italians have an almost amorous relationship with chocolate. Chocolates with hazelnuts or cherries may be bought at café counters. Chocolate Baci (Kisses)—chocolate wrapped in silver paper containing a love message—have helped to promote the Perugina firm since 1922. Finally, this family firm of Ferrero, with its ingenious marketing discoveries, has hoisted itself to fourth place in the world of chocolate products just behind the multinationals: Nestlé, Mars, and Kraft-Jacobs-Suchard.

In Italy chocolate is associated with a large number of desserts, like the zabaglione and the tart. Pan *pepato di cioccolato* is a brioche with chocolate, spices, and almonds, which is served in Ferraro as part of the midnight feast on New Year's Eve. Tiramisu, a cake comprising alternate layers of coffee-flavored cookies and mascarpone, is sprinkled with cocoa.

THE ORIGINAL CAFFAREL *GIANDUJA* BOX DEPICTED THE INDEPENDENCE
HERO WHO GAVE HIS NAME TO THIS SPECIALITY.

TAKING ITS CUE FROM HAUTE COUTURE, CAFFAREL CREATES TWO
COLLECTIONS EACH YEAR.

It was named after a traditional carnival character, *Gian d'la duja*. Since then the Gianduja has been around the world and has remained *the* symbol of Italian chocolate. Today Caffarel is one of the most prestigious trade names in Italy. The firm uses genuine taste stylists and designers to bring out two complete chocolate collections every year. Its metal tins with their relief lithography are always very stylish. Caffarel is now a part of the Lindt & Sprüngli group.

Iced desserts were certainly invented in southern Italy during the seventeenth century after the use of salt to conserve the ice had been discovered. The Italians make excellent ice creams, and these are both unctuous and tasty. The Italians were responsible for inventing chocolate profiteroles (in 1875) as well as *tartuffo*, the traditional dessert consisting of a large chocolate ice cream truffle. Chocolate and Gianduja are, needless to say, classic flavors offered by most ice cream merchants.

Ever since the eighteenth century Italy has maintained the custom of using chocolate in its kitchens, often in pasta or meat dishes. Macerata in 1786 evoked lasagne with almonds, with walnuts, and with chocolate. In Venice of today tagliatelli are sold flavored with cocoa, and in Ancona chocolate-filled ravioli are a specialty.

The chocolate hall of fame

ISIDORE CAFFAREL (1817–1867)
Isidore Caffarel's father established his chocolate business in Turin in 1826. His "tonic chocolate," flavored with cinnamon and recommended for all the family, quickly gained a solid reputation in Piedmont. In 1861 Isidore himself invented a fondant paste that mixed hazelnuts, walnuts or almonds, finely crushed, sugar, and chocolate, which he retailed in small trapezoidal ingots.

CAFFAREL CHOCOLATE SLABS DEPICT A BANK NOTE ON THE WRAPPER. IT USED TO BE IN LIRA, BUT NOW IT IS IN EUROS.

THE PROUD HISTORY OF VIENNA IS THE INSPIRATION FOR DEMEL'S CHOCOLATE WRAPPER, ILLUSTRATING EMPEROR FRANZ-JOSEF AND EMPRESS ELIZABETH.

In Austria

Austrians eat mainly milk chocolate in the form of small slabs or candies purchased individually. They are also fond of Rohkost, chocolate-coated fruits and nuts. But the preeminent symbol of Austrian chocolate is the Mozart Kügel, a chocolate candy made of pralines or *gianduja* in an almond paste, coated in dark chocolate in Salzburg and milk chocolate in Vienna. These candies are wrapped in paper embossed with Mozart's image, and their taste has given rise to a chocolate liqueur, the tiny flask of which also bears the composer's portrait. For chocolate-loving tourists these candies are found in a number of different presentations showing other Austrian celebrities such as Empress Elizabeth or Richard Strauss.

The drink known as "Viennese chocolate" is a great specialty. The traditional recipe specifies that it should thicken over a low heat because of the egg-yolk that is added to it. But in reality Viennese chocolate is now simply chocolate-flavored milk with a whipped-cream topping.

Few cities in the world can rival Vienna in its love of food. Its three passions are coffee, patisserie, and whipped cream. The Viennese observe a break mid-morning and another for their *jause*, or afternoon coffee, which is a time for cakes. These are often flavored with chocolate in either the cookie or cream-filling part or both. The most typical cakes are these:

• *Mohr im Hemd,* a chocolate cake topped with hot chocolate sauce and decorated with whipped vanilla cream;

• *Rehrücken,* a chocolate pastry studded with almonds, which is shaped like a saddle of venison (hence the name);

• *Dobos Torte,* a rich cake invented in Hungary in 1887 by the patissier Josef Dobos: alternate layers of soft pastry and chocolate cream beneath a caramel icing;

• *Imperial Torte,* a square cake invented by a patissier in service to Emperor Franz-Josef in which fine layers of almond paste and chocolate cream are laid on top of one another;

• *Indianerkrapfen*: choux pastry filled with chocolate whipped cream.

FRONT OF THE HOTEL-PATISSERIE IN VIENNA

BOX OF THE ORIGINAL DEMEL TORTE

Sacher versus Demel

The most celebrated of Austrian pastries remains the Sacher Torte, *invented in Vienna in 1832 by an apprentice to Prince Metternich. This chocolate cake with apricot jam is the finest possible demonstration to the world of the Viennese art of living. It was the occasion of a court battle between the descendants of Franz and Edward Sacher and the famous patisserie Demel's (founded in 1786). Both sides maintained that they had inherited the genuine recipe: the Sacher version had the jam layer in the middle of the cake, whereas the Demel version believed it should be under the icing. In 1962 the Supreme Court ruled in favor of the Sacher version, but the battle goes on. Demel's is nonetheless the best patisserie in all of Austria.*

In Germany

Germany today is the second largest producer of chocolate in the world. Huge consumers of confectionary, the Germans like sweet chocolates, non-filled slabs, and chocolate spreads. Recent interest in the finer points of wine making has prompted a discovery of crus in cocoa and enthusiasm for very bitter chocolate; it is worth recalling that it was the Germans who in 1920 invented brandy-flavored chocolate.

Hot chocolate in Germany was at one time made from cocoa dissolved in Spanish wine with pepper added. Tastes have gradually moved on; today liquid chocolate is mixed with milk, vanilla, sugar, cinnamon, salt, and pepper.

The Germans are extremely fond of chocolate pastries. Their best-known cake is Black Forest Gâteau. Originally from that region, so proud of its almond-scented bitter cherries, Black Forest Gâteau consists of chocolate génoise, small Morello cherries macerated in alcohol, and whipped cream.

PACK OF COCOA POWDER WITH ILLUSTRATION RECALLING LIOTARD'S FAMOUS PASTEL, *LA BELLE CHOCOLATIÈRE*.

In Great Britain

Great Britain is today the third largest producer of finished chocolate products in the world. Fry, Cadbury, and Rowntree are the three chocolate-making dynasties whose products have regaled the British since the nineteenth century. The rare chocolate craftsmen active in the country flavor their creations in a very traditional British way, and these do little to upstage the industrialized products, which are consumed in large volumes.

In general, the English like their chocolate oily and sweet. They eat lots of chocolate bars, slabs, and candies. They also produce a caramel milk chocolate (*crumb*). Cookie making is an English specialty that goes back a long way, and the British are masters in the lithographic decoration of packaging. Some of their desserts may be chocolate flavored and may even be accompanied by a chocolate sauce.

The chocolate hall of fame

JOSEPH FRY (1728–1787)

John Fry was a pharmacist in Bristol when in 1761 he bought a cocoa bean processing factory from one Walter Churchman. In 1847 Fry's succeeded in molding the first chocolate slab, and in 1866 he created its chocolate cream bar, which is still on the market. When Joseph Storrs Fry took over in 1878, Fry's was the largest chocolate manufacturer in Great Britain, making almost one quarter of the chocolate sold there. Cadbury bought out the firm Fry & Sons in 1920.

JOHN CADBURY (1801–1889)

John Cadbury opened a tea, coffee, and chocolate shop in Birmingham in 1824. Seven years later he began manufacturing chocolate himself. The partnership that he forged in 1847 with his brother Benjamin laid the foundations of what would become the leading trade name in confectionary in Great Britain. When Chocolate Essence was created in 1866, Cadbury received the highest praise from the medical authorities. John Cadbury, who dreamed of blazing a trail similar to the French industrialist Menier, copied his social policy by building a workers' township, Bournville. Dairy Milk, launched in 1905 and easily recognizable by its caramelized sugar taste, remains England's favorite milk chocolate. As for Cadbury's Chocolate

"I HEAR YOU ARE DASHING IT ON YOUR WAR BONUS!" IS THE CAPTION TO THIS POSTCARD EVOKING THE RESTRICTIONS OF THE SECOND WORLD WAR.

Fingers, they are probably to England what Camembert and *saucisson sec* are to France ...

JOSEPH ROWNTREE (1836–1925)

Joseph Rowntree founded the firm that bears his name in 1862, and in the very early twentieth century he constructed a workers' village on the outskirts of York. The firm remains famous for having created Smarties (1937) and After Eights (1962), thin sleeves of chocolate filled with mint cream.

Cadbury and Rowntree were instigators of a whole reorganization of world cocoa production. Their Quaker convictions, supported by their German and American allies, led them to boycott cocoa grown in countries that used slave labor.

In Spain

The Spanish have been drinkers of hot chocolate ever since the Conquest of the New World. This explains their large consumption of powdered cocoa, even if they do also enjoy solid chocolate bars. On the other hand, it is surprising that this country, which introduced chocolate to Europe and, in 1772, had 150 millers of chocolate, has not retained a chocolate making tradition.

THIS SLAB OF CREFER CHOCOLATE EVOKES WORKING WITH THE METATE, AS IN THE TIME OF THE AZTECS.

MARIJUANA-FLAVORED
CHOCOLATE, OPENLY SOLD
IN THE NETHERLANDS

In the Netherlands

In perfecting the manufacture of powdered cocoa in 1828, Coenraad Johannes Van Houten gave his country an importance in the world of chocolate that he could still take pride in today. The Netherlands is the second largest importer of cocoa beans in the world, and more cocoa passes through Amsterdam than through any other port. The Dutch drink a lot of hot chocolate, encouraged maybe by the harsh winters they have to endure. Powdered cocoa is sold in lithographed metal tins or carton packages illustrated with all the archaic charm of the nineteenth century.

In the Netherlands, chocolate is an integral part of social and religious life. A Saint Nicholas Day feast without chocolate is simply unthinkable. Christmas cakes, small crowns filled with chocolate, help to compensate for that time of the year when the days are so short. Children love to sprinkle their bread and butter with granules of either dark or milk chocolate (*hagelslag*), and chocolate coins in silver paper are greatly loved by them.

Although Koster, sometimes creates with the invention of movable type in printing, has a memorial in Haarlem, the inventor of chocolate letters is anonymous. The industrial production of this Dutch specialty is reminiscent of creative craftsmanship. With their original and varied forms, these chocolate letters combine aesthetics

Eternally Droste

Around 1904 Gérard Droste must have seen Jean-Étienne Liotard's painting La Belle Chocolatière, *the image of a perfect servant bearing a glass of water and a cup of chocolate on a tray. Hardly anyone knew the picture that inspired Droste, but everyone delighted in the version he had an unknown draftsman's make of it: a gleaming nurse whose tray bears no medicines, only chocolate. The slogan "Droste, eternally yours" on the cocoa box is conveyed by the picture of the nurse bearing a tray on which the same cocoa box sits depicting the same nurse, who is bearing a similar tray similarly bearing the same box. The implied message of this image is: there's no getting away from it. Once you've tasted Droste, you can't live without it!*

with pleasing the palate. Giving ... a sweetheart her (or his) name in chocolate letters is almost like saying, "I could eat you."

The Dutch have always had a certain taste for dark chocolate (Droste pastilles are the confectionary with the highest sales), but they are nevertheless large consumers of chocolate bars.

The chocolate hall of fame

COENRAAD JOHANNES VAN HOUTEN (1801–1887)

Van Houten settled in Amsterdam in 1815, where he was assisted by a German chocolate specialist. In 1828 he patented a process for making powdered chocolate. Inspired by a technique described as early as 1679 by Nicolas de Blégny, Van Houten designed a press capable of extracting cocoa butter. His invention meant that ordinary people could now enjoy hot chocolate, which hitherto had been the preserve of the rich. Ever since, the Netherlands has been the world specialist in bitter cocoa powder.

In the United States

The United States is the largest producer of chocolate in the world and is above all the nation of the chocolate bar. The Kraft-Jacobs-Suchard group comprises the names Suchard, Milka, Toblerone, Daim, and Côte d'Or, whereas Mars, M&Ms, Milky Way, Snickers, Twix, and Bounty belong to the Mars group. A vestige of the Prohibition era is the ban on chocolates filled with spirits or liqueurs, except in Kentucky and Tennessee (where bourbon, the local specialty, is used), as well as in Nevada. Brownies, dense cookies with chocolate and nuts (often pecans), are very popular. Americans like chocolate layer cake, which has the charm of an old-

HUNGRY, ANYONE?

During the world championship boxing match in 1997 Mike Tyson bit off a piece of Evander Holyfield's ear. Two Californian patissiers, the brothers Sepulveda, had the idea of making a chocolate version of the famous ear. Their slogan urged customers not to stop at one only.

fashioned cake and is made from a filled chocolate crumb cake, covered with chocolate icing. Devil's food cake, chocolate fudge, and chocolate chip cookies are also mainstream favorites throughout the country.

The chocolate hall of fame

MILTON SNAVELY HERSHEY (1857–1945)

Milton Hershey was born into a family of Swiss Mennonites who had settled in Pennsylvania in the early eighteenth century. Already a manufacturer of candies and milk caramels, he launched into cocoa-bean processing in 1900. In 1903 he began building his factory in Hersheyville, a genuine town that reproduces the world geography of cocoa on an urban scale. Today Hersheyville is home to six thousand workers' families and has a theme park dedicated to chocolate. There is even a beauty and health center at the Hershey Hotel where cocoa is used therapeutically in body treatments. Hershey Bars, made of thin dark chocolate, and Hershey's Kisses are the largest selling candies in the United States.

In Mexico

In Mexico's craft markets, *metate* and foamers still figure among the household utensils on sale. Thick rounds of raw chocolate, as hard as stone, are sold in all markets; once melted they yield a thick, rustic chocolate flavored with cinnamon and vanilla. Certain regions have retained their traditional recipes. *Champurrado*, for example, is a hot chocolate made of *atolle*, an age-old corn-based porridge, and chocolate, flavored with brown sugar and cinnamon, which is drunk in the region of Mitla. *Tejate* is an iced drink much appreciated in the markets and popular festivals of the region of Oaxaca; it is prepared in vast earthenware bowls with, among other ingredients, corn, cinder, peeled cocoa beans, cacao flowers, sugar, and oil palm seeds.

Mole poblano, which remains Mexico's national dish, was invented in the seventeenth century by Carmelite sisters in Puebla. The marriage of cooking and celestial voices no doubt explains the particular flavor of this pimento and chocolate sauce, which generally accompanies turkey or chicken. It is a dish that is hard to escape on Christmas Eve in Mexican households.

In Asia

Sweet flavors have long been ignored in Asia, and chocolate has only recently made an entry into Asian food habits. This has been because of chocolate bars, which symbolize, along with other things, the American way of life.

Japan: tradition ...

In Japan, food connoisseurs pay a lot for dark, not too sweet, chocolates, which they buy singly. French chocolate makers are much thought of; hence the success of the Salon du Chocolat, imported by the French agency Event International.

Chocolate sold on Saint Valentine's Day, a celebration launched in Japan by chocolate makers in the 1950s, represents currently more than sixty percent of the total consumption of chocolate in Japan. In this country, where social customs are highly codified, including those relating to matters of love, on February 14 each year female office workers give *giri choco*, the "chocolates of duty," to their male colleagues, and girls give their sweethearts *honmei choco*, the "chocolates that come from the heart." By rights, the happy beneficiaries of these gifts are supposed to respond with a small gift, exactly one month later, on the "white day."

China: a sweet tooth ...

China, too, has recently discovered a taste for sugar, confectionary, and chocolate. In large towns the growing consumption of bars, candies, and chocolate wafers reflects American influence. A new market is opening.

COCOA IN TWENTY-SIX LANGUAGES

French, Spanish, Italian, Romanian, Dutch: cacao

English: cocoa

Portuguese: cacau

German, Swedish, Danish, Norwegian, Polish, Czech, Serbo-Croatian, Hungarian, Turk, Esperanto, Russian: kakao

Finnish: kaakao

Indonesian: joklat bubuk

Greek: kakaio

Arabic: kakawe

Hebrew, Yiddish: kako

Japanese: kokoa

Swahili: mbegu za mti cacao

... AND TWENTY-SIX LANGUAGES FOR CHOCOLATE

French: chocolat

English, Spanish, Portuguese: chocolate

Italian: cioccolata

Romanian: ciocolata

German, Yiddish: schokolade

Dutch: chocolade

Swedish: choklad

Danish: chokolade

Norwegian: sjokolade

Polish: szekolada

Czech, Serbo-Croatian: cokolada

Hungarian: csokolade

Finnish: suklaa

Turkish: cikolata

Indonesian: tjoklat

Esperanto: cokolado

Russian: shokalat

Greek: sokola'ta

Arabic: shoukoulata

Hebrew: schokolad

Japanese: chokoreeto

Swahili: chokolati

5
chocolate, from fashionable to universal

the universality of chocolate makes it a unique food. Whether as an energy-giving breakfast drink, dessert, or snack, a symbol of pure pleasure, or a faithful friend in time of need, chocolate is with us throughout our lives, at any time of day or season of the year.

A food with a wealth of symbolism

CHOCOLATE AS A SYMBOL OF CHILDHOOD

At the end of the nineteenth century chocolate became democratized, largely owing to the wide distribution of products made by Menier and Poulain. At that point children discovered this

---

LULLABY

Go to sleep, my little brother Colas,
Go to sleep, you'll get some milk to drink.
Mama is upstairs making cake,
Papa is downstairs making chocolate ...

18th-century tune, 19th-century lyrics

highly versatile food, which soon became an essential part of their day. Their breakfast consisted of a bowl of hot chocolate enriched with powdered bananas. For their afternoon treat they had a bar of Menier chocolate either with plain bread or grated on to a piece of bread and butter. It was a snack for pure pleasure, which for several generations became a real "Proustian madeleine."

These days, children gobble their *pain au chocolat* on the way home from school, taking care to keep the precious chocolate center for the last mouthful so that the taste stays with them as long as possible. Chocolate bars are slipped into sports bags to be eaten after exercising—or indeed nibbled at any time of day when a teenager feels the pangs of hunger.

Since Choco BN cookies first appeared in 1933, every child has eaten them according to the same

ADVERTISEMENT FOR KOHLER CHOCOLATE PUBLISHED IN *L'ILLUSTRATION* (1930)

ritual. This involves delicately sliding off the cookie on top without breaking it in order to get to the chocolate cream underneath. Small teeth and tongues then move greedily into action, leaving no evidence behind but the inevitable smudge of chocolate on the nose.

Chocolate is also associated with happy times. A little mouse slips a piece of chocolate under the pillow of a child who has lost a milk tooth. Christmas trees are decorated with chocolate balls, fir trees, and Santa Clauses, and on Saint Nicholas' Day the same treats are slipped into every good child's shoes. At Easter, chocolate fishes, rabbits, hens, and eggs are hidden by parents in the garden and then frenetically searched for by children. A little magic square of chocolate dries every tear at the most painful moments of childhood. Every parent wants to pass on these precious memories. Chocolate is part of the imagery of childhood, evoking comfort snacks produced by mothers at the end of the school day and chocolate cakes, mousses, and other desserts lovingly prepared by grandmothers.

CHOCOLATE AS A SYMBOL OF LOVE

It was first the Aztecs and then later the mores of various royal courts that gave chocolate its reputation as an aphrodisiac. Although nowadays we tend to attribute this to the spices that were

COVER OF *PILOTE* MAGAZINE (1979, THE YEAR OF THE CHILD).
"THIS COVER AND THIS ISSUE ARE DEDICATED ... TO THE AFRICAN, OF COURSE, THAT THE WORLD OF CHOCOLATE IS DEVOURING ..."
EXTRACT FROM THE EDITORIAL BY CHIEF EDITOR GUY VIDAL.

added to the beverage, the essential idea is still universally accepted, and chocolate continues to be associated with love. Lovers offer chocolates as a special gift to be shared with the beloved, which may well explain why some hoteliers wish their guests a pleasant night by leaving a chocolate on each pillow.

A FOOD THAT MAKES LOVE
• Aztec emperor Moctezuma II habitually drank a cup of hot chocolate just before visiting his wives.
• The Marquis de Sade was an illustrious defender of "chocolate pleasure" and made a real cult of this food, to which he attributed aphrodisiac and "disinhibiting" properties.
• Chocolate is often quoted in the account of the gallant adventures of Giovanni Giacomo Casanova, who went so far as to claim: "Chocolate is a food that makes love."

On Wednesdays I go for a walk

With a straw in my lemonade

I go and upset vanilla skittles

And chocolate guys …

Alain Souchon, I am ten years old, 1974

CHOCO BN, "THE FRENCH CHILD'S AFTERNOON SNACK"
Created in 1933 by BN, the Biscuiterie Nantaise Company (Nantes Cookie Company), the Choco Cas'Croûte (Choco Snack) originally consisted of a mixture of vegetable fat, sugar, and cocoa sandwiched between two square, dry cookies. Its inventor, Pierre Cosse, intended it for sailors on long ocean voyages. He didn't bargain for the response of children, who after the war became a favorite target for food producers. The snack's name was changed to Choco BN in 1953. In 1976, European legislation prohibited the use of the word "chocolate" on packs of cookies filled with cocoa and not real chocolate, and as a result, BN removed the name "Choco" from its label. Despite many changes of name from then until the current "BN Filled Snacks," 157 million packs are still sold every year, which makes this cookie France's most popular snack.

BOX OF MON CHÉRI CHOCOLATES.

CHOCOLATE KISSES

Just like the Americans with their Hershey's Kisses, the Italians have for many years made a link between chocolate and love. The Italian company Ferrero is known throughout the world for its famous Mon Chéri chocolates, which have a whole cherry in the middle. In 1922, Perugina created chocolates filled with chopped hazelnuts, known at first as Cazotti ("knuckle dusters"). About ten years later, Giovanni Buitoni (whose family owned not only a pasta firm but also Perugina chocolates) decided to rename Cazotti as Baci ("Kisses") and hid a loving message for his mistress inside the box of chocolates he sent her. That led to the idea of hiding quotations to do with love under the silver paper the Baci were wrapped in. Designer Federico Seneca immortalized the couple embracing against a midnight blue background, who still sell more than half a billion Baci a day in all four corners of the world.

CARD DISTRIBUTED IN JEFF DE BRUGES STORES TO TEST THE INTENSITY OF CUS-TOMERS' PASSION FOR CHOCOLATE.
IT MAY BE TRUE THAT WE EAT CHOCOLATE TO MAKE UP FOR LACK OF LOVE, BUT WHAT IS FOR SURE IS THAT WE ARE ALL MADLY IN LOVE WITH CHOCOLATE (EXTRACT FROM WORDS ON BACK OF CARD).

CRAZY FOR CHOCOLATE

• In 1997, A New York couple celebrated their wedding on St. Valentine's Day by plunging into a bath filled with melted chocolate. The whole wedding was based on the theme of chocolate, including the bride's dress, the groom's suit, the cake, and the cocoa flowers. Even the champagne was chocolate-flavored.
• In the same year, a new variety of rose was invented; its name is Leonidas, and its flowers are the color of chocolate.
• For Easter 2000, Jeff de Bruges created a chocolate treat called Joyeuses PACS ("Happy Easter"), which consisted of a rabbit and a duck tenderly embracing as they emerged from the same egg.
• To celebrate the new millennium, two craftsmen had the idea of producing aphrodisiac chocolates. Paris chocolate maker Jean-Paul Hévin created the Dynamic Chocolate Bar, based on ginger, nutmeg, kola nuts, and Caribbean banded wood, while Bernard Dufoux of La Clayette (Saône-et-Loire) made his Bûchette Aphrodisiaque ("Aphrodisiac Stick") out of dark chocolate, pralines, chopped hazelnuts, pistachios, marzipan, and ginger.

DYNAMIC CHOCOLATE BARS CREATED BY JEAN-PAUL HÉVIN, PARIS CHOCOLATE MAKER.

Interestingly, a disappointment in love often brings on a craving for chocolate; the reason for this is that the phenyethylamine in chocolate is identical to the chemical substance produced in the brain when we fall in love. The antidepressant effect of this substance, along with that of theobromine, which alleviates sadness, makes chocolate an enormous source of comfort.

CHOCOLATE AS A SYMBOL OF GREED

Who knows whether eating chocolate is a sin of greed or just a human weakness? It may be that a feeling of guilt can still help us resist the pleasure that chocolate offers, but even so the very word "greed" stimulates the imagination and brings back childhood memories, and thanks to chocolate, adults can go on living out their greedy fantasies. These days, we sin openly and without shame; we scrape the saucepan or bowl with a spoon (or even better, a finger); we drain the sticky cocoa left at the bottom of a cup of hot chocolate to the last drop; we take a box of chocolates as a gift in the hope that we'll be offered one because, after all, doesn't politeness demand that the mistress of the house should share her chocolates with her guests?

Today the only remaining check on the sin of greed is our obsession with slimness, which is the modern form of sainthood in our secular societies. For both men and women fighting off the excess pounds, however, greed has become an internal conflict rather than a moral transgression.

Chocolate and advertising

Chocolate is not just an edible commodity. The passions that it generates give it power, and this is exploited by advertising to reach every generation.

LOVE, AFFECTION, AND CHOCOLATE

Chocolate is a source of pleasure and as a result can easily be associated with physical love. In 1999, an advertisement for Rocher Suchard alluded explicitly to sexual fantasies with a sensual, daring poster bearing the caption, "It's where he wants it, when he wants it!" and showing a shower stall, the back seat of a car, and an animal skin in front of a fire, all highly suggestive situations where the only sinful evidence left behind to make the link was a crumpled piece of paper.

-Tu crois qu'on ose?... C'est tellement bon....

-Oui, mais maman, qu'est-ce qu'elle dira? Sûr qu'on sera grondés...

-Non...... puisque c'est du *Frigor*

ORBA
KOHLER
CHOCOLAT
VER-BITTER

Le chocolat des messieurs

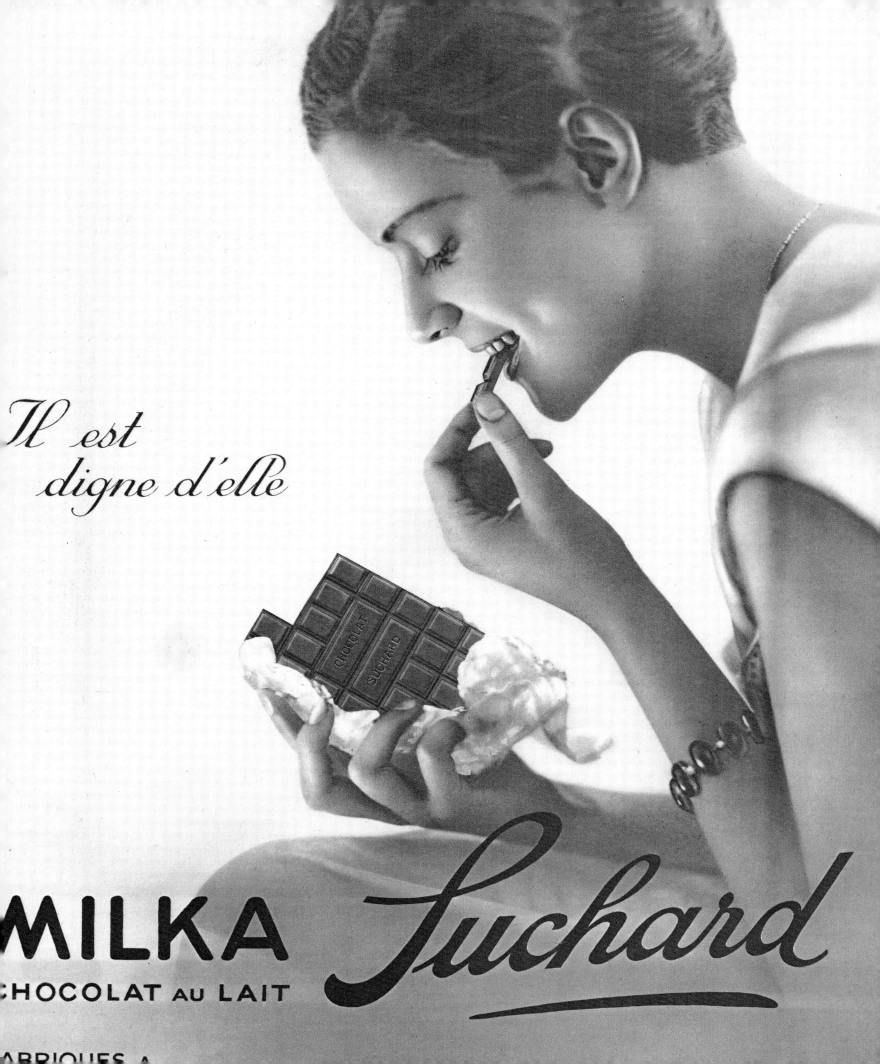

Nestlé dessert

C'EST FORT EN CHOCOLAT.

SINCE 1976, THIS PEAR COATED WITH MELTED CHOCOLATE HAS CONSISTENTLY MAINTAINED ITS HIGH POPULARITY RATINGS.

TELEVISION COMMERCIAL FOR LANVIN CHOCOLATE, FEATURING COLUMNIST STÉPHANE BERN.

The sauciest brand of chocolate, however, is undoubtedly Yves Thuriès. To gain wider publicity, this medium-sized company commissioned Richard Gotainer to create an eight-second commercial featuring the porn star Rocco Siffredi. Lying in a bed with rumpled sheets, he turns to his lady love and, in a deeply concerned yet somewhat complacent tone, asks the ritual question: "Well, feeling happy?" The lady puts on a doubtful face and retorts: "Mmm, yes, but it wasn't as good as Yves Thuriès chocolate." And a voice-over concludes: "Yves Thuriès gives eight inches of pleasure with every bar!"

SINS OF THE FLESH AND GREED

At Easter time in 1995, Rocher Suchard took a provocative line right in the middle of Holy Week. Wearing nothing but a few scraps of gold leaf, the black model Tyra Banks established a sensual parallel between carnal desire and the desire for chocolate. There were three different slogans: "To be forgiven, you've got to have sinned!"; "However much you say no, it sounds like yes!"; and "The good Lord sends these things to try us." It was an unqualified success (the actress was perceived as the exact incarnation of "the pinnacle of greed for chocolate"), but the brand was attacked by a feminist collective for incitement to rape, and the poster was withdrawn.

In 2000, the chain store E. Leclerc rehabilitated the sin of greed with a major sales drive offering vouchers in proportion to the value of goods purchased. To boost the accompanying publicity campaign, the company chose the image of two pairs of women's hands grappling for the same bar of Lindt chocolate, along with the caption: "Greed is a bad failing, except when it is rewarded. At E. Leclerc, chocolate makes you money."

LUXURY AND PLEASURE

Chocolate often comes wrapped in gold paper, and is thought of as a sort of gold bullion, with some brands even presenting their products in the form of little ingots. It could well be argued that this harks back to the Aztecs, who used cocoa beans as money.

It was no coincidence when, in 2000, Lanvin called on Stéphane Bern, the jet-set gossip columnist, to be the star of its TV commercial. Following in Salvador Dali's footsteps, he exclaimed, "Personally, I'm crazy about it!" after grabbing the one last Escargot Lanvin (Lanvin chocolate snail) off a silver tray. A voice-over then said: "Who can resist that kind of luxury?"

A FAR-OFF PLACE

For the consumer countries (with the exception of Switzerland, which has no colonial history), chocolate comes from a "far-off place" that is hot, sunny, and full of exoticism. Not only does chocolate warm the body by giving it calories, it also transports the mind—especially since the fashion began for cocoa of pure origin. We know where our chocolate bar comes from: Africa, Asia, Latin America. The advertisers are more than happy to show the plantations and the "cocoa gringos," as Jacques Vabre did for his coffee.

TO THE POINT OF MADNESS

Humor and chocolate go well together, as several brands have successfully demonstrated. To the tune of *La Mer* Charles Trenet sang the words: "Kohler, je suis fou de Kohler, pour la vie." ("Kohler, I'm crazy about Kohler, for my whole life.") Inspired by the so-called Singing Madman, Salvador Dalí exclaimed in 1974: "I'm crazy about Lanvin chocolate!" No one will ever forget the master's incredible moustache and the way he rolled his eyes. In the same humorous vein, Nestlé used a series of disaster movies to advertise Crunch, the "crispy, crunchy chocolate." Starting in 1971, their theme was simple; when you bite into a bar, everything around you collapses. The earliest ones were made by Jean-Jacques Annaud, and then Ridley Scott, Jean-Paul Goude, Edouard Molinaro, Jean-Paul Rappeneau, and Patrice Leconte followed on with an ever increasingly cataclysmic series of scenarios in which Adam and Eve, Napoleon, and even God the Father were subjected to the effects of the chocolate bar's bubbly rice filling.

The presentation of chocolate

PACKAGING WITH CHARM

At first, chocolates were wrapped in silver or tin foil. At the beginning of the nineteenth century the pharmacist Debauve was the first to sell his chocolates in wrappings with his name on them. The more supple aluminum foil was now used to protect chocolate bars and liqueur chocolates from heat and humidity.

The presentation of chocolates varies from country to country according to the type of commerce and the customs that exist there. Italian chocolates, for example, are wrapped individually for reasons of hygiene. The wife of Belgian chocolate maker Jean Neuhaus invented the cardboard box in 1915; this prevented the chocolates from being crushed, unlike the cornets that had been used previously. Nowadays, the boxes normally also contain fine sheets of paper to protect the different layers of chocolates, while the assortment boxes sold in supermarkets have separate compartments for each piece of chocolate.

The packaging of chocolates reflects the image of the manufacturer; those whose products are regarded as exceptional, in terms of quality or

THE MOST EXPENSIVE CHOCOLATES IN THE WORLD
For refined (and wealthy) lovers of chocolate, the French company J.-L. Hoffer produces the most expensive boxes of chocolates in the world. Prices vary from $32,000 to $84,000 and are justified by the use of rare types of wood, precious stones, diamonds, and gold for the presentations boxes. A range of spicy chocolates has been created by Serge Couzigou, who makes chocolate for the Henriet company in Biarritz, and Thierry Atlan, winner of the Best Workman in France award.

price, will use the same visual codes as other manufacturers of luxury goods. Robert Linxe, for example, chose Davoise Productions, who supply boxes and ribbons to Hermès, to create the image of La Maison du Chocolat (The House of Chocolate), the only French chocolate maker that is a member of the Colbert Committee. The keynote for top-of-the-line products is restraint, with the most frequently used colors being black and brown. In 1991, Primerose Bordier left her stamp on Weiss chocolate by creating a range of five colors in which to wrap five different chocolates. For Valrhona, Sonia Rykiel designed a presentation box for an assortment of their best chocolates in her favorite colors, black and red. Since then, manufacturers

---

BLACK PEOPLE AND CHOCOLATE
• *Around 1870, the word "chocolate" was used colloquially to denote a man of the black race. This analogy can still be seen today in the titles of various movies, which in every other respect have nothing at all to do with chocolate:* Bread and Chocolate *(1973),* Chocolate *(1988, starring Isaac de Bankole), and* Strawberry and Chocolate *(1994).*
• *In working-class French slang, a black who behaves like a white is called a "bounty," referring to a chocolate bar with a coconut filling called Bounty.*
• *A "nègre en chemise" ("Negro in a shirt") is a chocolate dessert served with crème chantilly (sweet whipped cream).*
• *Chocolate meringue balls were once known as "têtes de nègre" ("Negroes' heads"). Sale of the product under this name is now prohibited, but some bakeries and companies do not observe this ruling.*

PRESENTATION BOX CONTAINING THREE VARIETIES OF VALRHONA CHOCOLATE, DESIGNED BY SONIA RYKIEL.

VERT & RENOUAT HAVE CREATED A "CHOCOLATE-SCENTED" WIRED RIBBON WITH MICROCAPSULES THAT GIVE OFF A PLEASANT AROMA OF CHOCOLATE.

RIGHT, NUMBERED CHOCOLATE BY JOËL DURAND WITH ROSE PETALS (*ROSA CENTIFOLA*).

have frequently combined these two colors in the packaging for their chocolates.

TOPS AND FILLINGS

Chocolates have grown smaller, going in just a few years from quite a chunky size to a little one-fifth-ounce disc. Belgian chocolates, although often molded, are still generally larger than their French equivalents.

Craftsmen decorate the tops of their chocolates in various ways in order to distinguish between the fillings. Joël Durand of Rémy-de-Provence has invented numbered squares of chocolate. Some chocolate makers, such as Michel Richart of Lyons and Jean-Claude Briet of Prévenchères, decorate each chocolate with a transfer whose colors and motifs suggest its characteristic ingredients.

Chocolate in art

CHOCOLATE IN CLASSICAL PAINTING

One may wonder whether chocolate is a sufficiently serious or important subject to be the central theme of a painting.

Nevertheless the Spanish, who originally discovered it, devoted a number of sumptuous still lifes to it, in which it is the implements associated with chocolate that take pride of place: copper chocolate pots, porcelain cups, trembling cups and foamers, sometimes surrounded by *churros*, the long cookies or bread rolls that were dipped in the beverage. One painting by Luis Menendez contains an interesting detail; it shows chocolate pastilles, no doubt bought in town since, at that time, hot chocolate had to be made at home following an edict prohibiting its sale in the streets in order to prevent customers from flaunting their idleness. Here the chocolate pot was still made of copper, even though in an earlier canvas by the French painter Alexandre Desportes it was already in silver.

Paintings by later artists mainly showed meals or snacks being eaten in the drawing room or in a café and bringing together parents, children, and friends around a pot of hot chocolate. This highly prized drink represented an opportunity to share a moment of conviviality. The trembling cups were brought in on a tray by a maid, along with the usual glasses of water.

Artists also produced engravings and canvasses of a naughtier nature, however: tender tête-à-tête conversations as a prelude to more erotic games; passionate embraces in an alcove; a lover suddenly taking flight for fear of being discovered by a jealous husband; a bare-breasted beauty drinking a refreshing cup of chocolate first thing in the morning; a pretty marquise surrounded by visitors as she washes and gets ready, etc. In these works, where the whole emphasis is on flirtatious states of undress, negligees, scraps of lace, and suggestive, low-cut necklines, the chocolate pot presides over the private sphere of boudoirs and bedrooms. In some cases the subject appears to be innocent but is in fact loaded with erotic symbolism for those who know how to decode it. In Charles-Joseph Natoire's portrait of Mademoiselle Charolais, for example, she is making a knot with a cord, which has strongly suggestive symbolic overtones.

CHOCOLATE IN CONTEMPORARY ART

Famous poster designers put their talents at the service of the great chocolate manufacturers (Menier, the French Chocolate and Tea Company, Klaus, Poulain); these included Firmin Bouisset (1895–1925), Alphonse Mucha (1860–1939), and Leonetto Cappiello (1875–1942). The painter Degas (1834–1917) exhibited a painting, *The Cup of Chocolate*, in which a beautiful woman finishing getting ready is dipping a cookie into a cup of hot chocolate brought by a chambermaid (Öffentliche Kunstsammlung; Kunstmuseum, Basel).

In 1920, Kurt Schwitters included a chocolate bar wrapping in his composition *Miroir-collage (Mirror-*

> **STILL LIFES SHOWING CHOCOLATE**
> • Chocolate at lunch, *by Juàn de Zurburàn (1620–1649), son of Francisco de Zurburàn; Musée des Beaux-Arts, Besançon*
> • Still Life, *by Antonio de Pereda y Saldago (1652); The Hermitage, St. Petersburg*
> • Still Life, *by Alexandre Desportes (1661–1743)*
> • Still Life, *by Luis Menendez (1776); Prado Museum, Madrid*

CHOCOLATE AT LUNCH, BY JUÀN DE ZURBURÀN (1620–1649), SON OF FRANCISCO DE ZURBURÀN; MUSÉE DES BEAUX-ARTS, BESANÇON

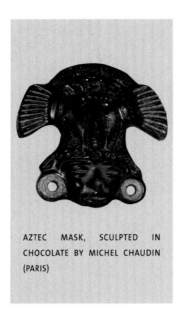

AZTEC MASK, SCULPTED IN CHOCOLATE BY MICHEL CHAUDIN (PARIS)

collage; Musée National d'Art Moderne, Paris). Still on a facetious note, Marcel Duchamp, having sketched two studies on the subject of *The Chocolate Grinder* (Düsseldorf Museum), used these as the basis for a work with the provocative title, *Bride Stripped Bare by Her Bachelors, Even, or The Large Glass* (1915–1923). The principal motif of this piece, which can be seen in the Philadelphia Museum of Art, is a chocolate-grinding mill based on one shown in an old engraving from the beginning of the century. In 1969, Fernando Botero painted a pastel still life of a chocolate pot that, as usual in this artist's work, had a plump, paunchy outline.

Now and again, chocolate appears in cartoons such as *Les Cent Métiers de Bécassine* (Bécassine's Hundred Jobs) by Caumery and Pinchon (1915) and *Les Cigares du Pharaon* (The Pharaoh's Cigars) by Hergé. Andrè Franquin used Spirou for an advertisement for Jacques chocolate bars; the Langues de Chat logo was created by Philippe Geluck in 1995; and Nicole Lambert's Triplés use chocolates to play practical jokes.

CHOCOLATE AND SCULPTURE

Chocolate can provide the theme for a work of art, but above all it is a material. This has tempted sculptors to work with it, even though in addition to the chisel it sometimes requires strange tools, such as a hair dryer. to give it a beautiful, smooth finish.

Daniel Spoeri (born in 1930) merely observed the material and captured for all time the remains of a meal in *Restaurant de la City-Galerie* (1965), which includes a leftover piece of chocolate cake. Diter Roth paints or sculpts with chocolate. He is

CHOCOLATE FLAVOR, PASTEL BY LOUIS J. (20TH CENTURY)

interested in the fact that it is perishable and inevitably evolves over the years, so his work becomes an exploration of the theme of decay through the gradual deterioration of the material. He also created *Ludwig van's Bath*, a scatological work showing a bath filled with chocolate, as an attack on the Germans, who listened to Beethoven in Switzerland during World War II.

In 1975, Jeanine Antoni exhibited *Beauty and the Beast* in Paris, which consisted of two busts, one made of lickable chocolate (even as an exhibit it remained a consumer object) and the other made of soap for getting clean.

César used chocolate for a sculpture whose motif is reminiscent of his classical compressions.

Many chocolate makers take courses in plastic art in order to become more skilled in creating chocolate sculptures, which they show at gastronomic exhibits. A test in sculpture also forms part of the competition for the title of Best Workman in the French Chocolate and Confectionery Industry.

Occasionally, scale models are made from chocolate. According to the *Guinness Book of Records*, the longest of these is thirty-three feet and weighs 2.2 tons; it was created in 1985 and represents the Olympic Village in Barcelona.

At the Salon du Chocolat (Chocolate Show) held in Paris in 2000, one of the pieces shown was an imposing model of Notre-Dame Cathedral. Every year this exhibit, run by Sylvie Douce and François Jeantet, puts on a fashion parade showing dresses designed by the top couturiers and made of chocolate by master chocolate makers. This has resulted in some remarkable creations by such pairings as Sherrer and Yves Thuriès, Chantal Thomass and Christian Constant, Balmain and Leroux, and Ungaro and Yannick Lefort.

CHOCOLATE IN LITERATURE

The earliest works on the subject of chocolate were those written by the doctors, churchmen, and chroniclers who traveled with the conquistadors. In the seventeenth century, writings about chocolate also discuss tea and coffee (de Blégny, Dufour, Spon). These are incomparable historical documents, but they are scientific works or travel accounts rather than literary texts. The first recipes for sweet or savory dishes using chocolate were created by Massialot (1691) and Menon (1755).

The peregrinations of chocolate at court are recounted in memoirs, chronicles, and letters such

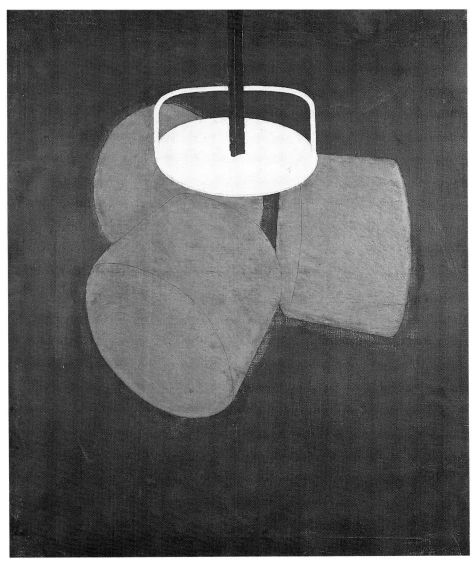

"THE CHOCOLATE FROM THE ROLLERS [OF THE GRINDER] COMING FROM WHO KNOWS WHERE, SETTLES AFTER THE GRINDING, LIKE CHOCOLAT AU LAIT [...] THE BACHELOR GRINDS HIS CHOCOLAT AU LAIT FOR HIMSELF" (MARCEL DUCHAMP).

PAINTINGS ON THE THEME OF LOVE AND CHOCOLATE

• A Gentleman and a Lady Drinking Chocolate, *by Nicolas Bonnart (late 17th century), Bibliothèque nationale de France*
• Portrait of Mademoiselle de Charolais, *by Charles-Joseph Natoire (1700–1777), Château de Versailles*
• Fear, *by Noël le Mire (1724–1800), after a painting by Jean-Baptiste Le Prince, Clark Art Institute, Williamstown, U.S.*
• Couple Drinking Chocolate, *by Martin Engelbrecht (1750), Kunstbibliothek, Berlin*
• Coffee and Chocolate, *by Johann Elias Ridinger (1698–1767), Bibliothèque royale Albert 1er, Brussels*
• Madame du Barry, *by Jacques-Fabien Gautier-Dagoty (1710–1781), Staatliches Museum, Berlin*
• The Lady's Visit, *by Pietro Longhi (c. 1778), Correr Museum, Venice*
• The Levée, *by Jean-Michel Moreau, known as Moreau the Younger (1741–1814), Musée du Petit Palais, Paris*
• The Morning, *by N. de Larmessin (18th century), Bibliothèque nationale de Paris*
• The Interrupted Lunch, *by L. Guyot after Mallet (18th century)*

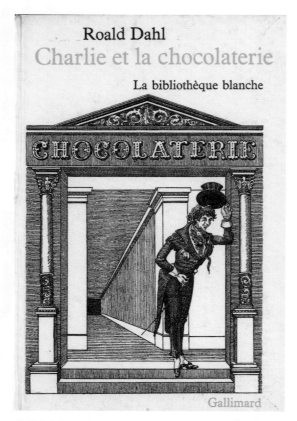

Roald Dahl
Charlie et la chocolaterie
La bibliothèque blanche
CHOCOLATERIE
Gallimard

CHARLIE AND THE CHOCOLATE FACTORY, BY ROALD DAHL (1964), 1967 EDITION

as those of Madame de Sévigné (sent from 1671 to 1675).

In the eighteenth century, an invitation to drink chocolate after supper left no room for doubt about the host's intentions. "Come now, don't play the innocent child; the chocolate is ready; follow me," writes de Sade in *La Nouvelle Justine*. Well-known for its aphrodisiac qualities, the drink of the gods was an essential for tête-à-têtes in alcoves, preparing the participants for love or restoring their strength after a passionate encounter. As a result, chocolate is much in evidence in novels of a licentious nature. It is associated with the pleasures of the mouth, most especially by Casanova (who found it "more effective than champagne") and de Sade, who gave it a prominent role in his ritual feasts: "[...] eight young sultanas appeared in the nude and served chocolate in that condition." Lesser-known writers, such as Godart d'Aucour, Argens, Chevrier, and Crébillon Junior, also expounded the suggestive virtues of the drink in their racy novels.

The Romantics enjoyed the beverage too; Goethe liked to drink his chocolate at the Café Florian on Saint Mark's Square in Venice, as did Alfred de Musset and Georges Sand at a later stage. Of all nineteenth-century authors, the one who wrote about chocolate with the most mouth-watering sensuality was Brillat-Savarin in his appreciative description of the advice he received from Madame d'Arestel, the Mother Superior of Belley convent, on how to make the best possible chocolate. Stendhal turned it into a poisoned beverage in *La Chartreuse de Parme* (The Charterhouse of Parma), and Voltaire mentioned it in *Candide*. In *Choses vues* (Things Seen) Victor Hugo told of his amusing encounter with Chateaubriand's wife, who managed, at a time when he was penniless, to sell him chocolate from her factory in rue de l'Enfer, Paris. With his genius for dabbling in everything, Alexandre Dumas added interesting details to the nineteenth-century's vision of chocolate in his monumental (and posthumous) *Grand Dictionnaire de Cuisine* (Complete Dictionary of Cooking).

Anatole France, Colette, Proust, and Aragon all mentioned chocolate in the course of their fictional works.

The Brazilian writer Jorge Amado went further by actually locating several of his novels in cocoa plantations (*Cocoa*, 1933; *Violent Earth*, 1942; *The Land of Fruits of Gold*, 1944; *The Lands at the Ends of the Earth*, 1946; *Tocaia Grande*, 1984; *The Cocoa Child*, 1982). In these works, he tells the harsh and bloody epic story of the planters.

A number of poems have been devoted to chocolate, notably some by Sapeck and Jules Beaucarne.

Jeanne Bourin and Irène Frain adore chocolate and frequently write prefaces in praise of it. In 2000, Joanne Harris published *Chocolat*, a novel that celebrates the pleasure of eating by describing the opening of a chocolate store in a little French village during Holy Week. The book was a great success and was adapted for the cinema a year later.

Also, in the world of Amélie Nothomb, frequent references are made to chocolate. She is disgusted by green chocolate (Japanese melon-flavored) in *Stupors and Shakes* but fascinated by white chocolate, which gives her a kind of rebirth in *The Metaphysics of Tubes*.

Notable children's books are *The Chocolate Castle* by Yvette Laforat, illustrated by Vatin, and, above all, the famous *Charlie and the Chocolate Factory* by Roald Dahl (1964), in which a child finds in a chocolate bar the golden ticket that enables him to visit Mr. Wonka's chocolate factory. In Irène Frain's *The Chocolate Fairy* (1995) the heroine is pursued by the King of Pebble Soup but marries the handsome, blond prince instead.

When chocolate becomes entertainment

CHOCOLATE AND THEATER

Not many plays feature chocolate, but the following are examples of ones that do.

• *The Little Chocolate Maker* by Paul Gavault is a comedy that was staged in 1909 by the Théâtre de la Renaissance in Paris. One critic at the time said of the play that it was "a creamy, fragrant soufflé; it contains nothing at all, but that nothing leaves behind a flavorsome impression."

• In 1995, *Love, Delight, and Chocolate* by Katherine Khodorowsky was put on by the La Marmite company in Malices. This comic opera used operatic melodies and literary and poetic texts to draw a parallel between the pleasures of love and chocolate. The Maison du Chocolat (House of Chocolate) molded a chocolate dinner service for the occasion, and Michel Cluizel lent his chocolate fountain for the finale. At the end of the show, the audience was invited on stage to nibble the set and props.

• *Choc*, first staged in 1998, is a musical drama by Philippe Mion, with a libretto by Claude Tabet.

Chocolate maker Mikhail Azouz appeared in the show.

CHOCOLATE AND BALLET

The year 1892 saw the first staging of *The Nutcracker*, a ballet by Lev Ivanov and Marius Petipa with music by Pyotor Ilich Tchaikovsky and a libretto based on a story by E.T.A. Hoffmann. One of the dances in this ballet refers to Spanish hot chocolate.

CHOCOLATE AND THE CIRCUS

In 1896, the circus entertainer Raphaël Padilla created a clown called "Chocolate" by smearing his face black. He formed a duo with the white clown Footit at the New Circus in Paris. Chocolate was always the one who lost out in these duo numbers, and this explains the origin of the expression "être chocolat" ("to be thwarted or foiled"), because the clown always finished his speeches with the words: "Je suis chocolat!" ("I am chocolate," or "Foiled again!").

CHOCOLATE AND THE CINEMA

In the U.S. the snack of choice at the movies has always been popcorn. But in Europe the real taste

CHOCOLATE ROSES: DESIGNS BY CHANTAL THOMASS, EMMANUEL LAPORTE, AND THIERRY BRIDRON. HAIR BY JACQUES DESSANGE. CHOCOLATE PARADE, SALON DU CHOCOLAT (CHOCOLATE SHOW), 2000.

THE COMIC OPERA *LOVE, DELIGHT, AND CHOCOLATE* WAS STAGED IN PARIS IN 1995 WITH EDIBLE SETS AND PROPS. THE EVOCATIVE COSTUMES, INCLUDING THIS DRESS DECORATED WITH LARGE CHOCOLATES, WERE CREATED BY JOSIANE PANCIATICI.

THE WORDS OF A STAR
My figure is the result of a life spent eating chocolate.
Katharine Hepburn

MOZART AND CHOCOLATE
Mozart liked chocolate so much that his operas contain numerous references to it. Don Giovanni, for example, asks for chocolate before he dies, while in Così fan tutte, *Despina, the maid, cannot resist tasting the chocolate she is frothing.*

COVER FOR LP RECORDING BY THE GROUP CHOCOLAT'S (1978), WHICH INCLUDES A TRACK CALLED *CHOCOLATE SAMBA*.

treats have been "choc-ices," the equivalent of Eskimo pies in the United States. Many still feel nostalgia for those slabs of ice cream covered in a fine layer of crunchy chocolate.

COCOA AT THE BEGINNINGS OF CALYPSO

It was a custom among slaves on the cocoa plantations of Trinidad to dance on the beans in order to separate them as they dried. They had no musical instruments, so they used bottles or cans to beat out a rhythm. And so began the steel band, which would later produce calypso.

SOMETING'S HAPPENING
"HERMAN'S HERMITS"

LUGLIO
"RICARDO DEL TURCO"

LE PETIT PAIN
AU CHOCOLAT
★★★★★★★★★★★★★★★★
JOE DASSIN
★★★★★★★★★★★★★★★★

"EVERY MORNING, HE BOUGHT HIS P'TIT PAIN AU CHOCOLAT, LA LA LA ..."

• In *Sherlock Junior*, directed by and starring Buster Keaton in 1924, the hero cannot decide whether to succumb to chocolate or to the pretty girl who is selling it.
• *Du sollst nicht stehlen* (Thou Shalt Not Steal), a 1927 movie starring Lilian Harvey, asks the following highly pertinent question: is the solitary, selfish consumption of chocolate a pleasure one can admit to?
• In George Cukor's 1935 movie *Dinner at Eight* Jean Harlow plays a true femme fatale who nevertheless cannot resist temptation when presented with a very Hollywood-style box of chocolates.
• *Love and Chocolate*, directed by Josée Dayan and starring Bo Derek (1992), tells the story of the recovery of a struggling chocolate factory belonging to Count Hubert de la Canelle.
• Tomàs Gutiérrez Alea's *Strawberry and Chocolate* (1993) tells how two great lovers of ice cream meet; one is a "rebel" who likes it strawberry-flavored, while the other is a "sheep" who prefers it tasting of chocolate.
• The plot of *Thank You for Chocolate*, directed by Claude Chabrol in 2000 and starring Isabelle Huppert and Jacques Dutronc, unfolds in a chocolate factory. A thermos of poisoned hot chocolate becomes a military weapon.
• The year 2000 saw the release of Lasse Hallström's latest film, *Chocolat*, starring Juliette Binoche.

UNE EXTRAORDINAIRE MÉLODIE TANGO
IMMENSE SUCCÈS INTERNATIONAL

WHETHER AS A THEME FOR PRE-1940S MUSICAL SCORES OR AS THE NAME OF A CONTEMPORARY GROUP RECORDING ON CD, CHOCOLATE HAS ALWAYS BEEN AN INSPIRATION TO ARTISTS.

Songs about chocolate

Discs
• Bitter Chocolate *by Joël Barret*
• A Good Hot Chocolate *by Carmen Campagne*
(children's star in Quebec)

... the songs ...
• Chokakao *and* Candies, caramels ... *(song from the movie* Boum sur Paris *[Party in Paris]) by Annie Cordy*
• Candies and Chocolates *by Dalida*
• *The* Petit pain au chocolat *by Joe Dassin*
• La Chocola, *a beguine sung by Odette Laure*
• Hard Mint Candies *by Sabine Paturel*

... the references ...
• *In a song by Jean Fusy, written by Jacques Dutronc:*
Oh, that cocoa from Cuba!
Morning, noon, and night ...
Lovely and hot, lovely and thick, right here in my cup ...

• *In* Uncle Cristobal *by Pierre Perret:*
In the morning after chocolate they chew tobacco
And spit six feet like in Mexico ...

• *In* Chocolate Tango *by Jean Varlez:*
Carried away by the intoxicating springtime,
I took her in my arms,
And to make her mouth water
We ate chocolate mouth to mouth.
Men do stupid things
For a lot less than that,
And that is why I am still haunted
By the sweet, lovely kisses we had then
When I think of their delicious flavor
Of love mixed with the taste of chocolate.

LE TANGO DU CHOCOLAT
(SCHENK MIR EIN TAFEL SHOKOLADE)
DAJOS BELA
DISQUE ODÉON DAJOS BELLA Nº 0.11.310 & COLUMBIA Nº D.W. 2.032

Chocolate and fashion

Chocolate is beautiful to look at because of its range of warm brown tones; it comes in a multitude of forms, smells good, makes us feel good, and even does our bodies good. It is hardly surprising, therefore, that the colors of chocolate are often used in fashion as the basis for cosmetic products and colorings. There are soaps, bath salts, luxury leather goods, and candles in the form of chocolate bars, single chocolates, and sometimes even liquid chocolate. In 1997, the Chocolatement Vôtre (Chocolately Yours) company was founded in Toulouse by Christiane Tixier. Once a pharmacist, she has a passion for chocolate and designs jewelry shaped like cacao fruit. Candles, perfumes, bath salts, and shampoos with a chocolate fragrance can be very sensual. Cocoa butter has always been used to heal chapped lips, but now it is regularly put into skin creams and some shampoos.

Along with that, chocolate is now also associated with our daily ablutions. Cocoa butter, a natural fat whose calming and healing properties were known to the Aztecs, is used as an ingredient not only in cosmetics but also in personal hygiene products. A chocolate-scented soap, sometimes shaped like a bar of chocolate, can arouse the senses. After treating herself to a mouth-watering, cocoa-scented bath, a woman tastes delicious.

Since 2001, the beauty and fitness center at the Hershey Hotel in Pennsylvania has been offering whipped cream and cocoa powder body wraps and baths. The director of the center is in no doubt about the benefits: "Chocolate contains caffeine, which is known to stimulate the circulation and indirectly prevent the formation of cellulite."

SPASCH COFFEE-DROP COOKIE, A CHOCOLATE CROWN SET ON A COFFEE CUP; DESIGNED BY ROBERT STADLER OF RADI DESIGNERS. "WHAT'S NEW IS THE COOKIE, NOT THE CUP!" THANKS TO ITS CONICAL SHAPE, IT WILL FIT MOST ESPRESSO CUPS. THE IDEA CAME FROM THE SPLASH CREATED BY A SUGAR LUMP FALLING INTO A CUP OF COFFEE; THE IMAGE WAS "FREEZE-FRAMED" AND TURNED INTO A COOKIE.

COFFEE CUP DECORATED WITH CACAO FRUIT; DESIGN BY PTS INTERNATIONAL

EXAMPLE OF AN ADVERTISEMENT USING CHOCOLATE TO SELL ANOTHER PRODUCT, IN THIS CASE SPEAKERS (BC ACOUSTICS FOR THE WORLD OF MUSIC [2001]; DESIGNED AND PRODUCED BY CURTIS & MCLUHAN)

2001 SALON DU CHOCOLAT CALENDAR; CARLA BRUNI WEARING YANNICK LEFORT MACAROONS AS JEWELRY, HAIR BY DESSANGES.

LONGCHAMPS SCARF DESIGNED IN 2001 ON THE THEME OF CHOCOLATE.

DESIGNS FOR "CHOCOLATE JEWELRY" (PARIS, 1998) BY MASTER JEWELER JEAN VENDÔME AND HIS SON THIERRY, WHO ARE BOTH GREAT LOVERS OF CHOCOLATE.

SHEET OF SWISS STAMPS ISSUED IN 2001 TO MARK THE CENTENARY OF CHOCOSUISSE, THE UNION OF SWISS CHOCOLATE MANUFACTURERS. THE STAMPS LOOK LIKE A CHOCOLATE BAR AND HAVE A SPECIAL VENEER THAT, WHEN SCRATCHED, GIVES OFF THE SCENT OF CHOCOLATE.

BROOCH IN THE FORM OF A CACAO FRUIT; DESIGNED BY CHRISTIANE TIXIER.

ORANGETTE CANDLE GIVING OFF THE AROMA OF A BERNARD LOISEAU DESSERT, *GYPSUM FLOWER WITH CHOCOLATE AND CANDIED ORANGE*; FRAGRANCE RECREATED BY B'PRIME.

THIS CREAMY, COCOA-SCENTED SHOWER GEL BY YVES ROCHER HAS THE COLOR, AROMA, AND CONSISTENCY OF A CHOCOLATE CREAM DESSERT.

CHOCO ROCK EAU DE TOILETTE CREATED BY CARREFOUR FOR TEENAGE GIRLS.

MOSCHINO BAG IN CHOCOLATE COLORS: THE BAG WAS A SUCCESS IN ITALY, WHERE IT WAS CREATED IN 1995, BUT THE FAMOUS COUTURE HOUSE HAS NEVER DARED TO MARKET IT IN FRANCE.

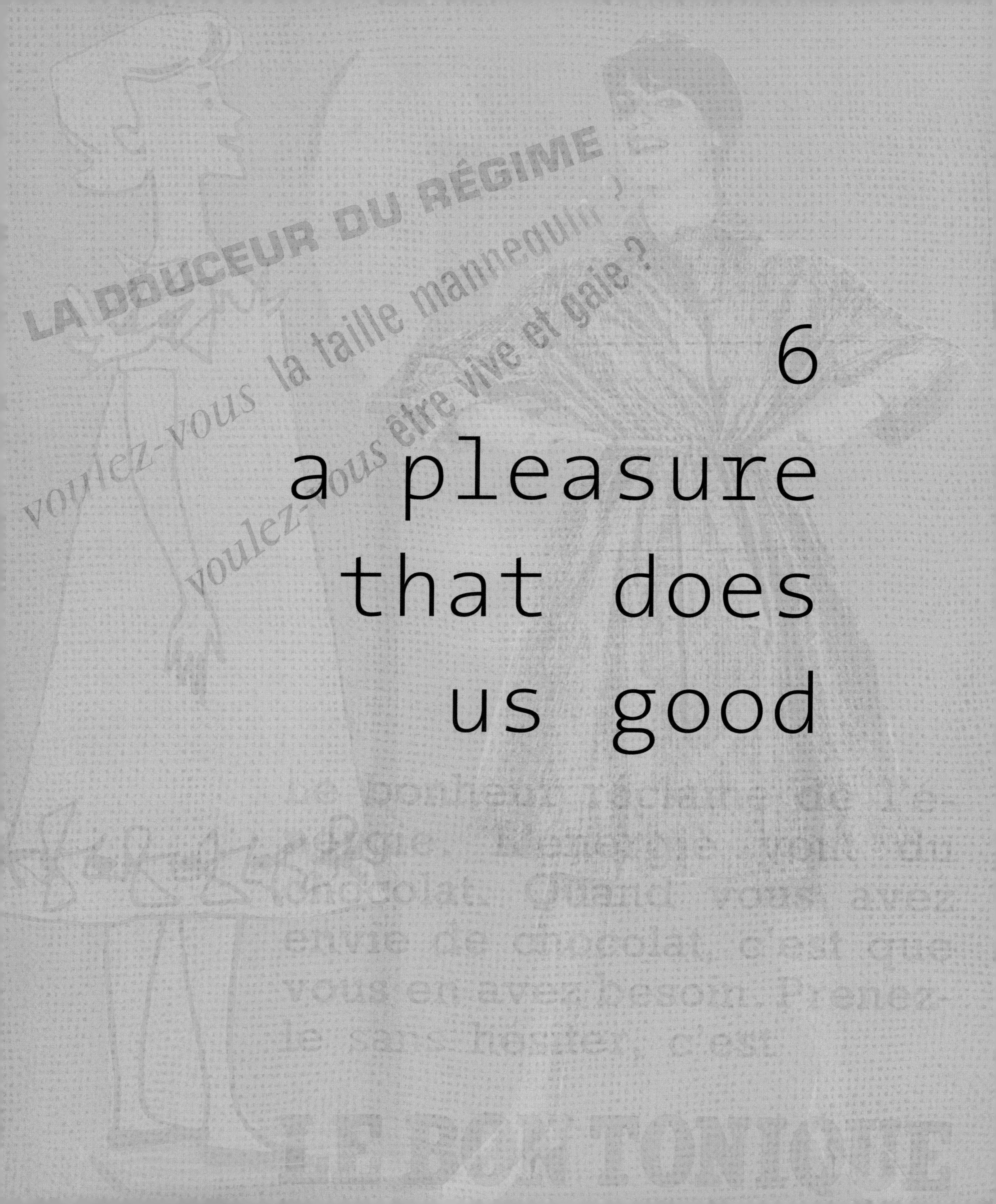

6

a pleasure
that does
us good

o appreciate the nutritional effects of chocolate and its impact on health, one needs to be aware of its composition. This differs according to its cru origins, percentage of cocoa, the presence or absence of milk, and the possible inclusion of other ingredients such as almonds, hazelnuts, or citrus fruits.

Composition of chocolate

As a food, chocolate is nutritionally very complete. It contains all the macronutrients (proteins, glucids, lipids, and fiber) and numerous micronutrients (vitamins, minerals, and oligoelements). Milk chocolate and white chocolate are sweeter and richer in calcium than dark chocolate. It is important to note that white chocolate contains no cocoa mass but only cocoa butter, milk, and sugar.

Received ideas about chocolate

As we have seen, doctors have been discussing the effects of chocolate upon health for centuries. By the end of the nineteenth century, they had all come to agree that chocolate had a tonic effect if it was consumed before meals and that it aided digestion if it was eaten after.

It is therefore very curious to discover that during the last half-century chocolate has been accused of a number of ills for which it is in no way responsible.

Perhaps the reason lies in the fact that chocolate is preeminently a childhood food. Do adults who eat it feel guilty about it? Are they afraid that they will be accused of going back to the oral stage and regressing to infancy? Is it a sin to seek pleasure in eating chocolate? There is no shortage of received

notions based on pseudoscience giving rise to popular myths. Despite the positive results of numerous studies, there remain many presuppositions about the effects of chocolate on health. Let's look at some of these.

"Chocolate is fattening"

The 530 kilocalories per one hundred grams of chocolate are terrifying for those watching their waistlines. Yet the idea that chocolate is fattening is a gross error. A little chocolate can be a perfect contribution to overall daily nutrition. Dieticians no longer demonize any food. It is permissible to eat anything, provided moderation is exercised; less concern is expressed about the quantitative aspect of nutrition (number of calories) now than to its qualitative aspect (nutritional composition). As we have seen, the calories provided by chocolate are not empty calories but contain some very valuable nutritional elements. Finally, chocolate is not the mainstay of our diet. A recent study of

AVERAGE COMPOSITION OF DARK CHOCOLATE (72% COCOA) PER ONE HUNDRED GRAMS	
Energy	529 kcal or 2.211 kJ
Proteins	9 g
Glucids	31 g
Lipids	41 g
Potassium	650 mg
Magnesium	200 mg
Phosphorus	240 mg
Sodium	70 mg
Calcium	60 mg
Iron	2 mg
Copper	0.7 mg
Vitamin A	40 IU
Vitamin D	50 IU
Vitamin B1	0.07 mg
Vitamin B2	0.08 mg
Vitamin B5	0.24 mg
Vitamin B6	0.08 mg
Vitamin B9	0.01 mg
Vitamin PP	0.78 mg
Vitamin E	2.4 mg
Vitamin C	1.2 mg
Vitamine C	1.2 mg

	PROTEINS	GLUCIDS	LIPIDS	CALCIUM
Per 100 g mild chocolate	7.5 g	57 g	32 g	220 mg
Per 100 g white chocolate	7.5 g	52 g	37 g	250 mg
Per 100 g dark chocolate (72% cocoa)	9 g	31 g	41 g	60 mg

ART DECO BILLBOARD

digestion takes depends on the quantity of fats absorbed. If at the end of a very rich meal (at Christmas, for example) a few chocolates are eaten, the impression may be created that the chocolate has caused the indigestion, whereas it is simply the straw that has broken the camel's back. But in any event the gallbladder adapts to the amount of fats ingested. Four candies provide only twelve grams of fats, two times less than a one-hundred-gram lamb chop.

"CHOCOLATE IS CONSTIPATING"
Another piece of enduring received wisdom. Yet radiologists have shown that chocolate actually has the opposite effect. Chocolate accelerates movement through the alimentary canal owing to the presence of certain tannins that stimulates the movements of the intestinal wall. A chocolate made of seventy-two percent cocoa also contains fifteen grams of fiber, which effectively fight constipation.

"CHOCOLATE CAUSES HIGH CHOLESTEROL"
Chocolate contains an oil, namely cocoa butter, which lowers the overall cholesterol rate and that of "bad cholesterol" (LDL cholesterol). It also raises the level of "good cholesterol" in the blood (HDL cholesterol), which is beneficial to health. Eating chocolate thus contributes to the prevention of arteriosclerosis.

"DIABETICS CAN'T EAT CHOCOLATE"
The rules relating to the diabetic diet have modified; a certain proportion of daily glucids is now allowed. The diabetic patient can manage his allowance as he sees fit, and this can include a small amount of chocolate. He will tend to choose a chocolate that is rich in cocoa (at least seventy percent) and has a low glycemic index (22) with little effect on the blood-sugar level. Foods containing glucids are nowadays ranked according to a glycemic index, which replaces the old classification into "slow" and "fast" sugars, now regarded as obsolete. The consumption of dark, cocoa-rich chocolate can be recommended to diabetics, with the guidance of their doctors, inasmuch as it can help to prevent cardiovascular disease.

"CHOCOLATE CAUSES MIGRAINES"
Chocolate contains tyramine, a chemical substance that can cause migraines, but it contains too little to be enough to precipate an attack on its own. It is necessary to consume several tyramine-rich foods

regular chocolate eaters shows that chocolate represents only five percent of their daily calorie intake and that there is no correlation between eating chocolate and obesity.

"CHOCOLATE CAUSES LIVER CRISES"
The liver crisis is a purely French invention, totally unknown in other parts of the world. To hear them, you might think the French had a special kind of liver. The reality is that only excessive alcohol consumption, poisonous fungi, and certain medicines are toxic to the liver.
Various studies have shown that the consumption of chocolate has no harmful effect on hepatic functioning, even when the liver has a viral hepatitis.

"CHOCOLATE IS INDIGESTIBLE"
Not true. When chocolate is eaten outside of mealtimes, it leaves the stomach after an hour—as quickly as a cup of tea. The length of time that

---

CONTRAINDICATIONS TO CONSUMING CHOCOLATE

Being rich in oxalic acid, chocolate should not be eaten to excess by persons who have suffered urinary lithiasis where the calculi have been composed of oxalic acid.

The theobromine, theophylline, and caffeine in chocolate lower the tone of the cardia, the lower sphincter to the esophagus. Persons who suffer from gastric reflux need, therefore, to monitor their consumption of chocolate.

balanced

during a meal (wine and cheese being prime candidates) for headaches to be triggered.

"CHOCOLATE CAUSES ALLERGIC REACTIONS"

This is very exceptional: only approximately 1.5 percent of sufferers from asthma, eczema, or rhinitis are allergic to chocolate proteins. Such an allergy needs to be evidenced by proper skin and blood tests carried out by an allergy specialist. More common are allergies to oleaginous fruits (such as hazelnuts or peanuts), which are often contained in filled chocolates and spreads.

"CHOCOLATE CAUSES ACNE"

Large U.S. studies on tens of thousands of subjects have definitively proved that nutrition has no effect on acne. Those who are afflicted by this complaint can console themselves—by having some chocolate.

"CHOCOLATE CAUSES CAVITIES"

Although chocolate contains sugar (thirty percent in a chocolate containing seventy percent cocoa, the cocoa mass contains fluoride, phosphates, and polyhydroxyphenol, substances that mitigate against cavities. Besides, eating chocolate does not prevent people from brushing their teeth.

"CHOCOLATE IS POLLUTED"

Some people fear ingesting pesticides when they eat chocolate. However, cacao-tree cultivation is still very artisan-based, being the province of small producers without the means to pay for phytosanitary treatments. The cocoa they produce is only very rarely chemically treated.

A number of producers in Santo Domingo, Madagascar, Bolivia, Peru, Togo, and Indonesia play the organic card, but obtaining the organic label costs money, and only large cooperatives and small, state-aided planters can afford it. It is true that, in theory at least, some chemical treatments are undertaken during shipment and storage of the beans; it would be difficult to exclude these without putting the crop at risk of insect or parasitic infestation. The manufacture of organic chocolate is as complex and constraining as that of

AN UNEXPECTED PROFILE?

A study of consumers of large daily amounts of dark chocolate (three pounds per day or more) has enabled psychiatrists to profile typical "chocoholics." They are single, have a normal social life, and are very sport-loving. They have an intense professional life, play hard, and like coffee. They do not suffer from insomnia or migraines and are not overweight.

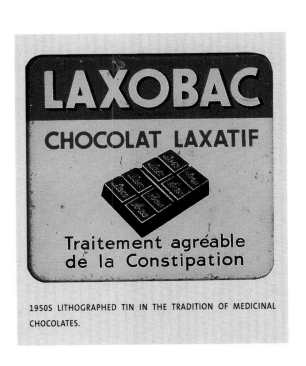

1950S LITHOGRAPHED TIN IN THE TRADITION OF MEDICINAL CHOCOLATES.

ALTHOUGH IN 1959 AN ADVERTISEMENT PROMOTED CHOCOLATE AS A SLIMMING AID, NOW THERE ARE DEVELOPMENTS TOWARD LINES OF FAT- AND SUGAR-REDUCED CHOCOLATE.

Kosher chocolate. Special lines of production have to be set up in chocolate factories to gain organic certification and authority to use labels like the French "AB" (Agriculture biologique) logo. However, certain coating makers do have organic lines, and some chocolate makers are already offering organic slabs that are finding their way into supermarkets.

"CHOCOLATE IS A DRUG"

The word "drug" implies habituation and addiction, yet this is not the case with chocolate. True lovers of chocolate, those who eat it for pleasure every day, can do without it when they have to, for example when they go on vacation to tropical countries where their divine product does not store well. Chocolate is thus not addictive like a hard drug or even tobacco and alcohol. An addicted smoker cannot do without a cigarette for several hours, let alone days, whereas a chocophile can easily do without chocolate and not suffer withdrawal symptoms.

A real drug addict tends to require larger and larger doses to achieve the same effect. But this is not the case for a chocolate lover, whose consumption tends to be constant from one day to another, unless it is simply occasional.

Chocolate contains anandamide, a substance also found in cannabis, but it has no effect at normal levels of consumption. You would need to consume more than twenty-four pounds per day for it to become active. Some anxious individuals have behavior problems centered around eating, with a tendency to bulimia. Some throw themselves at chocolate, while others go for cheese or cured sausage. People using chocolate in this way tend to choose the sweeter kind of chocolate such as white chocolate or milk chocolate. It is a known fact that sugar has a genuine traquilizing effect. It works as a true anxiolytic by promoting cerebral secretion of serotonin.

All of which goes to show that chocolate is absolutely not a drug. At the very most, it has a "come back" taste because of the pleasure it gives.

"CHOCOLATE IS AN APHRODISIAC"

This idea began during the time of the Aztecs, when the Spanish discovered that King Moctezuma II drank up to fifty cups of chocolate per day in order to satisfy his many wives. To this day, no substance stimulating the libido has been determined in cocoa mass. We know, on the other hand, that Aztec chocolate contained pepper and

CAN CHOCOLATE CONTAIN GMOS?

Chocolate sometimes contains 0.5 percent lecithin, a substance that facilitates the removal of chocolate slabs from molds, and some consumers worry that it may have come from genetically modified soya. However, lecithin is a lipid; only proteins contain genetically modified material. Companies that produce lecithin from soya guarantee their products to be GMO-free, but some admit that traces of soya protein may remain in the chocolate in the form of residual impurities. In order to totally reassure consumers, might it not be better to extract lecithin only from plants of which there are no genetically modified varieties?

  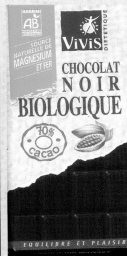 

pimento, spices which, if taken in large enough quantities, have been shown to have aphrodisiac qualities.

In the eighteenth century, chocolate perfumed with vanilla and ambergris was ever present in alcoves. In the nineteenth century, certain doctors, alarmed by Tissot's writings on "solitary pleasures," advised against eating chocolate, an ingredient judged overexciting for patients being treated for onanism.

Recent research has nevertheless shown that when chocolate is added to the diet of rats, their sexual activity increases, but no such research has been done on human beings. Perhaps the positive psychological effects of chocolate and its effect on blood circulation are enough to encourage sexual activity.

Let's leave the matter open and appreciate the poetry in Brillat-Savarin's writings: "Happy chocolate that, having traversed the world in the smiles of women, dies in the tasty, melting kisses of their mouths."

IN 2000, ON THE INITIATIVE OF THE ACADÉMIE FRANÇAISE DU CHOCOLAT ET DE LA CONFISERIE, THE FRENCH CONFÉDÉRATION DES ARTISANS CHOCO-LATIERS CREATED A LOGO AND ISSUED A GUARANTEE TO USE ONLY COCOA BUTTER TO THE EXCLUSION OF ALL OTHER VEGETABLE FAT.

SWISS CRAFT CHOCO-LATE MAKERS HAVE ANTICIPATED ADOP-TION OF THE EURO-PEAN DIRECTIVE BY CREATING THEIR OWN "QUALITY AND TRADITION PURE COCOA BUTTER" LOGO.

CHOCOLATE WITH VEGETABLE FAT?

In June 2000, at the request of certain member states, including Great Britain, the European Parliament voted a "cocoa directive" authorizing, beginning in 2003, the substitution of 5% of the cocoa butter present in chocolate by vegetable fat of tropical origin (karite, illipe, kokum, sal, mango kernel, palm oil). This measure may seem shocking because the cocoa-producing countries, most of them in the third world, are going to suffer economically from it, as palm oil is only one tenth of the price of cocoa butter. Moreover, the measure could open the door to other derivatives being used elsewhere: perhaps wine with 5% apple juice or butter with 5% oil. As for vegetable oils in chocolate, it will be impossible to check that the 5% limit is kept, since to date no reliable method of measurement is available. Why risk adulter-ating a noble product that has proved itself in the fields both of taste and of health? In the absence of scientific research, no one knows what consequences the new com-position of chocolate will have on blood-cholesterol levels, for example. In deference to the precautionary principle, some would have preferred research to have been carried out before a definitive decision was made.

The virtues of chocolate

Having looked at some popular misconceptions about chocolate, let's look at what scientists say on the basis of the many studies that have been undertaken. What emerges is that chocolate, especially the darker type, is innocent of the allegations made against it.

• Chocolate is rich in antioxydants: copper, vitamin E, and tannins (including epi-catechine, one of the polyphenols). These substances fight against free radicals (chemical forms of oxygen that degrade the cells as rust oxidizes iron); they slow down the aging of the cells, diminish the risk of cancer, and help prevent cardiovascular disease by preserving the artery walls.

• It has been proved that cocoa butter helps bring down the blood-cholesterol level.

• Finally, the high potassium content of chocolate reduces the risk of arterial hypertension.

A wild animal that is deficient or ill modifies its nutritional intake and searches in nature for the substance it needs. Behavioral specialists believe that we do the same. It is probable that every inveterate chocolate nibbler sometimes derives from his chocolate the support given by one or another of the many chemical substances it contains. A tired person doses himself with caffeine, theophylline, and theobromine, with undeniable tonic effects:

• The anxious and sick go for the sugar, which calms and diminishes pain sensitivity;

• The depressed find phenylethylamine, which lifts the mood;

• The stressed and spasmophilic gain magnesium in order to feel less vulnerable;

• The ill at ease find comfort in chocolate, thereby enhancing their secretion of endorphins (a genuine morphine manu-factured by our own metabolisms) and finding well-being and euphoria;

• The gourmet will simply enjoy the moment of pleasure.

Let's give the last word to Madame de Sévigné: "What I like about chocolate is that it delivers the desired effect."

Chocolate should no longer be thought of as a sweet little sin for it is a proper food, nutritionally rich and invigorating. It needs to be not simply rehabilitated but actually valued, especially because of its remarkable properties in helping to prevent cardio-vascular disease and its regulatory effect on the mood.

It remains true, however, that some chocolate makers still play on consumers' irrational fears and ignorance to market "diet chocolate" that "does not constipate," that is "well-tolerated by delicate livers and intestines," or where fructose or sweeteners (polyols) replace sugar.

REASSURING CONSUMERS ABOUT CHOCOLATE'S NATURALNESS AND PLACE IN THE DIET, THESE LABELS PROVE THAT THE TRADITION OF MEDICINAL CHOCOLATE PERSISTS.

IN 2000 LABORATOIRE NUXE LAUNCHED ITS ANTIAGING SKIN-CARE PRODUCT PHYTOCHOC, WHICH FOR THE FIRST TIME BLENDS POLYPHENOLS, INSAPONIFIABLES, AND COCOA PROTEINS.

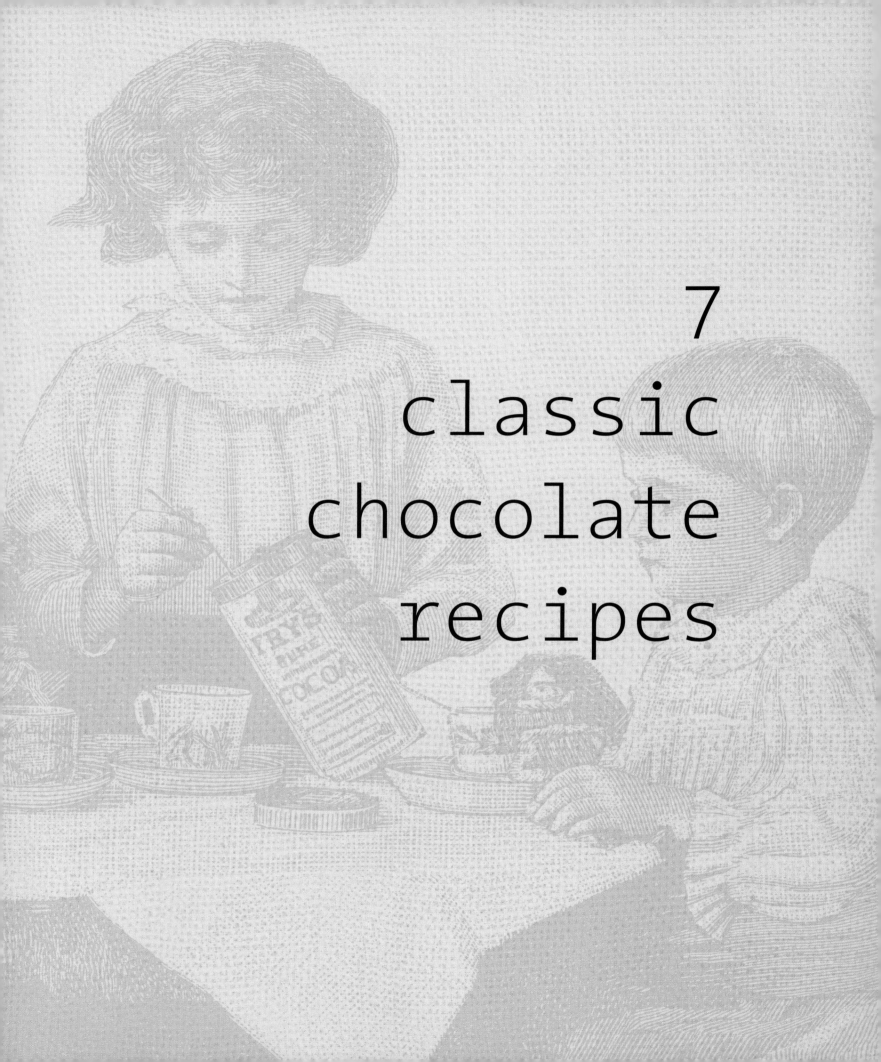

7
classic
chocolate
recipes

he recipes in this chapter are easy to make in any family kitchen and will delight all chocolate lovers.

Chocolate mousse

4 SERVINGS

8 ounces confectioners'
dark chocolate
(65% cocoa minimum)
3 tablespoons butter
8 egg whites
4 egg yolks
2 level tablespoons
powdered sugar
pinch of salt

Break the chocolate into small pieces and melt in a double boiler.

Dice and add the butter. Mix until smooth. Remove from the double boiler and leave to cool.

Add the pinch of salt to the egg whites and beat them until soft peaks are formed. As soon as this begins to stiffen, add the sugar and continue to beat until the whites become very stiff.

Fold the egg yolks into the chocolate-butter mixture. Then gently fold in the egg whites using a spatula.

Transfer to a bowl and keep in the refrigerator for at least 12 hours.

If you opt to freeze your chocolate mousse, take it out of the freezer 30 minutes before serving.

Hot chocolate

2 SERVINGS

4 ounces confectioners'
dark chocolate
(65% cocoa minimum)
2 cups fresh whole milk
1 cup water
1 tablespoon powdered
sugar (optional)

Pour the milk into a saucepan. Add the sugar (if any). Bring almost to the boil. During this time break the chocolate into small pieces.

Take the saucepan off the heat, add the chocolate, and stir until there are no lumps. The liquid should be smooth.

Return the pan to a very gentle heat, stir continuously without boiling, and add water until the desired consistency is obtained.

A particularly smooth version of this recipe may be made by whisking the mixture after it has been removed from the heat and serving it with a tablespoon of thick or whipped cream.

Chocolate soufflé

4 SERVINGS

5 ½ ounces confectioners'
dark chocolate
(65% cocoa minimum)
3 tablespoons cream
3 level tablespoons
powdered sugar
2 egg yolks
4 egg whites
slice of butter (for the mold)
fine salt

Soufflés should be prepared at the last moment. If they are kept waiting before serving, they will take revenge by collapsing. Do not overcook. A slightly liquid center inside the crustiness supplies a very pleasant contrast.

Heat oven to 350°. Break the chocolate into small pieces and melt them in a double boiler. Add the cream and remove the mixture from the double boiler.

Fold the egg yolks into the melted chocolate and chill.

Add the salt to the egg whites and whisk a little before adding the sugar. Continue to whisk until peaks are formed. Then very gently fold the whites into the prepared chocolate.

Butter a round, high-sided soufflé mold, lightly scattering it with powdered sugar. Pour in the prepared mixture and place in the oven. **C**ook for 20 minutes.

Do NOT open the oven door during cooking, as the inrush of air will prevent the soufflé from rising.

Serve immediately while still very slightly underdone.

Chocolate sausage

1 heaped tablespoon
nonsweetened cocoa powder
1 cup chopped walnuts
1 cup ground walnuts
½ cup powdered sugar
½ cup mild liquid honey
5 tablespoons rum
confectioners' sugar

This family recipe, from Katherine Khodorowsky's Russian grandmother, is a delicious piece of confectionery that looks like a genuine sausage.

Put the walnuts, honey, chocolate, rum, and half the sugar into a nonstick saucepan and mix well.

Over a low heat, using a wooden spoon and stirring continuously, mix the ingredients to a homogeneous paste.

Scatter the remainder of the powdered sugar over a smooth surface and place the prepared paste onto it. Incorporate the sugar into the paste as soon as its temperature permits.

Gently kneed the paste to lengthen it and roll it into a sausage shape. Dust with the confectioners' sugar, wrap in aluminum foil, and place in the refrigerator until solidified.

All that remains now is to cut it into thin slices like a genuine dry pork sausage.

Chocolate sauce

4 SERVINGS

*6 ounces confectioners'
dark chocolate
(65% cocoa minimum)
4 cups cream
1 cup water*

This sauce can be used to go over a vanilla ice cream, profiteroles, pear Belle-Hélène, pancakes, brioches, cookies, etc. Unfortunately, it cannot be reheated, but normally none is left over.

Pour the cream into a saucepan and bring it almost to the boil. During this time break the chocolate into very small pieces.

Remove the pan from the heat. Add the chocolate to the cream and stir with a spatula until the mixture is perfectly smooth and shiny.

Set over a very low heat, stirring all the time, then add water until the desired consistency is reached.

You can flavor this sauce by adding one or another of the following to the cold cream: powdered vanilla pod or extract; a teaspoon of powdered cinnamon; a pinch of nutmeg; two tablespoons of whiskey or rum. Be careful to mix the cream well when heating. It is also possible to use coffee as a flavoring. In that case, replace a part of the water with a small cup of very strong, black, unsweetened coffee.

As this chocolate sauce is fairly thick, it can be poured into an earthenware fondue dish and kept over a very gentle heat so that diners can dip in pieces of apples, pears, bananas, citrus fruit slices, dried fruits and nuts, or pieces of brioche, turning the end of the meal into a party.

Chocolate terrine

8 SERVINGS

18 ounces confectioners' dark chocolate
(65% cocoa minimum)
1 cup chilled cream
10 slices stale spice loaf
(French pain d'épice *or equivalent)*
2 tablespoons old rum
1 tablespoon vanilla sugar
1 teaspoon cinnamon powder

This quick recipe needs no cooking but has to be prepared the day before. If the age or preferences of your guests require it, the rum can be replaced by orange juice.

Break the chocolate into small pieces and melt them in a double boiler.

Mix together the vanilla sugar and the cinnamon. Grate or process the spice loaf into crumbs and soak these in the rum.

Remove the melted chocolate from the double boiler and allow it to cool down.

During this time beat the cream until stiff and fold it into the cooled chocolate. Then add the spice loaf crumbs.

Place the mixture in a cake mold, cover with plastic wrap, and keep in a cool place for at least 12 hours before removing from the mold.

Slice and serve with custard.

Spicy hot chocolate

2 SERVINGS

*4 ounces confectioners'
dark chocolate
(65% cocoa minimum)*
2 cups fresh whole milk
1 cup water
*1 level tablespoon
granulated sugar (optional)*
vanilla pod
cinnamon stick
½ teaspoon grated nutmeg
3 cloves
3 Chinese star anise stars

Break the chocolate into small pieces and put them in a large bowl. Split the vanilla pod in half lengthwise.

Pour the milk into a saucepan, add the spices together with the sugar, and bring to the boil, stirring continuously.

Pour the milk through a strainer onto the chocolate and mix until the liquid is perfectly smooth.

Return the pan to a very gentle heat. Stir continuously, do not allow to boil, and add water until the desired consistency is reached.

Bitter chocolate fondant

6 SERVINGS

*9 ounces confectioners'
dark chocolate
(65% cocoa minimum)
13 tablespoons butter
4 eggs
1/2 cup confectioners' sugar*

This amazing fondant is very easy to make. It earned Katherine Khodorowsky the special prize in the Rossini Competition at the Salon Gourmand de Fontainebleau, held in 1996. The judges included Bernard Loiseau, Pierre Hermé, and Lionel Poilâne.

Preheat the oven to 350°.

Break the chocolate into small pieces and melt in a double boiler. Cut the butter into small pieces, then gradually mix into the chocolate.

Remove from the double boiler. Add the confectioners' sugar and mix until a smooth, homogeneous paste is obtained.

Add the eggs one by one, mixing them in carefully.

Butter a cake mold and pour in the paste. Put in the oven and cook for about 25 minutes. To be sure that cooking is complete, slip the blade of a knife into the center of the cake: it should come out moist but with no traces of liquid paste sticking to it.

As soon as the cake is cooked, remove from the oven and cover in aluminum foil. It will be easy to remove from the mold once it has cooled.

This cake is delicious plain, with custard, or accompanied by a citrus fruit or berry fruit salad.

Chocolate potted creams

6 SMALL POTS

*8 ounces confectioners' dark chocolate
(65% cocoa minimum)
3 cups fresh whole milk
6 egg yolks
2 tablespoons powdered sugar
1 vanilla pod*

This childhood treat should be prepared the day before serving.

Pour the milk into a saucepan, split the vanilla pod in half along its entire length, and add it to the milk. Slowly bring to the boil, then remove from the heat and leave until lukewarm.

During this time beat the egg yolks with sugar until the mixture whitens.

Pour one-third of the boiled milk onto the whitened egg yolks and mix well. Pour this into the saucepan with the remainder of the milk and stir with a wooden spoon.

Place the saucepan over a gentle heat and let the cream thicken, stirring continuously.

When the cream coats the spoon, remove from the heat and filter it through a conical strainer (this procedure will also trap the vanilla pod).

Break the chocolate into small pieces and blend these into the filtered cream. Leave to stand for a minute, then stir until the mixture becomes smooth.

Distribute the chocolate cream among the small pots and keep them cool.

Brazilian creams

This variation on the previous recipe involves adding 2 tablespoons of instant coffee to the boiling milk. The rest of the recipe is unchanged, but the taste is altogether different.

Alexandra

2 COCKTAILS

2 ounces crème de cacao
4 ounces cognac
2 tablespoons crème fraîche
Several ice cubes

Put the cream, the cognac, the crème de cacao, and the ice cubes in a shaker.
Shake vigorously for 45 seconds, then distribute the contents between two ice-cold glasses, retaining the ice cubes in the shaker.

Turkey with cocoa

6–8 SERVINGS

2 ¼ pounds turkey fillets
1 ounce unsweetened cocoa powder
2 red peppers
2 green peppers
1 small mild green Spanish pepper
1 tablespoon powdered Espelette pepper
2 onions
1 clove of garlic
1 small can of tomato paste
4 ounces peanuts
½ teaspoon whole cloves
½ teaspoon coriander seeds
½ teaspoon cinnamon
1 teaspoon aniseed
3 tablespoons sesame seeds
2 cups chicken stock
4 tablespoons oil
salt and pepper

This recipe comes from the Yucatán region of Mexico. The sauce of the original recipe is extremely hot, although the quantities of pepper indicated here have actually been somewhat moderated. This dish can also be made using chicken rather than turkey.

Peel and chop the onions and garlic. Brown in a pan with two tablespoons of oil, adding the cinnamon, cloves, coriander, and aniseed, then simmer for five minutes.

Add the powdered Espelette pepper, the red and green peppers (chopped), and mild Spanish pepper (also chopped), together with the tomato paste and stock. Add salt and pepper and cook for 20 minutes on a low heat.

Remove from the heat. Add the cocoa and peanuts and stir well.

In a high-sided frying pan or shallow casserole, brown the turkey fillets in the remainder of the oil. Add salt and pepper, cover, and cook over a low heat for 20 minutes.

Pour the sauce over the turkey. Cover and continue cooking for 10 minutes.

Scatter the sesame seeds over the dish just before serving and accompany with rice.

Tasty snack recipes for children

Cooking is a fun, educational activity for children, but it can be hazardous. The following recipes are easy, but they need adult supervision.

Brioche surprise

4 SERVINGS

4 ounces unsweetened bitter cocoa powder
4 small brioches with heads
4 eggs
1/4 cup cream
4 tablespoons soft butter
4 tablespoons powdered sugar

Break the eggs and separate the yolks from the whites. (Put them in two separate, quite large, mixing bowls.)

Pour the cream and butter into the bowl containing the yolks. Beat with a whisk, gradually adding the cocoa.

Whisk the whites using an electric mixer. When they start to stiffen, gradually add the sugar and continue to beat them until they are firm and shiny.

Take 1 tablespoon of the whites and very carefully blend it into the cocoa mixture.

Continue to fold in the remaining whites, 1 tablespoonful at a time. Store overnight in a refrigerator.

The next day, at least two hours before serving, remove the heads from the brioches and scoop out the crumbs, using your fingers. Using a teaspoon, fill the brioches with the chocolate mousse and put them in the refrigerator until snacktime.

Don't forget: the chocolate mousse for these small brioches needs to be made the day before.

Chocolate-flavored petits-suisses

4 SERVINGS

1 ounce unsweetened cocoa powder
8 plain petits-suisses (individual portions of triple cream cheese)
3/4 cup powdered sugar

In a bowl mix together the petits-suisses, the sugar, and the cocoa.

Spoon the mixture into four ramekins and keep in the refrigerator until serving.

A hint for budding cooks: always wash your hands well before cooking.

Chocolate truffles

YIELDS ABOUT 70 TRUFFLES

10 ½ ounces dark chocolate
½ cup crème fraîche
1 cup powdered cocoa
(or grated coconut)

Break the chocolate into small pieces in a bowl.

Bring the cream to the boil and pour it over the chocolate, mixing continuously until the mixture is perfectly smooth. Allow to cool for 1 hour, then cover the bowl with plastic wrap and keep in the refrigerator for at least 10 hours.

The next day, remove from the refrigerator half an hour before continuing the recipe. Put the cocoa (or coconut) into a shallow bowl.

Make little balls of truffle paste using a teaspoon and roll them in the cocoa powder or grated coconut.

Truffles don't keep for more than several days. Keep them cool and in an airtight container.

Yuletide chocolate decorations

1 tablespoon unsweetened cocoa powder
6 egg whites at room temperature
fine salt
¾ cup confectioners' sugar
3 tablespoons powdered sugar
1 roll wax paper

This meringue mixture is capable of producing any number of different shapes, which will keep for several days, long enough to enjoy their appearance before eating them. These cookies can be hung on the Christmas tree with golden thread. They will look as good as they will taste.

Sift the confectioners' sugar and the cocoa into a mixing bowl and blend well together.

Put the egg whites into a separate and beat using an electric mixer. As they begin to foam add the powdered sugar and continue to whisk until the whites are well stiffened.

Gently add the blended cocoa and confectioners' sugar to the whites, mixing in an upward direction from the bottom of the mixing bowl to the top using a spatula.

Heat the oven to 300°. During this time cut the wax paper to fit your oven tray and use black crayon to draw the shapes you want to make: circles, stars, birds, angels, etc. Turn the paper over so that you can see the shapes through it.

Having filled a pastry bag fitted with a ½-inch nozzle with the meringue mixture, you can trace your designs by following the lines showing transparently through the paper. The nozzle needs to stay in contact with the paper at the same time as the mixture is released. Make sure you close up the shape of each subject.

Put the tray in the oven and cook for half an hour. Remove from the oven and allow to cool before carefully detaching the shapes from the wax paper.

Sweet recipes by prestigious patissiers and chocolate makers

Bison grass chocolates

YIELDS 2 POUNDS OF CHOCOLATES

1 cup milk

*4 ounces bison grass
(Bouteloua, from a herbalist)*

1/2 pound milk chocolate

*9 ounces confectioners' dark
chocolate (65% cocoa
minimum)*

2 ounces praline paste

1 1/2 tablespoons mild honey

5 tablespoons butter

*2 tablespoons vodka
zubrowka*

*8 ounces unsweetened bitter
cocoa powder*

RECIPE BY JEAN-CLAUDE BRIET,
CHOCOLATE MAKER AT LA
CHOCOLATIÈRE, PRÉVENCHÈRES,
LOZÈRE, FRANCE

Bring the milk to the boil. Remove from the heat, put the bison grass in it to infuse until it cools down, and then strain it to remove the herb.

Cut the two types of chocolate into small pieces in a bowl. Melt them in a double boiler with the praline paste and honey and mix together.

Remove the bowl from the double boiler and blend the butter into the chocolate as soon as the chocolate cools to room temperature. Add the vodka, mix, and keep cool for some 12 hours.

The next day remove this ganache from the refrigerator and allow it to stand for half an hour at room temperature before finishing off the truffles.

Create balls of ganache using a small warm spoon, fashion them manually, and roll them in the powdered cocoa.

Basque chocolate cake

2 CAKES OF 6 SERVINGS EACH

Basque pastry

½ pound softened butter

10 ounces granulated sugar

3 whole eggs (yolks and whites)

½ teaspoon salt

1 cup plain flour

2 ounces unsweetened cocoa powder

1 tablespoon baking powder

2 teaspoons vanilla extract

2 pinches cinnamon powder

Chocolate cream filling

2 cups whole milk

3 small eggs

⅓ cup powdered sugar

4 ounces good bitter chocolate (65% cocoa minimum)

3 tablespoons flour

For the molds and glaze

1 tablespoon butter

1 egg

RECIPE BY SERGE COUZIGOU, CHOCOLATE CONFECTIONER AT THE CHOCOLATERIE HENRIET, BIARRITZ, PYRÉNÉES-ATLANTIQUES, FRANCE; MEMBER OF THE ACADÉMIE FRANÇAISE DU CHOCOLAT ET DE LA CONFISERIE

Begin by preparing the Basque pastry mixture. In a bowl work the butter and granulated sugar together until they form a supple, homogeneous mass. Add the eggs, salt, vanilla, and cinnamon. Mix well. Sift together the flour, the cocoa, and the baking powder. Add these to the mixture, working it well, then cover with a damp cloth or plastic wrap, and place in a refrigerator for 12 hours.

The next day make the chocolate cream filling. Pour the milk into a saucepan and bring it to the boil. During this time whisk the sugar and eggs in a bowl until the mixture whitens; then add the flour and mix well. Little by little, pour the boiling milk into the bowl, whisking vigorously. Transfer the mixture back to the saucepan and cook it over a moderate heat for 5 minutes, stirring continuously. Chop up the chocolate, put it into the hot cream, and stir well. Then let the cream cool before working it with a spatula to make it smooth.

Preheat the oven to 350°. Roll out the Basque pastry to a thickness of about ¼ inch and separate it into two identical disks for each cake (i.e., four in all) about 10 inches in diameter. Brush two sponge cake molds with a little melted butter. Place a circle of pastry in each mold, topping each with approximately half of the chocolate cream mixture, taking care that the cream does not go too near the edge of the pastry. Then take the 2 remaining circles of pastry and, without applying pressure, place one on top of each sauce-covered circle. Glaze with lightly whisked whole egg, decorate the surface of each cake by tracing across with a fork, and cook in the oven for 35–40 minutes.

Chocolate fondant caramels

YIELDS 2 ½ POUNDS OF CARAMELS

1 ¼ pounds powdered sugar
2 ¼ cups cream
2 tablespoons honey (optional)
10 ½ ounces dark chocolate (70–80% cocoa)
2 tablespoons unsalted butter

RECIPE BY HENRI LEROUX, CARAMEL AND CHOCOLATE MAKER AT QUIBERON, MORBIHAN, FRANCE; MEMBER OF THE ACADÉMIE FRANÇAISE DU CHOCOLAT ET DE LA CONFISERIE

Cut the chocolate up into tiny pieces and melt these in a double boiler. Pour the cream into a small saucepan and heat it. Place another saucepan on a gentle heat, put in three tablespoons of the sugar, and let it melt: it should turn into a light-colored caramel. Add one tablespoon of sugar and mix until this, too, is melted. Continue in this way, spoonful by spoonful, until all the sugar has turned to caramel.

Gradually add the warm cream, continuing to stir and taking care not to get splashed, then add the honey.

Take the saucepan off the heat and add half the melted chocolate. Use a damp brush to clean the sides of the saucepan, return to a gentle heat and continue the cooking, stirring continuously.

Stop the cooking as soon as the mixture reaches 235° in winter and 237° in summer. (If you do not have a candy thermometer, test by putting a small amount of the caramel on a cold but not icy plate and letting it cool down to see from the touch whether it has the correct consistency.)

Remove from the heat. Add the butter (diced), then the remainder of the melted chocolate. Mix well and pour into a Flexiplan mold, or, failing that, a square or rectangular metal cookie sheet can be used.

Allow to cool before cutting the caramel into squares. Wrap each square in a piece of cellophane or plastic wrap and store in a cool, dry place.

Mendiants

YIELDS 10 MENDIANTS

6 ounces confectioners' chocolate (65% cocoa minimum)
10 whole hazelnuts
10 Provençal almonds
20 white raisins
10 pistacchios
10 pieces of crystallized orange peel

RECIPE BY THIERRY LALET, CHOCOLATE MAKER AT THE SAUNION CHOCOLATERIE, BORDEAUX, FRANCE

Cut the chocolate into small pieces and melt twothirds of it in a double boiler.

Remove from the double boiler, add the remainder of the chocolate, and stir until all of it is melted.

Cover a tray with aluminum foil and place a heaped teaspoon of the melted chocolate on the foil. Repeat until you have 10 disks of chocolate, spaced so as not to touch.

Pat the tray a little so that the chocolate spreads slightly farther, then immediately place on each chocolate disk 2 raisins, 1 piece of crystallized orange, 1 hazelnut, 1 almond, and 1 pistacchio, pressing each slightly into the chocolate.

Place the tray in the refrigerator for several minutes before delicately detaching the mendicants from the foil. Store out of the refrigerator in a cool, dry place.

Tarte fridoline

2 TARTS OF 6 PORTIONS EACH

1 cup flour
1/2 pound butter
*4 tablespoons tant-pour-tant
(equal quantities of ground
almonds and powdered
sugar)*
*4 tablespoons confectioners'
sugar*
1/4 teaspoon salt
1 egg
1 cup cream
*2 1/2 tablespoons raspberry
purée*
2 1/2 tablespoons mild honey
*10 1/2 ounces Valrhona
Manjari coating chocolate*
2 1/4 cups berry fruits
*2 thin (1/4 inch) slices of
chocolate layer
(see page 143)*
3 tablespoons berry fruit jelly

RECIPE BY THIERRY MULHAUPT,
PATISSIER AND CHOCOLATE MAKER AT
STRASBOURG, ALSACE, FRANCE

Dice 4 tablespoons of butter, add the flour, and mix. Using your fingers, rub the butter into the flour until the mixture resembles grains of sand.

Add the tant-pour-tant and the confectioners' sugar, followed by the egg and salt. Mix together until you have a homogeneous pastry: don't overwork it. Put to one side for 12 hours.

Bring the cream to the boil in a small saucepan. In another saucepan boil the raspberry purée. Chop the chocolate into small pieces using a knife.

Pour the cream onto the chocolate, mix, and add the boiling raspberry purée and the honey.

Mix until smooth and add the remainder of the butter, diced. Leave this ganache to thicken.

Line two rectangular pastry molds (with 1-inch sides) with the pastry and put aside for 1 hour.

Preheat the oven to 350°. As soon as it is hot, put the molds in to bake for 12–15 minutes. When the pastry bases have cooled, line them with a thin layer of ganache. Over this place the chocolate layer and then over this put another layer of ganache. Make a smooth surface using a flexible spatula.

Decorate the tarts with red fruits that are in season and glaze these with the (slightly warmed) fruit jelly.

This tart is best eaten at around 70° and may be accompanied by port, sherry, or a year-dated Maury.

Conserve Belle-Hélène

2 ½ pounds William pears, ripe but firm

1 ¾ pounds granulated sugar

1 orange

1 small lemon

9 ounces chocolate (68% cocoa)

RECIPE BY CHRISTINE FERBER, PATISSIER AND CONFECTIONER AT NIEDERMORSCHWIHR IN ALSACE, FRANCE. HER PRESERVES ARE WORLD-FAMOUS.

Peel the pears, remove the stalks, cut in half, remove the core contents, and slice finely.

Mix the sugar with the juice of the orange and lemon in a preserving pan; add the sliced pears and gently mix.

Heat until the preparation simmers, then pour into a bowl. Add the chocolate (grated) and mix. As soon as the chocolate has melted, cover with wax paper and keep cool overnight.

The next day return the preparation to the preserving pan and bring to the boil. Skim off any foam and cook over a medium heat for half an hour, delicately stirring.

Skim again, if necessary, and give another quick boil before testing for setting: the temperature should be 220°. If you don't own a candy thermometer, put a few drops on a cold plate and check its consistency; if it does not gel, boil a little longer until it does.

Pour immediately into jars that have been sterilized for several minutes in boiling water. Then put on the lids. Turn the pots upside down and leave them standing on their lids until they are completely cold.

Charlemagne's Almoner

4 SERVINGS

7 ounces dark chocolate (70% cocoa minimum)

3 tablespoons bitter cocoa powder (unsweetened)

8 brik leaves

4 vine peaches or white Provençal peaches

5 tablespoons powdered sugar

1 tablespoon vanilla sugar

3 teaspoons softened butter

1 pinch cinnamon powder

dash of powdered clove

½ cup water

small rose or bay leaves

RECIPE BY DENISE COURANT
BELLEFROID, CHOCOLATERIE
CHARLEMAGNE, HERSTAL, BELGIUM

Preheat the oven to 450°. Plunge the peaches in boiling water for 1 minute, then remove skins. Cut them in half and remove the pits.

Blend 2 teaspoons of softened butter with 1 tablespoon of sugar, the pinch of cinnamon, 1 teaspoon of bitter cocoa, and the dash of powdered clove.

Stuff each half-peach with this mixture and wrap it in a brik leaf. Put the almoners in the oven and cook for 10 minutes.

Cut up the chocolate into small pieces and melt in a double boiler together with the water, the remainder of the powdered sugar, and the vanilla sugar, mixing continuously.

When the chocolate sauce coats the spoon well, add the remainder of the butter and mix.

Place the small rose (or bay) leaves on the rim of each plate, dust them with bitter cocoa powder using a sieve or tea strainer, then very carefully remove the leaves.

Cover the center of each plate with the chocolate sauce, then place 2 almoners in the center of each.

Black Forest cake

8 SERVINGS

Chocolate layer

5 egg yolks
5 egg whites
³/₄ cup sugar
²/₃ cup flour
*1 ¹/₂ tablespoons
unsweetened cocoa powder*
1 ¹/₂ tablespoons cornstarch
³/₄ cup water

Chantilly (whipped cream)

*1 ¹/₂ cups very cold whipping
cream*
2 tablespoons fine sugar

Chocolate cream

1 cup whole milk
³/₄ cups fine sugar
1 tablespoon cornstarch
3 egg yolks
*4 ounces confectioners'
chocolate
(70% cocoa minimum)*
3 tablespoons butter

Kirsch syrup

¹/₂ cup water
¹/₂ pound fine sugar
4 tablespoons kirsch

Decoration

8 ounces milk chocolate slab
Confectioners' sugar

RECIPE BY JEAN JARRIGES,
CHOCOLATE MAKER AT THE PALETS
D'OR, MOULINS, ALLIER, FRANCE;
AND MEMBER OF THE ACADÉMIE
FRANÇAISE DU CHOCOLAT ET DE LA
CONFISERIE

Begin by preparing the chocolate layers. Put the eggs yolks and half the sugar in a bowl; beat the mixture for several minutes until it froths. Then add the water and mix. Sift together (in another bowl) the flour, cocoa powder, and cornstarch, then fold this into the previous mixture spoonful by spoonful.

Preheat the oven to 350°. Whisk the egg whites until stiff, gradually adding the rest of the sugar; continue to whisk for 1 minute. Delicately add one half of this egg-white mix to the mixture obtained in the previous paragraph. Mix carefully a little, then add the second half and mix.

Pour the completed layer mix thus obtained into a nonstick mold 10 inches in diameter. Cook in the oven for approximately 40 minutes. Before removing from the oven, make sure it is cooked by slipping a knife into the center: if the mixture is cooked, the blade should come out clean. Remove from the oven, leave for 12 hours in a cool place, then cut into three circles of equal thickness.

For the chantilly, whip the cream, adding the 2 tablespoons of sugar in the middle of the operation. Continue whisking until the chantilly is good and stiff.

Now prepare the chocolate cream. Beat the sugar with the egg yolks until the mixture whitens; add 1 tablespoon of milk, mix, and add the cornstarch. Place the rest of the milk in a saucepan. Bring it to the boil and then pour it gently onto the egg and sugar mix.

Transfer the mixture thus obtained to the saucepan and bring to the boil, stirring continuously. Remove from the heat, stir in the butter (diced), then leave the cream thus obtained to cool down a little. During this time cut the chocolate into small pieces and melt it in a double boiler. As soon as it is perfectly melted, fold it into the cream.

To make the kirsch syrup, bring the water and the ¹/₂ pound of fine sugar to the boil in a saucepan. Let it cool down, then add the kirsch. Brush the three chocolate layer circles with this mixture until they are soaked with it.

Spread the bottom circle with chocolate cream and place a second circle on top of it. Spread this circle generously with the chantilly and place the third circle on top of this. Using a flexible spatula, cover the whole of the top of the cake and sides with chantilly. Grate the milk chocolate over the whole cake, lightly pressing them into the chantilly—use a paring knife to obtain quite substantial shavings—and dusting them with confectioners' sugar.

Iced truffles with fresh thyme

4 SERVINGS

Fresh thyme ice cream
1 ½ cups whole milk
¾ cup cream
1 sprig fresh thyme
7 egg yolks
½ cup powdered sugar

Soft ganache
4 ounces confectioners'
chocolate (Guanaja by
Valrhona, 70% cocoa)
½ cup whole milk
⅔ cup cream
3 tablespoons granulated
sugar
1 egg white

Decoration
¼ cup unsweetened bitter
cocoa powder

RECIPE BY CHRISTOPHE FELDER,
HEAD PATISSIER AT THE HÔTEL DE
CRILLON, PARIS, FRANCE

Begin by preparing the thyme ice cream. Pour the milk and cream into a small saucepan, bring to the boil, and then shut off the heat immediately. Add the sprig of thyme and allow to infuse for 10 minutes (do not exceed this, or the thyme flavor will be too pronounced).

Whisk the egg yolks and sugar in a mixing bowl until the mixture whitens. Pour this mixture into the thyme-flavored milk and cream. Mix well and heat over a slow flame. Cook, stirring continuously with a wooden spoon until it properly covers the spoon (i.e., it should lightly coat the spoon without dripping). Transfer the cream to a mixing bowl, where it should be left to cool to room temperature. When cool, pour this cream into a sorbet maker and turn it until the ice cream sets, then freeze it.

Prepare the soft ganache. Break the chocolate into small pieces or, better yet, grate it. Put it in a large bowl. Pour the sugar onto the egg yolk and mix with a whisk, turning it slowly so that the mix becomes homogeneous without whitening.

Put the milk and cream into a saucepan, bring to the boil, and pour the boiling liquid onto the mixture of egg yolk and sugar.

Transfer to a saucepan and cook slowly, stirring continuously with a wooden spoon until the mixture thickens and coats the spoon.

Pour this cream onto the grated chocolate and stir gently with the wooden spoon until the mixture becomes perfectly smooth, then allow to cool to room temperature.

Put the plates into the freezer; you should leave them there until you are ready to serve. Pour an even layer of ganache onto the center of each plate and, using the handle of a teaspoon, draw curves to decorate. Scoop out four round, smooth balls of thyme-flavored ice cream and place them on the ganache in the center of the plates. Put some cocoa into a very fine strainer and scatter it over them to give the appearance of big truffles. Serve immediately.

This very refined dessert is not difficult to make: the decor simply needs a bit of precision. Don't rush things: prepare the ice cream and the ganache the day before. You will then just need to get the ganache out of the refrigerator 1 hour or so before you pour it onto the plates so that it has a smooth texture.

Rich chocolate truffles

YIELDS 2 1/4 POUNDS

1 1/4 cups cream (40% fat)
1/4 Bourbon vanilla pod
*1 1/2 pounds confectioners'
chocolate (70% cocoa
minimum)*
*3 tablespoons softened
butter (room temperature)*
*1 cup unsweetened cocoa
powder*

RECIPE BY MICHEL CHAUDUN,
CHOCOLATE MAKER, PARIS, FRANCE

Using a knife, chop the chocolate into pieces. Slice the piece of vanilla pod along its length. Pour the cream into a heavy-bottomed saucepan, add the vanilla, bring to the boil, and remove immediately until the boiling ceases. Bring to the boil again and yet again withdraw from the heat. Do the same again one more time.

Carefully remove the vanilla pod, pour the hot cream onto the broken chocolate, and mix with a whisk until you have a cream with the same consistency as mayonnaise. Then fold in the butter and mix well to form a ganache.

Cover a metal cookie sheet with tin foil and pour the truffle mixture onto it once it is lukewarm (105°). Distribute the mixture over the sheet, smoothing it with a spatula. Give it 1 hour to cool down further, then refrigerate overnight.

The next day transfer the truffle mixture onto a sheet of wax paper. Cut into 1 1/2-inch squares using a ruler and fine-bladed knife. Put the foil-wrapped sheet containing the squares back in the refrigerator.

Break 10 1/2 ounces of chocolate into small pieces and melt them in a double boiler. Remove the chocolate from the double boiler, let it cool to 78°, then reheat to 90°.

Using a fork, spike one of the squares of truffle mixture, plunge it in the molten chocolate, then roll it in the cocoa powder. Do the same with the rest of the pieces. Put the truffles on a plate and refrigerate them for 2 hours before removing any excess cocoa powder by shaking them in a sieve or colander.

You can enjoy these delicious truffles for 10 days. Keep them cool, at a temperature of 50–62° maximum, but do not refrigerate.

Orange and chocolate pancakes

3/4 cup flour

3 tablespoons unsweetened cocoa powder

1/2 cup fine sugar

9 eggs

6 tablespoons bière brune (a dark, sweetish beer)

2 cups whole milk

9 ounces dark chocolate (65% cocoa)

10 tablespoons butter

2 oranges

RECIPE OF YANNICK LEFORT, PATISSIER, FOUNDER OF THE SOCIÉTÉ MACARONS GOURMANDS, YERRES, ESSONNE, FRANCE

Melt 4 tablespoons of butter in a double boiler and let it cool.

Sift the flour and cocoa into a mixing bowl. Add 3 tablespoons of fine sugar and 4 eggs, one after the other, working the mixture in order to remove lumps.

Add the beer, then the milk, and finally the cold melted butter, mixing continuously. Put this pancake mixture to one side to stand.

Work the rest of the butter in a bowl in a double boiler until it has a creamy appearance.

Cut the chocolate into small pieces, melt them in the double boiler, and mix the resulting chocolate with the creamy butter.

Grate the oranges with a fine grater so that you obtain a fine peel, avoiding the white part, that has more bitterness than aroma. Squeeze the oranges.

Break the eggs, separate the yolks from the whites, and beat the whites until stiff, adding the remainder of the sugar a little at a time.

Pour the egg yolks, the orange juice, and the grated peel into the mixture of butter and chocolate. Mix, adding the beaten egg whites and folding them in gently with a wooden spoon.

Preheat the oven to 400°.

Fry the pancakes in a nonstick pan with a little butter. Spread each of these with some of the chocolate and orange preparation and fold them in half and then again into triangles. Arrange them in an oven dish, and place them in the oven for 3 to 4 minutes.

Serve the pancakes as soon as they come out of the oven, accompanied by whipped cream or a scoop of vanilla ice cream.

Azteca truffles

YIELDS 2 1/2 POUNDS

2 1/4 cups cream

14 ounces confectioners' dark chocolate (65% cocoa minimum)

4 ounces cocoa grué (cocoa nibs)

6 cups unsweetenend cocoa powder

RECIPE BY NICOLAS NESSI, CHOCOLATE MAKER IN LAUSANNE (SWITZERLAND)

Grate the chocolate finely into a mixing bowl.

Pour the cream into a small saucepan; bring it to the boil and pour it onto the chocolate. Mix with a whisk to obtain a perfectly homogeneous mass.

Add the splintered cocoa beans, cover the bowl, and cool in the refrigerator.

As soon as the preparation is thoroughly cooled down and hardened, use a teaspoon to form small balls, fashion them manually, and roll them in the cocoa powder.

Cocoa nibs (grué) may not be easy to find in stores, but a well-disposed craft chocolate maker will be able to supply these splintered beans.

Citrus nobilis

MAKES 2 CAKES OF 8 SERVINGS EACH

Dacquoise

1 ¼ cups egg whites

1 ½ tablespoons sugar

2 ounces roasted hazelnuts

2 ounces roasted almonds

½ orange

Chocolate parfait

9 ounces confectioners'
chocolate
(70% cocoa minimum)

1 ½ tablespoons unsweetened
bitter cocoa powder

1 cup egg yolks

4 ounces sugar

¼ cup milk

1 ounce leaf gelatin

1 ½ cups cream

Citrus syrup

⅔ cup mandarin orange juice
(frozen concentrate)

1 ¼ cup sugar

⅔ cup water

1 ½ tablespoons grenadine
syrup

2 oranges

Mandarin cream

¼ cup water

⅔ cup mandarin orange juice
(frozen concentrate)

1 teaspoon orange-flower water

9 tablespoons butter

½ cup sugar

1 cup eggs

¼ cup grated orange zest

2 ounces leaf gelatin

2 ¼ cups cream

RECIPE BY GÉRARD GATHERON,
LENÔTRE'S SUGAR DEPARTMENT CHIEF
AND A HOLDER OF THE MEILLEUR
OUVRIER DE FRANCE AWARD

Preheat the oven to 340°. Take the peel from the half orange for the dacquoise and grate it together with the nuts. Beat the egg whites with the sugar, then delicately add the grated peel and nuts. Divide the preparation between 2 circles 8 inches in diameter, placing them on an oven tray covered in wax paper. Put the tray in the oven, reducing the temperature immediately to 300°. Cook with the oven door slightly ajar for about half an hour.

Now prepare the chocolate parfait. Mix the egg yolks with the sugar and milk, heating the mixture to 180°. Cut the chocolate into small pieces and melt these in a double boiler. Vigorously whisk the egg mixture with the chocolate, cocoa, and gelatin (the leaves should be softened first in water). Continue whisking until the mixture has completely cooled down. Whisk the cream until stiff and fold it gently into the chocolate mixture.

Peel the 2 oranges intended for the syrup and divide them into segments. Remove all pith and skin, leaving only the orange flesh. Pour the water, the sugar, the mandarin juice, and the grenadine syrup into a small saucepan and bring to the boil. Remove from the heat, stir in the orange flesh, and allow to cool.

Drench the round dacquoises with the citrus syrup. Cover each one with half the chocolate parfait and put in the freezer to solidify for half an hour.

To make the mandarin cream, begin by boiling the water, the mandarin juice, the orange-flower water, the butter, the sugar, and the grated zest. Remove from the heat. Add the eggs and bring back to the boil, stirring continuously with a wooden spoon. Remove from the heat entirely and add the gelatin previously softened in cold water. Beat the cream until whipped and fold it into the mandarin mixture as soon as this is totally cooled down.

When the parfait is completely solidified, cover each circular layer with mandarin cream and allow to harden in the freezer for half an hour.

Citrus nobilis is the name botanists give to the mandarin orange tree, which came from China and is associated with long life and nobility.   *Gérard Gatheron*

Orange chocolate roulade

8 SERVINGS

Chocolate fat-free layer

4 eggs
1/2 cup sugar
1/3 cup flour
*1 1/2 tablespoons
unsweetened cocoa powder*

Orange truffle cream

*8 ounces confectioners'
chocolate
(60% cocoa minimum)*
1 orange
1/4 cup whole milk
*2 tablespoons unsweetened
bitter cocoa powder*

Chocolate mousseuse

2 1/4 cups cream
*8 ounces confectioners'
chocolate (70% minimum)*

Orange syrup

*3 chemically untreated
oranges*
3/4 cup sugar

RECIPE BY MICHEL BELIN,
CHOCOLATE MAKER AT ALBI,
TARN, FRANCE; MEMBER OF
THE ACADÉMIE FRANÇAISE DU
CHOCOLAT ET DE LA CONFISERIE

Begin by making the layer. Break the eggs, separating the whites from the yolks. Beat the yolks with the sugar until the mixture whitens. Then sift the flour and cocoa together and gently fold into the previous mixture. Preheat the oven to 425°.

Beat the whites until stiff and blend them carefully into the previous preparation. Cover an oven tray with wax paper, spread the layer mixture on it, put it in the oven, and cook for 8–10 minutes. Remove the tray from the oven and cool the layer on a rack covered with a clean cloth.

Now make the orange truffle cream. Finely remove the zest from the orange and squeeze the fruit. Pour the milk into a small saucepan and bring it to the boil; then add the orange zest and allow it to infuse for 2 minutes off the heat. Use a knife to chop up the chocolate and pour the milk over it through a strainer. Add 8 tablespoons of orange juice and mix together, then process in a microwave oven for 2 minutes on maximum. Mix well and pour this truffle cream onto the silver paper from the chocolate slab, checking that it forms a regular layer 1/2 inch thick. Put in the freezer.

To make the chocolate mousseuse, bring 3/4 cup of the cream to the boil in a small saucepan. Add the chocolate (grated), mix to a smooth texture, and allow to cool.

Whip the rest of the cream until it froths, then blend it into the previous mixture to form the mousseuse.

To make the orange syrup, take the zest of 2 oranges and poach for 20 minutes in a syrup made up of 1/2 cup of sugar and 1/2 cup of water.

Bring to the boil the juice from the 3 oranges together with the rest of the sugar, then remove from the heat and allow to cool.

Place the layer on some plastic wrap and moisten it with the cooled-down syrup, then spread half the mousseuse over its entire surface. Take the truffle cream out of the freezer, cut into small cubes, and sprinkle them over the mousseuse, taking care to retain a few for decoration. Roll up in the form of a log, applying sufficient pressure, and put into the refrigerator for at least 1 hour.

Remove the plastic wrap and cover the log with the remainder of the mousseuse. To decorate, make lines with a fork and sprinkle the log with the reserved cubes of truffle cream and parings of the orange zest previously poached in the syrup.

Jivara

MAKES 2 CAKES OF 6 SERVINGS
EACH

Brownies

*4 ounces confectioners' dark
chocolate (65% cocoa
minimum)*

*10 tablespoons softened
butter*

3 eggs

2/3 cup sugar

1/3 cup superfine flour

*2/3 cup mixed walnuts and
hazelnuts*

Vanilla crème brûlée

1 1/4 cups milk

1/4 cups cream

1/2 cup egg yolks

5 tablespoons sugar

1 vanilla pod

Jivara milk chocolate
mousse

*14 ounces confectioners' milk
chocolate (Jivara by
Valrhona)*

5 tablespoons sugar

1/4 cup water

1 egg

5 egg yolks

1 ounce leaf gelatin

1 2/3 cups cream

Decoration

*4 ounces confectioners' milk
chocolate (Jivara by
Valrhona)*

1 vanilla pod

RECIPE BY FRÉDÉRIC CASSEL,
PATISSIER AND CHOCOLATE MAKER,
FONTAINEBLEAU, NEAR PARIS,
FRANCE

Preheat the oven to 350°. Cut the chocolate into small pieces, melt in a double boiler, then blend with the softened butter. Fold in the eggs and sugar, then the sifted flour, and lastly mix in the nuts (coarsely chopped). Divide the mixture between 2 round straight-sided molds 28 inches in diameter, put in the oven, and cook for 10–15 minutes; the mixture should still be very slightly frothy. Remove from the oven and reset the temperature to 200°.

Now prepare the vanilla crème brûlée. Bring the milk to the boil in a small saucepan. Remove from the heat, add the vanilla pod, split in half lengthwise, and infuse for at least 30 minutes. Add the cream and stir. Mix, though do not beat, the egg yolks with the sugar, then add the milk and cream mixture, filtering it through a conical sieve. Pour the cream into 2 round molds 8 inches in diameter with detachable, nonstick bottoms. Put in the oven and cook for 75 minutes.

To make the chocolate mousse, begin by heating the sugar and water to 250°. Pour the mixture obtained onto the egg and egg yolks. Whisk to increase the volume and allow to cool before adding the gelatin (softened in cold water prior to use). Cut the chocolate up into small pieces and melt in a double boiler. Whip the cream until stiff. Add the chocolate to the egg mixture, then fold in the beaten cream, stirring gently and carefully with a spatula.

Set one of the layer rounds within a high-sided circle 8 inches in diameter. Spread over it a 1 1/2-cup layer of crème brûlée, followed by a 1-cup layer of chocolate mousse. Repeat the procedure to make a second cake. Put both in a cool place to set.

Decorate with grated milk chocolate and a vanilla pod split into half lengthwise. Remove the circles just before serving.

Desert roses

MAKES APPROXIMATELY 60 CHOCOLATES

12 ounces confectioners dark chocolate (70% cocoa)
2 tablespoons cornflakes glazed with sugar
2 tablespoons puffed and toasted rice grains
4 tablespoons crystallized orange peel
4 tablespoons soft yellow raisins

RECIPE BY FRANCIS BOUCHER, CHOCOLATE MAKER, PARIS; MEMBER OF THE ACADÉMIE FRANÇAISE DU CHOCOLAT ET DE LA CONFISERIE

Finely dice the orange peel and put the small cubes into a wide bowl. Add the raisins and mix together. Then add the cornflakes and puffed rice grains. Mix well and put to one side.

Chop 8 ounces of chocolate into small pieces, put these into a mixing bowl, and melt them over a double boiler, stirring from time to time with a spatula. When the temperature reaches 110°, remove from the double boiler. Finely grate the rest of the chocolate, add to the mixing bowl, and mix.

Reheat the chocolate preparation with a hairdryer, so that it liquefies and becomes homogeneous while remaining somewhat cold to the touch (88°). If you do not have a candy thermometer, put a trace of chocolate on a knife blade: the chocolate should cool down quickly and look dark and shiny.

Now add the other ingredients to the chocolate preparation, delicately mixing this material to throughly coat it with the chocolate. Be careful not to crumble the cornflakes.

Prepare a tray, covering it with plastic wrap. Using a teaspoon, take a desired amount of the mixture and place it on the plastic wrap. Continue until all the mixture has been used up in this manner. Allow the chocolates to harden and transfer to a cool place prior to serving.

Alpine supreme

MAKES 2 DESSERTS OF 8 SERVINGS

Joconde nut layer
1 ¹/₂ cups flaked white almonds
1 ¹/₄ cups confectioners' sugar
2 cups eggs
¹/₂ cup flour
¹/₂ cup pralines
¹/₃ cup grated roast hazelnuts
1 ¹/₄ cup egg whites

Cointreau syrup
³/₄ cup water
¹/₄ cup sugar
¹/₄ cup Cointreau

Custard
²/₃ cup crème fraîche, 35% fat
²/₃ cup whole milk
¹/₄ cup egg yolks
¹/₄ cup sugar
2 ounces leaf gelatin

White chocolate supremes
1 ³/₄ cups custard
1 ³/₄ cups cream, 35% fat
18 ounces white chocolate

Milk chocolate mousse
9 ounces milk chocolate (40% cocoa)
1 ¹/₄ cups cream (35% fat)
2 cups whipped cream

RECIPE BY RÉMI BELDAME, CHOCOLATE MAKER, LAUSANNE, SWITZERLAND

Begin by preparing the Joconde layer. Crush the almonds with the icing sugar, then add the 2 cups of eggs and whip until the mixture froths. Add the flour and mix for 1 minute, then blend in the pralines. In a separate bowl whisk the egg whites until stiff, then add to the previous mixture, folding in delicately. Preheat the oven to 450°. On cooking parchment paper place 2 circles of the cake mixture ¹/₂-inch thick and 10 inches in diameter, plus 2 others just ¹/₄-inch thick and 8 inches in diameter. Spread the remainder of the mixture in strips ¹/₄-inch wide and ¹/₄-inch thick. Put into the oven and cook for 4 minutes.

Now for the Cointreau syrup. Pour the water into a small saucepan, add the sugar, and bring to the boil. Remove from the heat and allow to cool before adding the Cointreau.

To make the custard, begin by bringing the milk to the boil together with the cream. Separately, beat the egg yolks with the sugar until the mixture foams. Gradually pour the milk and cream mixture onto the egg and sugar mixture, transfer the new mixture to a saucepan, and heat to 180°, stirring continuously.

Pour the mixture through a conical sieve into a bowl to cool. Take several tablespoons of the hot custard, pour it onto the gelatin to soften it, and blend this into the rest.

Now make the supremes. Cut the white chocolate into small pieces and melt in a double boiler at 100°. Whip the cream until stiff, blend it into the 1 ³/₄ cups of cold custard, add the melted white chocolate, and mix all thoroughly to obtain a creamy texture. Take

the 2 thin circles of Joconde layer (¹/₄ by 8 inches) made previously and place each inside an 8-inch ring mold. Cover with the creamy mixture and freeze.

To make the milk chocolate mousse, bring the cream to the boil in a saucepan, then remove from the heat and add the chocolate (chopped). Mix until the preparation is shiny, then add the whipped cream, and fold delicately into the warm ganache.

Take two 10-inch diameter rings and dress the sides with the strips of Joconde layer, placing the thick circles of Joconde layer in the base. Pour in the chocolate mousse to midheight of the ring molds, then place the frozen supremes on top. Finish off by spreading on the remainder of the milk chocolate mousse. Now freeze in order to stabilize the different textures and decorate as you like. Remove from the freezer approximately 15 minutes before serving.

Chocolate mousse with crystallized orange peel

10 SERVINGS

18 eggs
2 ¹/₄ cups powdered sugar
1 ¹/₂ pounds confectioners'
dark chocolate
(65% cocoa minimum)
1 ¹/₂ cups crystallized orange
peel

RECIPE BY STÉPHANE BONNAT,
CHOCOLATE MAKER, MAISON
BONNAT, VOIRON, ISÈRE, FRANCE

Break the eggs and separate into whites and yolks. Hand-whisk the yolks with 1 ¹/₂ cups of sugar, then clean the whisk, and mix the whites with the remainder of the sugar. Make sure that in either case the sugar is totally dissolved. You could place the bowls over hot water to ensure this as long as the eggs do not cook.

Cut the chocolate in small pieces, melt them in a double boiler, and retain the molten chocolate there, ensuring that the temperature stays at 95–105°.

Beat the egg whites and sugar until stiff, then let them stand long enough to have time to mix together the yolks and melted chocolate using a whisk or spatula. Fold the beaten egg white mix into the chocolate preparation. Take care not to flatten the whites.

Dice into small pieces the crystallized orange peel, reserving some for decoration, then add the remainder to the mousse, mixing gently.

If you wish, divide the mousse among individual ramekins, slipping around the surface of each with a knife previously warmed in hot water. Scatter the mousses with small cubes of crystallized orange and keep them cool until serving.

Warszawa

10 SERVINGS

Chocolate génoise

1/3 cup unsweetened bitter cocoa powder
10 eggs
1 1/2 cups sugar
1 cup flour
3 tablespoons cornstarch

Vodka-flavored chocolate cream

3/4 cup confectioners' dark chocolate
(70% cocoa minimum)
3 cups cream
3 ounces vodka

Vodka syrup

1/2 cup water
1 1/4 cups sugar
4 tablespoons vodka

Icing

1 1/2 pounds confectioners' dark chocolate
(70% cocoa minimum)
2 1/2 cups confectioners' sugar
1 tablespoon crème fraîche

RECIPE BY MARCEL BONNIAUD, PATISSIER AND CHOCOLATE MAKER, LYON, FRANCE

Begin by making the chocolate génoise. Preheat the oven to 350°. Put the sugar and eggs in a mixing bowl over hot water (as if in a double boiler) and whisk the mixture for 1 minute. Remove from the heat and continue whisking until the mixture is cold and forms a strip.

Now very carefully add the flour (sifted), the cornstarch, and the cocoa powder, mix, and then transfer to a buttered and floured sandwich mold. Put in the oven and cook for half an hour. Remove the génoise from the mold as soon as it leaves the oven, but do not cut it before garnishing, when it is completely cold.

Next make the vodka-flavored chocolate cream. Whip the chilled cream until stiff and add the vodka to it. Cut the chocolate in small pieces, melt it in a double boiler, and blend it into the vodka-flavored whites, mixing quickly.

Bring to the boil the water and sugar to make the syrup. Remove from the heat, allow to cool, and add the vodka.

Cut the génoise into 3 disks of equal thickness and drench all of them in the syrup, using a brush. Spread the first disk with half the cream, place the second on top, spread this with the remainder of the cream, then place the third and final disk of génoise on the very top. Place in a cold refrigerator for the whole to solidify.

To make the icing, cut into pieces the chocolate intended for this and melt in a double boiler. Remove from the heat, then blend in the crème fraîche and confectioners' sugar (sifted), stirring this ganache well to ensure there are no lumps.

When the cake has perfectly solidified, cover it with the icing ganache, smoothing it well with a spatula. Keep cool until serving.

Warszawa *is the Polish form of Warsaw, and this cake was created in memory of a trip to Poland.*

Marcel Bonniaud

Truffettes Katherine

MAKES 1 POUND OF TRUFFLES

1 ¼ cups crème fraîche

4 ounces confectioners' dark chocolate (70–80% cocoa)

1 tablespoon small cubes of crystallized orange peel

3 tablespoons Grand Marnier

½ cup milk chocolate (coating grade)

RECIPE BY BERNARD DUFOUX,
CHOCOLATE MAKER AT LA CLAYETTE,
SAÔNE-ET-LOIRE, FRANCE

Pour the Grand Marnier into a bowl, add the cubes of cystallized orange peel, and allow to macerate for 12 hours.

The next day chop the dark chocolate into small pieces and drain the orange peel cubes.

Bring the cream to the boil in a small saucepan. Take off the heat and add the chocolate, then stir well to obtain a smooth, well-homogenized cream.

When the mixture has cooled, add the cubes of orange peel and mix together, introducing plenty of air to lighten the mixture.

Use a teaspoon to form small balls of the mixture, roll them between your fingers, and dip them briefly in the milk chocolate (already melted in a double boiler for this purpose).

Place the truffles on a tray covered in wax paper and allow to harden before sampling. They will keep for up to 10 days but should be stored in an airtight container and kept cool.

Prune truffles

MAKES 2 POUNDS OF TRUFFLES

8 ounces prunes (pitted)

2 cups rum

1 ½ cups cream

13 ounces confectioners' dark chocolate (70% cocoa minimum)

2 ½ tablespoons glucose

7 ounces unsweetened bitter cocoa

RECIPE BY HUBERT MASSE,
CHOCOLATE MAKER AT CACAOTIER,
ENGHIEN-LES-BAINS, VAL D'OISE,
FRANCE

Soak the prunes in the rum overnight.

The next day put the cream and glucose in a small saucepan and bring the mixture to the boil over a low heat.

During this time chop the chocolate into small pieces using a large knife.

Take the cream off the heat and add the chopped chocolate, then mix well to obtain a smooth ganache.

Drain the prunes, reduce them to a purée using a food processor, and blend this purée with the ganache. Keep in the refrigerator for about 12 hours.

Bring back to room temperature, then use a warmed spoon to form little balls of ganache. Fashion them manually, then roll them in the unsweetened cocoa powder. These truffles will keep in the refrigerator for up to 10 days.

Soft chocolate cake

6 SERVINGS

3 eggs
½ cups powdered sugar
8 tablespoons fresh butter (softened)
12 ounces confectioners' dark chocolate (70% cocoa minimum)
⅓ cup flour
⅛ cup potato starch
1 cup cream
1 teaspoon unsweetened bitter cocoa powder

RECIPE BY JEAN-PAUL HÉVIN, CHOCOLATE MAKER AND PATISSIER, PARIS; AWARDED MEILLEUR OUVRIER DE FRANCE; MEMBER OF THE ACADÉMIE FRANÇAISE DU CHOCOLAT ET DE LA CONFISERIE

Cut 4 ounces of chocolate into small pieces and melt them in a double boiler. Preheat the oven to 350°.

Break the eggs into a mixing bowl, add the sugar, and whip until it dissolves and the mixture whitens. Then blend in the soft butter and chocolate. Sift the flour and potato starch together and add them to the chocolate preparation. Mix carefully, then divide the mixture between 2 sandwich molds, which have been previously greased and floured.

Put the molds in the double boiler, then put them in the oven and cook for 35 minutes.

Remove the molds from the oven, allow the contents to cool, and take them out of the molds.

Pour the cream into a saucepan, add the cocoa, and bring to the boil, whisking vigorously.

Cut the remainder of the chocolate into pieces in a mixing bowl, pour over the boiling cocoa-flavored cream, mix well until smooth, then allow to cool.

Spread a good amount of ganache over the first layer, place the second layer on it and finally spread the remainder of the ganache over the top. Smooth with a flexible spatula and sprinkle cocoa powder over the cake.

Oven-crystallized mint leaves

2 ¼ pounds granulated
sugar
1 egg white
1 bunch fresh mint
2 ¼ pounds confectioners'
chocolate (60% cocoa
minimum)

RECIPE BY RÉMI HENRY, CHOCOLATE
CONFECTIONER AT THE ATELIER DU
CONFISEUR, COLOMBES, PARIS,
FRANCE

All varieties of mint are suitable for this recipe. Rémi Henry buys Moroccan mint at the supermarket in the winter and is supplied by local Paris-region market gardeners in the summer.

Wash the sprigs of mint well under running water, shake the water off, and place them to dry on paper towels. Then remove the leaves from the stems.

Put the egg white in a bowl and beat it lightly. Using a brush, dab the mint leaves on both sides with the egg white, place them on the paper towels, and wait 2 minutes.

Preheat the oven to 180°.

Pour the sugar into another bowl and dip the mint leaves in it one by one, shaking them afterward to remove any excess sugar.

Cover an oven tray with cooking parchment paper or else with aluminum foil. Place the leaves on the tray and put it into the oven for 3 hours. A few bubbles should appear on the leaves during this time, but if they become covered with bubbles, then the oven is too hot.

Cut the chocolate into small pieces and melt it in a double boiler.

When the mint leaves have cooled down, choose the smallest ones—the larger ones will be good to eat as they are or as cake decoration—and, with the aid of a fork, drench them quickly in the molten chocolate. Drain them and place them on a sheet of aluminum foil to harden.

Successful oven-crystallized mint leaves will keep for 6 months in a container in a damp-free atmosphere. The same method can be applied to produce crystallized rose petals, provided insecticides have not been used.

Savory recipes by prestigious chefs

Wherever cocoa has been known, it has been used as a spice. As such, it is found in the making of the Mexican national dish, Mole Poblano de Guajolote, *and also in the creation of Catalan-style crayfish or Bordeaux-style lamprey. I would not hesitate to introduce its use in wine sauces, whether for marinated meats or for fish in a matelote sauce. Associated with fresh ginger, it will color preparations and enrich their aromatic range with a warm, discrete spiciness.*

Christian Constant

The following savory recipes, in which cocoa is used as a spice, are recommended to experienced cooks.

Sautéed lamb with chocolate

4 SERVINGS

2 teaspoons unsweetened bitter cocoa powder
1 ounce half-bitter dark chocolate
1 $^2/_3$ pounds shoulder of lamb
1 $^1/_2$ tablespoons butter
2 tablespoons oil
2 shallots (finely chopped)
1 $^1/_2$ cups red wine
1 bouquet garni
salt and pepper

RECIPE BY EMMANUEL LAPORTE, CHEF OF THE RESTAURANT LES FEUILLES LIBRES, NEUILLY-SUR-SEINE, PARIS, FRANCE

Cut up the meat into approximately 2-ounce pieces. Heat the butter and oil in a pan; when the butter foams, add the pieces of meat and seal them. Add the chopped shallots, drench with the wine, salt and pepper, and add the bouquet garni. Cover the pan and simmer for 50 minutes. When the meat is cooked, use a skimmer to remove the lamb pieces and keep them hot. Put the pan back on the heat to reduce the juices, then strain it off and mix it with the cocoa powder and dark chocolate (finely chopped). Whip this sauce for a good length of time and strain it again. Spoon the lamb into soup plates and cover the individual portions with the sauce.

Garnish with pickled red cabbage, chestnuts, or diced apple.

Parisian round of beef with dark chocolate sauce

6 SERVINGS

6 squares dark chocolate containing cocoa bean nibs
2 $^1/_2$ pounds round of beef
1 $^1/_2$ liters red wine
2 shallots
2 tablespoons olive oil
2 tablespoons flour
1 bouquet garni
3 tablespoons butter

In a large bowl prepare a marinade of red wine, olive oil, finely chopped shallots, salt, pepper, and a bouquet garni. Cut the meat into slices, lay them in the dish, and marinate for 12 hours.
Place a little butter in a frying pan and heat it. When it foams, add the slices of beef and fry them several minutes on either side, enough to brown the outsides. Use a skimmer to remove the slices and keep them hot.
Add the bouquet garni, salt, and pepper to the juices left by the meat after its quick fry.

Make a roux with a little flour and cook the sauce for several minutes, then add the dark chocolate squares. If the sauce is too thick, add a little wine from the marinade and continue cooking for 5 minutes over a slow heat to produce a thinner texture.
Pour the sauce into the base of a serving dish, arrange the slices of beef on it, and serve immediately.

Langoustines and shrimp swimming awry in their own cocoa-spiced juices

2 SERVINGS

4 tablespoons unsweetened bitter chocolate powder
1 ½ tablespoons cocoa nibs (coarsely crushed cocoa beans, available from a craft chocolate maker)
6 very large langoustines or shrimp or crayfish
12 very large shrimp
4 ounces butter
3 leeks
2 shallots
½ cup crème fraîche
5 tablespoons butter
½ cup dry white wine
1 cup water
several drops Worcestershire sauce
Tabasco
olive oil
salt, ground pepper

RECIPE BY DANIEL GIRAUD, AWARDED MEILLEUR OUVRIER DE FRANCE; CHOCOLATE MAKER AND CATERER, VALENCE, DRÔME, FRANCE; MEMBER OF THE ACADÉMIE FRANÇAISE DU CHOCOLAT ET DE LA CONFISERIE

Seal the langoustines, shrimp, and finely chopped shallots in 2 tablespoons of butter and a little olive oil for 1 minute. Season with salt and pepper, then remove the shellfish from the pan, peel them, and put the shells to one side, keeping them slightly warm.

Add a large slice of butter to the pan in order not to lose the initial cooking juices, throw in the heads and shells, and lightly pan-roast.

Beat and crush the shells and heads once these and the butter start to brown; then pour the white wine and water over them into the pan and bring to the boil. At this point, remove the pan from the heat and pour the contents through a conical sieve to trap the shells, which should then be discarded. Return the juice to the heat and reduce.

During this time wash the leeks, slice them finely, and blanch them. Drain and season them in the remainder of the butter before dividing between 2 heated plates, arranging the leeks in a nest on each plate. In the middle of each nest place the langoustines and shrimp.

Finish cooking the sauce by seasoning it: add a splash of Tabasco, the drops of Worcestershire sauce, the tiny crushed chocolate nibs, and the cream. Pour this sauce, very hot, over the shellfish and scatter a few cocoa nibs over the dish.

If you prefer, you could replace the strands of leek with fresh pasta.

Bordeaux-style Lamprey

4 SERVINGS

2 ounces dark chocolate (70% cocoa)
1 live lamprey
(or a medium-size eel)
1 large onion (chopped)
3 carrots (diced)
1 clove garlic (crushed)
4 leeks (white parts only, diced)
2 thick slices of Bayonne ham (diced)
2 tablespoons flour
12 tablespoons butter
salt and pepper
fresh ginger (grated)
1 bouquet garni (thyme, bay leaves, parsley sprigs)
1 bottle red Bordeaux wine
4 slices plain white bread (for croutons)

Bleed the lamprey and keep the blood; this will serve to thicken the sauce. Scald the fish for 3 minutes in order to remove the skin, then cut off the head and tail, and remove the spine from the length of the fish. Cut into steaks.

In a large, high-sided frying pan, brown onion and carrots in butter, then add the pieces of fish, the garlic, the bouquet garni, and the ginger. Pour the wine over the mixture and cook for 6 minutes only. Drain the pieces of lamprey and keep them warm.

While the fish is cooking, sauté the leeks with the Bayonne ham, then keep warm.

Prepare a roux with the flour and butter in a saucepan. Add the juices from the cooking of the fish and reduce. Strain the sauce through a conical strainer and, off the heat, whisk in the chocolate and blood.

Arrange the leeks on a heated serving dish with the lamprey pieces on top. Then pour the sauce over the lamprey and accompany the dish with croutons fried in butter.

RECIPE BY CHRISTIAN CONSTANT, CHOCOLATE MAKER, PARIS, FRANCE; MEMBER OF THE ACADÉMIE FRANÇAISE DU CHOCOLAT ET DE LA CONFISERIE

Pan-roasted shrimp in a chocolate-flavored American red pepper and dried mango tapenade

6 SERVINGS

4 ounces dark chocolate (65% cocoa minimum)
18–24 peeled shrimp
2 roots of salsify
1 pound red peppers
4 ounces dried mango
10 tablespoons extra-virgin olive oil
10 tablespoons hot sauce
²/₃ cups olive oil
1 ¹/₂ cups cooking oil
1 teaspoon paprika powder
Tabasco
salt and ground pepper

RECIPE BY ÉTIENNE KREPS, HEAD CHEF OF THE RESTAURANT L'HERMITAGE, MONTREUX-CLARENS, SWITZERLAND

Cut the salsify into strips like tagliatelli, fry these in oil, and salt them. Then keep them warm. Cut the dried mango into small sticks 1-inch long; put these to one side.

Preheat the oven to 425°. Place the red peppers on an oven tray and heat them until they color. Then remove them, cover them in aluminum foil, and let them cool down. When the peppers are cold, peel them, remove the seeds, and cut into fine slices. Process them for an instant in a food processor together with ¹/₂ cup of olive oil, salt, a splash of Tabasco, and the paprika. Add the sticks of mango and keep warm.

Cook the red pepper mixture over a low heat and gradually add the chocolate (chopped small), whisking well so that the sauce is perfectly smooth and light (possibly giving it a short spin in the food processor). Season with salt and pepper.

Season the peeled shrimp and pan-roast them in olive oil. Distribute the red pepper tapenade among 6 plates, and place the shrimp on top. Surround each portion with a stream of sauce and add a few strips of fried salsify. Serve immediately.

Breasts of game birds, cocoa-spiced, with cabbage-wrapped thighs

4 SERVINGS

4 Cornish game hens, squabs, or partridges
4 ounces green cabbage leaves (Savoy-style)
1 carrot
1 onion
1/2 cup Banyuls
1/2 cup chicken stock
allspice
unsweetened bitter cocoa powder
4 ounces spice loaf (French pain d'épice)
1/2 pound salt pork
9 tablespoons sunflower oil
5 tablespoons butter
salt and pepper

RECIPE BY YVES THURIÈS, TWO TIMES AWARDED MEILLEUR OUVRIER DE FRANCE, CHEF OF THE RESTAURANT LE GRAND ÉCUYER, CORDES-SUR-CIEL, TARN, FRANCE; MEMBER OF THE ACADÉMIE FRANÇAISE DU CHOCOLAT ET DE LA CONFISERIE

Remove the thighs and breasts from the birds, season them and sprinkle them very lightly with bitter cocoa powder.

Discard the ridges from the cabbage leaves and blanch the leaves in boiling water.

Chop the carrot into small cubes and very thinly slice the onion. Soften these in 1 1/2 tablespoons of butter and 1 tablespoon of oil in a high-sided frying pan without browning, then add the cabbage leaves. Cover and cook over low heat. When the cabbage is thoroughly cooked, turn off the heat and season.

Cut the spice loaf into fine slices. Pour 1 tablespoon of oil into a pan and heat it. As soon as it smokes, put the slices of spice loaf in the pan and quickly brown each side, drying off the excess oil afterward on a cloth.

Remove the bones from the fleshy part of the 8 thighs, roll each thigh in a cooked cabbage leaf, and then in a slice of salt pork that has been thoroughly blanched.

Fry the breasts and thighs in the remainder of the oil and foaming butter, then keep them hot.

Pour the Banyuls into a small saucepan, adding a pinch of allspice and a pinch of bitter cocoa, and reduce by one third. Add the stock and then reduce until the sauce barely drops off the spoon. Season with salt and freshly ground pepper.

Slice the breasts and divide them, together with the thighs, among the ready-heated plates. Scatter the fine slices of spice loaf, and pour the sauce over each serving.

To accompany this dish, in which spices and vegetable flavors marry the rich flavor of the game birds, choose a fruity, powerful Banyuls, a Banyuls Vintage (or Rimage) 1993, for example.

8

for true lovers of chocolate

hoosing chocolate well is a real art. For single chocolates it is always best to shop at a good specialist chocolate store. In the case of chocolate bars you can buy them in supermarkets, where you will find every type from the best to the worst. The only way to choose is to try out the different brands for yourself.

Choosing chocolate

SINGLE CHOCOLATES
These should be bought in small quantities from a good chocolate maker. Word of mouth and specialist guides can point you in the right direction, but even so a chocolate maker should be tried several times to test his creativity and the freshness and reliability of his product. When you recommend a good store to a gourmet, it is not only an act of friendship, it also guides new customers to the craftsman of talent, which means that he can produce even fresher chocolates.

Be careful with the descriptions "homemade," "proprietor's own," and "local produce;" these are not legal terms. Case law does indicate, however, that they are only permitted for products made at the place of sale and sold directly to the consumer.

CHOCOLATE FOR CHRISTMAS
Gone is the time when boxes of chocolates were chosen in supermarkets for their packaging rather than their contents. It used to be that there were two criteria for choosing a box of chocolates: the size of the box—after the lean post-war years it had to be big—and the illustration on the lid (more often than not a Currier & Ives scene). Nowadays the pictures and decorations on boxes focus mainly on the variety of cocoa used. It should be pointed out, however, that these industrially produced chocolates are manufactured several months in advance and that their taste can only be stabilized by adding alcohol or preservatives.

Furthermore, the weight of the chocolates is usually less than might be expected for the size of the box. You can avoid disasters by choosing a well-known brand; although even then it is essential and often highly instructive to read the list of ingredients very closely. It is often wiser to buy a small box for the same price from a gifted craftsman rather than a large box whose contents turn out to be disappointing.

CHOCOLATE BARS
The quality of industrially manufactured bars has greatly improved over the last few years, but the consumer now has the problem of being faced with a bewildering profusion of different brands, products, and advertising messages.

Where dark chocolate is concerned, the choice has been complicated by the ever increasing focus on percentage of cocoa content, as a result of which the uninformed consumer tends to think: "The higher the cocoa content, the better the chocolate." If only it were that simple. A bar with eighty percent cocoa content will taste eighty percent bad if the beans used are not of high quality or if they have been badly handled. A bar containing only sixty-four percent cocoa, for which the beans have been selected and well treated, will have a significantly better taste. The current fashion for bitter chocolate means that a powerful flavor is frequently being confused with a burnt taste (due to badly roasted beans) or excessive acidity.

Even so the best criterion of choice for every consumer is still personal taste, which does of course evolve with experience but which should never succumb to the allure of snobbery or fashion.

EASTER CHOCOLATE
The plated chocolate used for molding Easter eggs, bunnies, and so on will be more or less glossy depending on how carefully it has been worked. That is the first criterion of choice, especially for dark chocolate (milk chocolate has more of a matte appearance). It is always best to go for gifts created by craftsmen using high-quality ingredients.

CHOCOLATE POWDER
The return to "authentic" flavors has brought chocolate shavings back into fashion. Melted over a low heat with water or milk depending on the brand, they will give you a much more tasty beverage than instant blends. For breakfast, use an unsweetened bitter cocoa (the best of these are still made in the Netherlands) to guarantee a tasty drink.

How to store chocolate

Chocolate needs to be stored well if it is to retain its full flavor. This is not quite as simple as it seems since, although it goes well with many things, chocolate has three implacable enemies: heat, damp, and proximity to other odors.

WHERE TO KEEP IT
Chocolate should be kept in its original packaging, away from light, and in a place that is cool (less than sixty-five degrees), dry, and airy. The wine cellar is ideal throughout the year unless it is damp. It is not a good idea to put it in the refrigerator since chocolate does not like sudden changes in temperature and will react by turning white. Note, however, that this does not

---

IN A GOOD CHOCOLATE STORE

• A clean smell of cocoa greets you as soon as you open the door.

• The merchandise is protected, not just from customers' hands but from strong electric lights as well.

• The color of the chocolates is clean, and their surface is glossy with no sign of whitening (which would show that they had been badly kept).

• The products are handled with a gloved hand or a pair of tongs.

• The chocolate maker is passionate about his craft, loves to talk about his products and explain in detail what ingredients they contain, and does not object if you ask to sample them.

• He prefers to produce little and often to guarantee that his chocolates are fresh.

The best way to judge, of course, is always by the taste ...

As the chocolate makes contact with the tongue it may be delicate, creamy, pasty, rough, sandy, silky, coarse, tender, gritty, light, full, soft, supple, powdery, grainy, floury, smooth, rich, dry, clingy, melting, fine ...

make the chocolate unfit to eat or change its taste in any way; it is simply a chemical reaction produced by cocoa butter or sugar crystals rising back to the surface.

If you have no option but to keep your chocolates in the refrigerator, place them in an airtight metal container. This will protect them from other food smells, which are easily picked up by chocolate fats. Always remember to bring them out a short time before eating them so that their temperature can gradually rise to about seventy degrees.

HOW LONG SHOULD IT BE KEPT?

Unopened chocolate bars will keep for several months, and just to be sure, there is always a use-by date on the wrapper. Filled chocolates, on the other hand, need to be eaten within one month of purchase, while those containing cream or butter, such as ganaches and truffles, should be consumed within two weeks, otherwise they may develop a rancid taste.

Sugar and alcohol are nature's preservatives, which means that bitter ganaches will keep less well because they contain very little sugar, whereas chocolates that contain alcohol will last longer, as will pralines, because they are sweeter. One piece of advice for gourmets: to be sure that your chocolates don't go bad, buy them often and in small quantities. Big eaters should have no problem since they will no doubt have finished their little box well before the fateful two-week (or one-month) deadline.

How to eat chocolate

A bar of chocolate can of course be gobbled down in no time to satisfy an uncontrollable urge; and of course it is possible to empty a box in a series of mechanical gestures, with those greedy fingers not stopping until they reach the bottom. Nevertheless, ever since it entered the upper echelons of gastronomy chocolate has shared with wine the privilege of being ceremoniously tasted by fine gourmet palates. Brillant-Savarin had anticipated this when he emphasized that eating chocolate offered "a mouthwatering harmony of colors, smells, and sounds, which mingle, accumulate, and create pleasure." All five senses of the gourmet—or just the hungry eater—come into play and complement each other as they orchestrate the art of tasting.

THE PREPARATION

Because eating chocolate is a moment of pleasure that demands concentration, it also requires a certain amount of preparation. It is a good idea to have an empty stomach and settle down in a light, fairly cool room. Start by eating the least bitter chocolate and then build up to the one with the highest cocoa content. Likewise, milk chocolate should go before dark chocolate and filled chocolate before pure chocolate.

LOOKS ARE IMPORTANT

Consciously or unconsciously, someone eating chocolate will be affected from the start by the appearance of the finished product. If this first impression fulfills expectations, it will create the right conditions for maximum enjoyment of the chocolate. If not, the remainder of the tasting may be colored by initial prejudice.

TOUCHING, FOR SENSUALITY

A high-quality plated chocolate is smooth and soft; one should feel like stroking it, even if prolonged contact is to be avoided for obvious reasons to do with temperature.

Contact with the tongue enables the taster to appreciate the texture; once the silky coating has melted (it should not be bitten into), the filling underneath will be revealed. Grinding and conching are the key stages in the production of chocolate, which ensure that "there is no grainy feeling on the tongue."

SMELLING, THE FIRST STEP TO ECSTASY

The smell begins by tickling the mucous membrane, and with this fragrant moment the pleasure begins. In order to get the most out of a chocolate's olfactive qualities, it is best to start by just sniffing it two or three times before "inhaling" it deeply. If powerful aromas are released, they should be clean, natural, pleasant, and appetizing.

HEARING, FOR THE PLEASURE OF IMAGINING

The darker the chocolate and the better its quality, the drier and crisper the sound will be when you bite into it. With a rich milk chocolate you will hear less. Like the sound of a cork coming out of a bottle, the noise that chocolate makes is a pleasure that whets the appetite.

TASTING, FOR THE JOURNEY TO THE LAND OF FLAVORS

After stimulating the nose chocolate then goes on to release its flavors in the mouth as soon as it makes contact with the tongue. The flavors should be clean, straightforward, fresh, pure, authentic, and well blended. They develop in several phases: first there is the attack when the chocolate spreads over the tongue just after being placed there; then, as chewing releases the "taste molecules," the flavors open out, moving at this point to the back of the throat; next, the finish, when the chocolate reveals its deepest flavors; and finally the best chocolates show "good length" by leaving the imprint of their natural ingredients everywhere in the mouth (if nothing is left but the taste of sugar, change your supplier).

What should you drink with chocolate?

The drink to accompany chocolate needs to be chosen with care. The richer the chocolate's flavors, the subtler the choice will be. When various types of chocolate are being compared, only still spring water at room temperature and with the most neutral flavor possible should be used to cleanse the palate. Some professionals who make a point of tasting their products every day drink milk to freshen their taste buds. Bread can also be relied upon for this because of its neutral taste and clean, chewy quality.

The choice of a drink to go with chocolates or a chocolate dessert is of course subjective. It is based in principle on two types of criteria:

TASTING HOT CHOCOLATE

Hot chocolate deserves to be celebrated by all five of our senses if we are to gain maximum pleasure from it. It is a good idea to drink a glass of water at room temperature first; this "wakes up" the palate and prepares it for the taste of the beverage.

• **HEARING** *The foamer beats out a rhythm as it forces air into the chocolate to make it froth; "choco, choco," gurgles the defenseless beverage. But by the time it is being poured out, it is perfectly silent; it knows it is where it belongs in the smooth, round contours of a china cup.*

• **SIGHT** *The light froth on the chocolate whets the appetite just by its appearance. The Aztecs even thought that foaming their hot chocolate brought them closer to the gods. The sweet liquid may have an infinite variety of colors, some darker, some lighter, some brown, reddish, or even almost black. The surface will be matte if the cocoa is fat-free, or if it contains cocoa butter, it will be shiny, thus providing a mirror in which the drinker can see the reflected image of his own desire.*

• **TOUCH** *As the cup nestles between both hands its warmth passes into the tips of the fingers and then spreads like a caress right up the arms. At the same time the nerve endings in the palms are sending their message to the brain: "Look out, there's a treat on the way!"*

• **SMELL** *The piping hot aromas from the chocolate make the nostrils twitch and the mouth water. It is deeply tempting to plunge your nose right into the froth, feel its tickling caress, and then have the embarrassment of wiping it off with the back of your hand.*

• **TASTE** *The taste buds are now fully primed, and at last their long wait is rewarded. Half-liquid, half-creamy, the drink of the gods first impregnates every taste bud and then fills the palate. The hot beverage flows down your throat. Your eyes are closed. Time has come to a halt.*

AN EPICUREAN INITIATION

Among family or friends comparative tasting can become a game that is both educational and convivial. Michel Cluizel was the first to produce boxes of chocolate disks that vary in terms of origin or cocoa content. Just by the way they are decorated these boxes are enough to start anyone dreaming about exotic places, but actually discovering the different flavors becomes a real epicurean initiation.

It must have been the same idea of playing a game that motivated Régis Bouet to create his colored chocolates, which have to be tasted "blind" since no information is given as to their flavor apart from the words "carmine," "iodine," and "leaf."

• the match may be synergetic or complementary, enabling each flavor to express itself without overwhelming the other;

• it may be a match between two similar flavors that come together and mutually reinforce each other.

But there are so many tastes and colors ...

CHOCOLATE AND COFFEE

Broadly speaking coffee and chocolate obviously come from the same stable; they grow in the same equatorial climate and often on the same plantations. Although this geographical coincidence might be enough to justify a marriage of convenience, it hardly explains the inseparable love bond that exists between the two products. Perhaps the baptism by fire that they both undergo (roasting) brings their flavors closer together.

The custom we have adopted from Italy of offering a piece of chocolate with a cup of coffee gives us the pleasure of a tasting experience using all five senses on an everyday basis. The wrapping is often in the colors of a brand of coffee; the little one-ounce square is solid, smooth, and cold when it is placed on the tongue before we experience the first wave of coffee flavor. At this point there is a confrontation not only between consistencies (solid and liquid) but also between temperatures (cold and piping hot). The chocolate quickly surrenders and turns into a luscious paste in which its own flavor mingles with the flavor of the coffee, and the two complement each other perfectly.

CHOCOLATE AND TEA

This is the most difficult combination to succeed with since, when tea has been brewed for too long, its tannins get in the way of the taste of chocolate, while green tea, on the other hand, is not a particularly good accompaniment to chocolate at any time. Like wine, tea can only go well with chocolate if it is low in tannins, mild, and very smooth.

CHOCOLATE AND WINE

"Wine cannot be drunk with chocolate," was the dogmatic view expressed by Courtine. In fact the combination is possible, although not easy to achieve. The quality of both products depends on a subtle balance of flavors (sweet and acidic) and on compatibility of texture. It is always best to taste the wine first so that it fills the palate. If you start with the chocolate, it will prevent the flavor of the wine from opening out fully.

Red wines

The tannins in red wine fill the mucous membranes in the mouth, and this normally prevents the chocolate from developing its flavors. The only red wines that will go well with chocolate are ones that have been mellowed by the sun or by the maturing process, such as a Côte-Rôtie or a Châteauneuf-du-pape that is at least five years old.

White wines

Not all white wines by any means will be a good accompaniment to chocolate. One might imagine, for example, that champagne would be the perfect drink to go with a chocolate dessert, but in fact quite the opposite is true; the cold, acidic bubbles in champagne numb the taste buds and thus take away all the flavor from the chocolate. Dry white wines are not recommended either since their acidity is reinforced by the sweet flavor of the chocolate.

Vins doux naturels (naturally sweet wines)

A sweet wine, such as a Muscat, a Banyuls, or a Maury, will go very well with a chocolate dessert as long as it is not too sweet. This is because these wines have a silky structure, are rich, and develop aromas that suggest citrus and dried fruits—and sometimes even chocolate.

CHOCOLATE AND SPIRITS

Generally speaking the tannins in spirits interfere with those of chocolate. This means that spirits to accompany chocolate must be chosen with care.

Brandy, for example, needs to be old so that it has lost most of its tannins and astringency; it will dominate the chocolate just a little as its flavors develop, and the finish will be fresh and smooth. A pink Pineau des Charentes that has been matured in oak for more than five years will give flavors of red berries, honey, and sweet almonds and will then release chocolate notes on the finish. A rum matured in oak for at least three years loses some of its alcohol content and takes on a wonderful amber color that suggests cocoa and vanilla—a magical combination. Finally, when a chocolate dessert already contains some added spirits, it can be accompanied—in moderation, needless to say—by the same drink that has been used as an ingredient.

Drinks that go well with chocolate

RECOMMENDED WINES

The selection of wines that follows is not exhaustive. These are *crus* whose flavor is known to enhance the taste of chocolate, but there is nothing to prevent you experimenting for yourself.

• CÔTE-RÔTIE GUIGAL "LA MOULINE," 69420 Ampuis
• CÔTE-RÔTIE SEIGNEUR-DE-MAUGIRON, Delas Frères, 07300 Saint-Jean-de-Muzols
• CHÂTEAU-LA-NERTHE 1991, 84230 Châteauneuf-du-pape
• CHÂTEAU-DE-LA-GARDINE, 84230 Châteauneuf-du-pape

ODD COMBINATIONS

Sweet or acidic flavors are those most commonly used along with chocolate, but there are other combinations that can produce interesting taste sensations.

• Chocolate and salt: a buttered piece of bread covered in dark, grated chocolate, as our grandmothers remember, is given a new lease on life if the butter is salted and is especially delicious when sprinkled with salt crystals.

• Chocolate and spices: the same bread and chocolate snack (with unsalted butter) will transport you to faraway places if the chocolate is seasoned with a little freshly milled Szechuan pepper or a pinch of grated nutmeg.

THE PLEASURE OF SHARING

People do of course eat chocolate on their own even if they feel slightly ashamed and worried that they are being greedy. But the idea of sharing the experience with fellow chocolate lovers and translating one's feelings into words is attractive and lends an extra dimension to the ceremonies of gourmet tasting—hence the current growth of tasting clubs in the main consumer countries throughout the world.

Chocolate can be satiny, silky, dull, matte, smooth, grainy, shiny, powdery, glowing, spotted ... The colors of dark chocolate: tobacco brown, mahogany, brown, reddish-brown, brownish-ocher, purple ... The colors of milk chocolate: pale ocher, sienna, light caramel ...

Chocolate can have a rancid smell or a smell of licorice, honey, tea, tobacco, a citrus fruit, leather, dust, vanilla, spices, smoke, caramel, burning, roasting, coffee, wood ...

- Jurançon domaine-cauhapé "Symphonie de Novembre" 1999
- Muscat-de-rivesaltes domaine-cazes, 66600 Rivesaltes
- Muscat-de-beaumes-de-venise "La Pastourelle" 1995, Delas Frères, 07300 Saint-Jean-de-Muzols
- Rasteau rouge "Cuvée Signature 93," 84110 Rasteau
- Banyuls astell-des-hospices 1982, 66650 Banyuls-sur-Mer
- Banyuls christian-reynal 1985, 66650 Banyuls-sur-Mer
- Banyuls l'étoile select-vieux 1983, 66650 Banyuls-sur-Mer
- Banyuls vial-magnères al-tragou-rancio-très-vieux 1976, 66650 Banyuls-sur-Mer
- Banyuls domaine-la-tour-vieille "Cuvée Francis Cantié" 1990, 66190 Collioure
- Banyuls domaine-de-la-rectorie "Cuvée Léon Parcé" 1991, 66650 Banyuls-sur-Mer
- Maury mas-amiel "Cuvée spéciale," 66460 Maury
- Les-vignerons-de-maury chabert-de-barbera 1979, 66460 Maury
- Jerez de la frontera (sherry)
- Forty-year-old fonseca port (tawny)
- Kagor 1989 (Crimean wine)
- Château-martin-de-kincsem tokay 1988
- Rum from the Montagne-Pelée Plantation, Chantal Comte, 30900 Nimes

Some crucial tips for cooking with chocolate

Making chocolate is not easy; it takes several years to train a professional chocolate maker, and any gourmet who wants to cook with it needs to stick to certain rules in order to achieve at least satisfactory results. It should be remembered that although there is always room in cooking for some creative variations, the basic rules of baking and cake making are subject to very precise and exacting laws of chemistry. When it comes to using chocolate, some even talk of alchemy.

Quality is the key

All cooks and confectioners will tell you the same: you can only make something good with good ingredients. Always choose high-quality, very fresh produce.
Butter and cream are particularly risky, and only the best will do. There is nothing to compare with the taste you get by using full cream and fresh milk. Current recipes use less sugar than was used before to mask the flavor of the other ingredients. This is all for the best but, even so, high quality is still of the essence.

Choosing the right chocolate

Dark eating chocolate is not ideal for cooking. The plated chocolate that professionals use is rich in butter and cocoa and gives the dish a smooth quality.
Cocoa content is not the priority; chocolate that consists of seventy percent bad cocoa will not produce a good cake. A bitter taste, often confused with the burnt flavor that results from bad roasting, should be avoided. It is better to choose chocolate with a lower cocoa content but with a pleasant taste of fruity spices. The cocoa flavor becomes more important for dishes, such as chocolate mousse, that do not require baking.

Choosing the right cocoa

The powdered cocoa used in cooking and baking needs to be unsweetened so that the flavors are concentrated. Dutch brands are still the best in the world.

How to melt chocolate

Most recipes for chocolate involve melting it, but it is important to note that it should never be placed in a saucepan directly over the flame but should be allowed to heat up gently in a double boiler. The chocolate should be grated or broken into small pieces of the same size and then placed in a bowl set in a saucepan of simmering but not boiling water (130 degrees at the most). It is then important to ensure that all the chocolate is completely melted. A microwave oven may also be used at low temperature (set at defrosting). Once melted, the chocolate must be used immediately. Particular care should be taken when melting plated and milk chocolate, which are extremely sensitive to heat.

Chocolate and water do not mix

When melting chocolate in a double boiler, it is essential to prevent any water from splashing into it. The slightest drop of water is liable to impair the fluidity of the chocolate, making it solidify and turn grainy. Once it is melted you can add milk, cream, or butter; the fat they contain will prevent the chocolate's texture from being broken. Only after that should you pour in any alcohol or coffee.

Coffee and chocolate: a love story

Coffee will give a pleasant flavor to chocolate desserts or mousses. It should be very concentrated and added to the melted chocolate after the cream, milk, or butter has been mixed in.

Icing

Plated chocolate is ideal for icing. Even though it contains more than seventy percent cocoa, by the time the cake is cut the icing will be supple and will not break.
Choose high-quality chocolate because this will be the first part of the cake to release its flavors on the palate.

The simplest way to make a really glossy icing is to melt seven ounces of plated dark chocolate, add one tablespoonful of oil with a neutral flavor, and stir them together away from the double boiler until the mixture is smooth and shiny. Use a metal spatula to spread it evenly over the surface and sides of the cake and then leave it to cool at room temperature (chilling in the refrigerator will spoil its appearance).

Stencil decorations

Cakes can be decorated with unsweetened cocoa powder sifted through a small sieve. To create a pattern, make a stencil by cutting out the desired shape (a candle, a heart, etc.) in the middle of a piece of cardboard. Sprinkle the whole surface of the cake with cocoa and then place the stencil on the cake and sprinkle with sieved confectioner's sugar before delicately removing the cardboard.

Writing with chocolate

Cut a triangular piece of greaseproof paper and roll it very tightly into a cone. Fill the cone one third full with melted chocolate and then fold it over at the top so that the chocolate cannot escape. Cut the point of the cone with scissors to the desired width. You can now decorate your cake with swirls or write words such as "Long live chocolate!"

Dark chocolate in sauces

An added square of dark chocolate will thicken and give extra flavor to all kinds of stews and casseroles made with wine sauces.

HUNGARIAN TOKAY

Louis XIV named Tokay "the king of wines and the wine of kings." It was also the favorite wine of Mozart, Goethe, Schubert, Rossini, and Elisabeth of Wittelsbach or "Sissi," who was empress of Austria.

This wine still graces the most prestigious tables today and is only produced in two or three years out of every ten, which explains its rarity and high price.

With its amber-yellow color, smoothness on the palate, and complex symphony of honey, dried fruit, and crystallized apricot flavors, this outstanding wine has every possible asset. It is more or less sweet depending on the number of puttonyos (baskets) indicated on the label.

KAGOR, "THE BLOOD OF CHRIST"

In the Crimea the noble Muscatel grape produces a dark wine with shades of dark chocolate, coffee, and tobacco. It used to be served as a communion wine in the Russian Orthodox Church and was also the favorite wine of Czar Nicholas II.

Drinks to complement chocolate

WITH MILK CHOCOLATE OR A MILK CHOCOLATE DESSERT	An early-harvest Darjeeling tea (with flavors suggesting muscatel and green almonds), a Yunnan (the king of Chinese teas with an aroma of honey and flowers), a white tea, or a green tea A Santo Domingo Barahona coffee (fruity and subtly acidic) An oak-matured pink Pineau des Charentes, an old Poire Williams brandy, or an old cognac
With caramel-flavored milk chocolate	A late-harvest Gewurztraminer (a high-quality wine that is balanced and elegant, with aromas of flowers and fruit)
With milk chocolate and dried fruits **With a ganache coated in milk chocolate**	A white port A Hungarian Tokay
WITH SWEET DARK CHOCOLATE OR A DESSERT MADE WITH NOT PARTICULARLY DARK CHOCOLATE	A Costa Rican San Marcos de Tarrazu coffee (with longlasting flavor) A first flush Assam tea (with spice flavors) A late-harvest Gewurztraminer, a *grand cru* Banyuls (with flavors of stewed fruit, spices, mocca, tobacco, and notes of roasting), or a Maury (with notes of roasting [coffee and cocoa], undergrowth and tobacco, licorice or *pain d'épice*, or even dark berries [blackcurrants, blueberries]) A ruby port (with fruit and berry flavors) An oak-matured pink Pineau des Charentes
With a chocolate dessert topped with vanilla egg custard	A Rivesaltes Muscatel (with ripe fruit flavors and aromas of exotic fruit, mint, and lemon), or a Beaumes-de-Venise Muscatel (whose flavors suggest all the citrus fruits)
With a plain ganache **With a chocolate macaroon**	A Hungarian Tokay An old Mirabelle brandy or a kirsch
WITH BITTER DARK CHOCOLATE OR A BITTER DARK CHOCOLATE DESSERT	A Yunnan tea A Jurançon (sweet wine with flavors of dried fruits, especially currants, and honey) A ten- to twenty-year-old tawny port (with extraordinary flavors of dried fruits, orange peel, cinnamon, and spices) An old rum
With African dark chocolate	A mocha coffee from the Sarsell Estate, Zimbabwe (high-quality bitter variety)
With a criollo-type chocolate	A Venezuelan Tachira coffee (highest-quality Arabica with flower aromas)
With Asian chocolate	A Papuan coffee (with flavors of dried fruits and cocoa)
With a ganache coated in bitter chocolate	A Java Blue Tawar coffee (rich and strong with chocolate notes) A Lapsang Souchon tea (with a smoky, oaky taste) A Hungarian Tokay A pure malt whisky at least ten years old
WITH PRALINE-FLAVORED CHOCOLATE	An Indian Mysore coffee (both velvety and subtle with hazelnut and almond flavors) An Oolong tea (with chestnut and honey notes) A yellow Jura wine (with powerful, fresh, nutty flavors) A Maury A tawny port at least ten to twenty years old A pure malt whisky at least ten years old
With an almond praline	A Darjeeling tea (with flavors suggesting muscatel and green almonds) or a Maté (a Brazilian tea made from an infusion of roasted holly and very high in caffeine)
WITH A CHOCOLATE MOUSSE	A five- or six-year-old Côte-Rôtie (with flavors of red berries and sometimes even licorice, spices, and cocoa) or a Châteauneuf-du-pape (with flavors of citrus fruits and red berries, which lose their tannins as the wine matures) A yellow Jura wine (with powerful, fresh, nutty flavors) A vintage port (with very fruity, floral, and sometimes resinous flavors) An old cognac
With a bitter chocolate mousse	A Brazilian Sul Minas coffee (strong, smooth, and with longlasting flavor) A Rivesaltes Muscatel or a Beaumes-de-Venise Muscatel A ten- to twenty-year-old port A Grand Marnier

WITH CHOCOLATE ICE CREAM	A Honduran coffee (mild and balanced) A sherry (this sweet Andalusian wine with peppery, cherry flavors counteracts the cold of the ice cream)
With a cocoa sorbet	A Costa Rican Bella Vista coffee (with a hint of bitterness at the finish) A sherry
WITH A BLACK FOREST CAKE	A Columbian Causa coffee (smooth and slightly bitter with red berry flavors) A Rasteau (wine with flavors of crystallized red berries and figs) A sherry or ruby port (with fruit and berry flavors) A kirsch
WITH A HOT CHOCOLATE SOUFFLÉ OR A HOT CHOCOLATE DESSERT	A Javan Macassar coffee (with aromas of spices and cocoa) A five- or six-year-old Côte-Rôtie or a Châteauneuf-du-pape A yellow Jura wine A sherry (Andalusian wine with peppery, cherry flavors) or a vintage port An old cognac
WITH A CHOCOLATE AND FRUIT DESSERT	A Kenyan AA coffee (refined Arabica with fresh and slightly acid notes suggesting citrus fruits) A five- or six-year-old Côte-Rôtie or a Châteauneuf-du-pape A Grand Marnier
With a slightly fruity dark chocolate	An Oolong tea (with chestnut and honey notes)
With citrus fruit chocolate	A Rivesaltes Muscatel or a Beaumes-de-Venise Muscatel
With crystallized oranges	A ten- to twenty-year-old tawny port A Grand Marnier
With a fruit ganache	An oak-matured pink Pineau des Charentes
With Poires Belle-Hélène	An old Poire Williams brandy
WITH SPICY CHOCOLATE OR A DESSERT COMBINING CHOCOLATE AND SPICES	A five- or six-year-old Côte-Rôtie or a Châteauneuf-du-pape A Lapsang Souchon tea A ten- to- twenty-year-old tawny port A yellow Jura wine
With a spicy ganache	A first flush Assam tea A Maury
With ginger chocolate	A Rivesaltes Muscatel or a Beaumes-de-Venise Muscatel
WITH CHOCOLATE CONTAINING DRIED FRUIT	A Yunnan tea A *grand cru* Banyuls A Hungarian Tokay An oak-matured pink Pineau des Charentes
With pistachio chocolate	A late-harvest Gewurztraminer A ten- to twenty-year-old tawny port
With milk chocolate accompanied by dried fruit	A white port
WITH CHOCOLATE WITH A CARAMEL FLAVOR OR FILLING	A Yunnan tea, white tea, or green tea A Hungarian Tokay
With caramel-flavored milk chocolate	A late-harvest Gewurztraminer
WITH A COFFEE AND CHOCOLATE DESSERT	A Maté tea A Rasteau A *grand cru* Banyuls A vintage port

Chocolate has exactly the same effect on men, babies, and old people; it melts them into a state of ecstasy and is irresistibly tempting because it combines all the charm, glamour and grace that stand for luxury and easy living.

Jean-Paul Aron

Where to find the best specialist chocolate makers

IN PARIS AND THE SURROUNDING AREA

LA FONTAINE AU CHOCOLAT
201 rue Saint-Honoré, 75001 Paris
JEAN-PAUL HÉVIN (+ pâtisserie and salon de chocolat)
231 rue Saint-Honoré, 75001 Paris
(two other stores in Paris)
CHRISTIAN CONSTANT (+ pâtisserie and salon de chocolat)
37 rue d'Assas, 75006 Paris
GÉRARD MULOT (+ pâtisserie)
76 rue de Seine, 75006 Paris
CHOCOLATS PUYRICARD
106 rue du Cherche-Midi, 75006 Paris
PIERRE HERMÉ (+ pâtisserie)
72 rue Bonaparte, 75006 Paris
(one other store in Paris)
MICHEL CHAUDUN
149 rue de l'Université, 75007 Paris
DEBAUVE & GALLAIS
30 rue des Saints-Pères, 75007 Paris
(two other stores in Paris)
RICHART DESIGN ET CHOCOLAT
258 boulevard Saint-Germain,
75007 Paris (one other store in Paris)
FAUCHON (+ pâtisserie)
26-30 place de la Madeleine,
75008 Paris
LA MAISON DU CHOCOLAT (+ pâtisserie and salon de chocolat)
52 rue François-Ier, 75008 Paris
(five other stores in Paris)
FOUQUET
22 rue François-Ier, 75008 Paris
(one other store in Paris)
À LA MÈRE DE FAMILLE
35 rue du Faubourg-Montmartre,
75009 Paris
DALLOYAU (+ pâtisserie and salon de chocolat)
93 rue de Provence, 75009 Paris
J.- L. HOFFER, LAFAYETTE GOURMET
46 boulevard Haussmann, 75009 Paris

FRANCIS BOUCHER
202 rue de la Convention, 75015 Paris
LENÔTRE
44 rue d'Auteuil, 75016 Paris
JEAN-YVES MALITOURNE (+ pâtisserie)
30 rue de Chaillot, 75016 Paris
(one other store in Paris)
PIERRETTE CHARPENTIER
87 rue de Courcelles, 75017 Paris
ARNAUD LARHER
53 rue de Caulaincourt, 75018 Paris
L'ATELIER DU CHOCOLAT
rue de l'Église, 95510 Vétheuil
LE CACAOTIER
14 rue Mora, 95880 Enghien-les-Bains
FRÉDÉRIC CASSEL (+ pâtisserie)
71 rue Grande, 77300 Fontainebleau
DAUBOS SAINT LOUIS (+ pâtisserie)
35 rue Royale, 78000 Versailles
(two other stores in the region)
JEAN-LUC PELÉ (+ pâtisserie)
8 rue de Pologne,
78100 Saint-Germain-en-Laye
(three other stores in the region)
PATRICK ROGER
47 rue Houdan, 92330 Sceaux
RÉMI HENRY, L'ATELIER DU CONFISEUR
3 avenue Jean Jaurès, 92700 Colombes

OUTSIDE THE PARIS AREA

AU PALET D'OR
136 boulevard de la Rochelle,
55000 Bar-le-Duc
CHOCOLATERIE DE BEUSSENT LACHELLE
66 route de Desvres, 62170
Beussent
(*cordonnier* chocolate spread)
MICKAÉL AZOUZ (+ pâtisserie)
22 rue d'Alsace-Lorraine, 70000 Vesoul
AU PARRAIN GÉNÉREUX
21, rue du Bourg, 21000 Dijon
BENOÎT
77 rue de la Monnaie, 59800 Lille

MARCEL BONNIAUD
64 avenue des Frères-Lumière,
69008 Lyon
MICHEL BELIN (+ PÂTISSERIE)
9 rue du Taur 31000 Toulouse
(one other store in Albi)
BÉLINE CHOCOLATERIE
5 place Saint-Nicolas, 72000 Le
Mans
BERNACHON
42 cours Franklin-Roosevelt, 69006
Lyon
JEAN-CLAUDE BRIET
La Chocolatière, 48800 Prévenchères
BONNAT (+ pâtisserie and salon de chocolat)
8 cours Sénozan, 38500 Voiron
PHILIPPE BOUVIER
5 rue de la Parchemenerie, 35000
Rennes
JEAN-FRANÇOIS CASTAGNÉ
quai Charles Cazenavenue,
81200 Mazamet
JEAN-PHILIPPE CHARPOT
11 rue de la Cité, 10000 Troyes
LA CHOCOLATIÈRE
6 rue de la Scellerie, 37000 Tours
VINCENT DALLET
26 rue du Général-Leclerc, 51200
ÉPERNAY
Bernard Dufoux
32 rue Centrale, 71800 La Clayette
JOËL DURAND
3 boulevard Victor-Hugo,
13210 Saint-Rémy-de-Provence
CHRISTINE FERBER
18 rue des Trois-Épis,
68230 Niedermorschwihr
JEAN-CLAUDE FRESSON
37 avenue Jean-Jaurès, 54800 Jarny
GIRAUD (+ pâtisserie)
5 place de la République,
26000 Valence
ÉDOUARD HIRSINGER
38 place de la Liberté, 39600 Arbois

HISTOIRE DE CHOCOLAT
60 rue de Siam, 29200 Brest
FRÉDÉRIC JOUVAUD
40 rue de l'Évêché, 84200 Carpentras
PIERRE JOUVENAL
25 rue de la République,
38260 La Côte-Saint-André
HENRI LEROUX
18 rue de Port-Maria, 56170
Quiberon
LES PALETS D'OR
11 rue de Paris, 03000 Moulins
MORAND CHOCOLATERIE
immeuble Carrefour, 74220 La
Clusaz
HENRIET
place Clémenceau, 64200 Biarritz
DANIEL MICHEL
1 rue de Gunsbach,
67400 Illkirch Graffenstaden
MORAND
Le Pas-du-Roc, 74220 La Clusaz
THIERRY MULHAUPT (+ pâtisserie)
18 rue du Vieux-Marché-aux-Poissons,
67000 Strasbourg
(one other store in Strasbourg)
PATISSERIE JACQUES
50 avenue Altkirch, 68100 Mulhouse
RENÉ PILLON
2 rue Ozenne, 31000 Toulouse
PRALUS
8 rue Charles-de-Gaulle,
42300 Roanne
(two other stores in France)
DANIEL REBERT
7 place du Marché-aux-Choux,
67160 Wissembourg
REYNALD (+ pâtisserie)
13 rue Saint-Jacques, 27200 Vernon
SAUNION
56 cours Georges-Clémenceau,
33000 Bordeaux
CHOCOLAT YVES THURIÈS
place de la Cathédrale, 81000 Albi
(+ fifteen stores in France)

ELSEWHERE IN EUROPE

MANON
9a chaussée de Louvain,
1030 Brussels (Belgium)

CHOCOLATS DE LEAUCOUR
35D chaussée d'Audenaerde,
7742 Herinnes (Italy)

CHARLEMAGNE
8 place Jacques-Brel,
4040 Herstal (Belgium)

WITTAMER
12 place du Grand-Sablon,
1000 Brussels (Belgium)

ENRIC ROVIRA
Sant Geroni 17, 08296 Castellbelli
el Vilar Barcelona (Spain)

VALL D'OR
calle Mestre Cellers, 27570 Tora (Spain)

DOLCE & AMARO
via Barba 6 bis, 12030 Pagno CN (Italy)

NICOLAS NESSI LA SALLAZ
avenue du Temple 65, 1012 Lausanne
(Switzerland)

RÉMI BELDAME
avenue Églantine 2, 1006 Lausanne
(Switzerland)

L'HEURE DU CHOCOLAT
Grand'Rue 56, 1820 Montreux
(Switzerland)

IN JAPAN AND THE UNITED STATES

MARY'S CHOCOLATE
1-14 Ohmori-Nishi 7, Chome, Ohta-ku
Tokyo 143-8508 (Japan)

SELIMA SALAUN (eyeglasses and
chocolates by Maribel Lieberman)
25 Prince St, New York, N.Y. (United
States)

The best places to drink hot chocolate

IN PARIS

LA MUSCADE
36 rue de Montpensier, 75001 Paris

ANGÉLINA
226 rue de Rivoli, 75001 Paris

JEAN-PAUL HÉVIN
231 rue Saint-Honoré, 75001 Paris

MAISON STEIGER
20 rue des Capucines, 75002 Paris

LA CHARLOTTE DE L'ISLE
24 rue Saint-Louis-en-l'Ile, 75004
Paris

LA MAISON DE LA VANILLE
18 rue du Cardinal-Lemoine, 75005
Paris

LE CAFÉ DE FLORE
172 boulevard Saint-Germain,
75006 Paris

CLARA RESTAURATION
9 rue Christine, 75006 Paris

CHRISTIAN CONSTANT
37 rue d'Assas, 75006 Paris

L'HEURE GOURMANDE
22 passage Dauphine, 75006 Paris

BRASSERIE LUTÉTIA
45 boulevard Raspail, 75006 Paris

MARIE THÉ
102 rue du Cherche-Midi, 75006 Paris

RESTAURATION VIENNOISE
8 rue de l'École-de-Médecine, 75006
Paris

LES DEUX ABEILLES
189 rue de l'Université, 75007
Paris

LE CRILLON
10 place de la Concorde, 75008
Paris

LA MAISON DU CHOCOLAT
52 rue François-Ier, 75008 Paris

LE SALON DU CHOCOLAT
11 boulevard de Courcelles, 75008
Paris

L'ART HOME CAFE
44 boulevard Arago, 75013 Paris

LE STÜBLI
11 rue Poncelet, 75017 Paris

CHOCOLAT VIENNOIS
118 rue des Dames, 75017 Paris

ELSEWHERE IN FRANCE

BONNAT
8 cours Sénozan, 38500 Voiron

ELSEWHERE IN EUROPE

CAFFE BARATTI & MILANO
piazza Castello, 29, Turin (Italy)

CAFFE FLORIAN (opened 1720)
piazza San Marco, 56/59, Venice (Italy)

RIVOIRE
piazza della Signoria, 5 Florence (Italy)

GILLI
piazza della Repubblica 39/R, Florence
(Italy)

GREENWOODS SINGEL
103 Amsterdam (the Netherlands)

KÖNIG
Lichtentaler Strasse 2, Baden-Baden
(Germany)

GORROTXATEGI
Letxuga Kalea 3, 20 400 Tolosa (Spain)

VIADER
Xuclà 4-6, Barcelona (Spain)

CAFE FÜRST
13 Brodg, Salzburg (Austria)

DEMEL
1 Kohlmarkt, Vienna (Austria)

HOTEL SACHER
4 Philharmonikerstrasse, Vienna
(Austria)

CAFE POUCHKINE
place Pouchkine, Moscow (Russia)

IN MEXICO

THE COFFEE BEANS
5 de Mayo, 114 Oaxaca (Mexico)

Ice cream makers

IN FRANCE

BERTHILLON
31 rue Saint-Louis-en-l'Ile, 75004 Paris
(many places on the l'Ile Saint-Louis
sell Berthillon ice cream)

LA GELATERIA D'ALBERTO
45 rue Mouffetard, 75005 Paris

OCTAVENUE
138 rue Mouffetard, 75005 Paris

BATISTELLI
24 allée Vivaldi, 75012 Paris

PASCAL LE GLACIER
17 rue Bois-le-Vent, 75016 Paris

MISTER ICE
6 rue Descombes, 75017 Paris

DEL PRETE GLACIER
48 rue de la Justice, 95300 Pontoise

GELATI MARSALA
4 rue du Chemin-de-Fer,
93800 Épinay-sur-Seine

LE PIC À GLACE
141 rue Moslard, 92700 Colombes

LE SORBET DE PARIS
22 rue Condorcet,
93100 Montreuil-sous-Bois

LES SORBETS DE SAINT-MANDÉ
47 rue Germaine-et-Roger-Lefèvre,
91550 Paray-Vieille-Poste

MANIVA
17 rue Constant Coquelin,
94400 Vitry-sur-Seine

PEDONE GLACIER
7 rue Marat, 94400 Vitry-sur-Seine

MARTINE LAMBERT
76 bis, rue Eugène-Colas,
14800 Deauville
(one other store in Trouville)

ELSEWHERE IN EUROPE

SAN CRISPINO (open until midnight)
via della Panetteria 42, Rome (Italy)

FESTIVAL DEL FREDO
via Principe Eugenio 17, Rome (Italy)

EREDI GIOLITTI SILVANO
via Uffici del Vicario 40, Rome (Italy)

FIOCCO DI NEVE
via del Pantheon, Rome (Italy)

TRE SCALINI
piazza Navona 38, Rome (Italy)

PERCHE NON
via Tavolini 19, Florence (Italy)

VIVOLI PIERO IL GELATO
via Isola delle Stinche 7/R, Florence
(Italy)

HELADERIA RAYAS
calle Almirante Apodaca, Seville
(Spain)

IN MEXICO

LA ESPECIAL DE PARIS
Insurgentes Centro 117, Loc B Col.,
San Rafael, Mexico City (Mexico)

Restaurants with exciting new ideas for chocolate

Menus may change from season to
season, but these restaurants will
never disappoint with the daring ways
in which they use cocoa and chocolate.

SAVORY DISHES

LE GRAND VÉFOUR
17 rue de Beaujolais, 75001 Paris

À LA MEXICAINE
68 rue Quincampoix, 75003 Paris

SALON DE THÉ FAUCHON
26 place de la Madeleine, 75008 Paris

APICIUS
122 avenue de Villiers, 75007 Paris

L'HERMITAGE
rue du Lac 75, 1815 Montreux-Clarens
(Switzerland)

SWEET DISHES

HÉLICES ET DÉLICES
8 rue Thénard, 75005 Paris

L'ARPÈGE (ALAIN PASSARD)
84 rue de Varenne, 75007 Paris

LES GRANDES MARCHES
6 place de la Bastille, 75012 Paris

JAMIN
32 rue de Longchamp, 75016 Paris

LES FEUILLES LIBRES (Emmanuel Laporte)
34 rue Perronet,
92200 Neuilly-sur-Seine

LE GRAND ÉCUYER (Yves Thuriès)
grand-rue Raymond-VII,
81170 Cordes-sur-Ciel

Clubs

LA MARMITE À MALICES
12 place de Séoul,
75014 Paris
The Marmite consists of a tasting club
(for chocolate and other gastronomic
products) and a theater company
(activities include food exhibits, meals
for chocolate-makers' guilds, and
shows based on the theme of the art
of eating and drinking). It also exhibits
on request a large collection of
advertisements and old objects on the
theme of "chocolate, from advertising
it to enjoying it."

CLUB DU CHOCOLAT AUX PALAIS
62 rue de Rennes, 75006 Paris
This club was founded by three
lawyers and a doctor and is limited to
members of the Palais de Justice, the
Palais du Luxembourg, and the Palais-
Bourbon. Meetings, tastings, etc.

CLUB DES CROQUEURS DE CHOCOLAT
68 bis, boulevard Péreire, 75017 Paris
The club was founded by Jean-Paul
Aron, Nicolas de Rabaudy, and Claude
Lebey in 1980. It is limited to five
hundred members, who must be
nominated for admission. This club
produces the *Guide des croqueurs de
chocolat* (*Chocolate-Eaters' Guide*).

CLUB DU CHOCOLAT
Hôtel Mercure, 1 rue Saint-Jérôme,
31000 Toulouse

CLUB DES MORDUS DU CHOCOLAT
42 cours Pierre-Puget, 13006 Marseille

CLUB DES PASSIONNÉS DU CHOCOLAT
7 rue Hermann-Frenkel,
69364 Lyon Cedex 07

CLUB NESTLÉ (the club does not hold
meetings but has its own small
newspaper and offers special benefits
to members)
Nestlé France, 7 boulevard Pierre-
Carle, BP 900 Noisiel, 77446 Marne-la-
Vallèe Cedex 2

France also has other clubs with more
limited memberships:

LE CACAOE (Comité d'action du
chocolat amer et ouvertement
européen) (Action group for bitter,
unashamedly European chocolate)

LE CACAO (Confrérie des amateurs de
chocolat à l'arôme "otentique")

(Society for lovers of chocolate with an authentic flavor)
LA CITÉ DU CHOCOLAT

CLUB DES PASSIONNÉS DU CHOCOLAT
rue de la Cité 19, CH 1204 Geneva, Switzerland

THE CHOCOLATE SOCIETY
Bar Lane, Roecliffe, York, North Yorkshire, Great Britain

THE CHOCOLATE CLUB
Unit 9, St. Pancreas Commercial Center, 63 Pratt Street, London, Great Britain

CLUB DES MORDUS DU CHOCOLAT
CP 35026, 1221, rue Fleury, East Montreal, H2C3K4 Quebec, Canada

Museums

MUSÉE DU CHOCOLAT
14 avenue Beaurivage, 64200 Biarritz
A remarkable private collection created by chocolate maker Serge Couzigou.

MUSÉE DE L'HÔTELLERIE DU DOMAINE DE CHANTEPERDRIX
26400 Allex
Private collection of master chocolate maker Daniel Giraud (MOF).

LE PALAIS DU CHOCOLAT
25 rue de la République, 38260 La Côte-Saint-André
Private collection of chocolate maker Pierre Jouvenal.

MUSÉE MUNICIPAL
5 place du Collège, 41400 Pontlevoy
The collection is mainly concerned with Poulain chocolate.

MUSÉE ROYBET-FOULD
178 boulevard Saint-Denis, 92400 Courbevoie
The collection focuses primarily on everything to do with Banania.

MUSÉE BASQUE ET DE L'HISTOIRE DE BAYONNE
(Museum of the Basque region and the history of Bayonne)
maison Dagourette
37 rue des Corsaires
64100 Bayonne

LA MAISON DU CACAO
Grand Plaine, 97116 Pointe-Noire, Guadeloupe

MUSÉE DU CACAO ET DU CHOCOLAT
13 Grand-Place, 1000 Brussels, Belgium

MUSÉE DE LA CHOCOLATERIE JACQUES
rue de l'Industrie 16, 4700 Eupen, Belgium

MUSEUM OF CONFECTIONERY
(José Mari Gorrotxategi)

7 plaza Zarra, 20400 Tolosa (Gipuzkoa), Spain

IMHOFF-STOLLWERCK MUSEUM
Rheinauhafen, 50678 Cologne, Germany
A prestigious collection that includes rare pieces; the museum publishes two catalogs in book form.

CADBURY'S MUSEUM
Linden Road, Bournville, Birmingham, Great Britain

CAFFAREL MUSEUM
via Gianavello 41, 10062 Luserna San Giovanni (near Turin), Italy
A private museum that can be visited by appointment.

THE WORLD OF CHOCOLATE
Schoko-Land, Alprose, 6987 Lugano, Switzerland

Events

LE MARCHÉ AUX CHOCOLATS (Chocolate Market)
This takes place at the end of October in Paris and is a gathering for the specialist chocolate makers of the Union professionnelle des confiseurs de Paris et d'Ile-de-France (Professional Association of Confectioners in Paris and Ile-de-France) 103 rue La Fayette, 75481 Paris Cedex 10.

LE SALON DU CHOCOLAT (The Chocolate Show)
This event, organized since 1995 by Sylvie Douce and François Jeantet (Event International: 70 rue de la Tour, 75116 Paris), brings together craftsmen and manufacturers in Paris and usually takes place at the end of October. The star attraction is a fashion parade of chocolate dresses, which is now taken abroad every year to the Chocolate Show in New York at Thanksgiving and to Tokyo on Saint Valentine's Day.

BAYONNE EN CHOCOLAT
An event organized by the chocolate makers of Bayonne on Ascension Day. Information from the office du tourisme, place des Basques, 64100 Bayonne.

THE CATALAN XICOLATADA
A hot chocolate aperitif is offered to the public in August by the inhabitants of Palau, dressed in traditional costumes (66800 Palau-de-Cerdagne).

LA FÊTE DU CHOCOLAT (The Festival of Chocolate)
Founded in 1992 by Michail Azouz, this takes place in October and consists of various events outside of Paris.

INTERSUC
The International Exhibit of chocolate making, confectionery, baking, cookie

making, and gourmet products (limited to professionals) is held in Paris in January (Intersuc, 103 rue La Fayette, 75010 Paris).

SALON INTERNATIONAL DE LA CONFISERIE DE COLOGNE (ISM) (International Confectionery Exhibit at the Salon de Cologne)
This event, held in January, brings together more than 1,500 exhibitors from seventy countries (René Wodetzki, Salon de Cologne, 12 rue Chernoviz, 75782 Paris Cedex 16).

EUROCHOCOLATE
An event organized until 1999 in Perugia, then moved in April 2000 to Turin (Direzione e Ufficio Stampa, 19 via Ruggero d'Andreotto, 06124 Perugia, Italy).

Bookstores specializing in food and cuisine

LA LIBRAIRIE DES GOURMETS
98 rue Monge, 75005 Paris
LA LIBRAIRIE GOURMANDE
4 rue Dante, 75005 Paris
ALLALEIGH HOUSE
Blackawton, Totnes, TQ9 7DL, Great Britain
KITCHEN ARTS & LETTERS
1435 Lexington Avenue, New York, NY 10128, U.S.A.

ANTIQUARIAN BOOKS
RÉMI FLACHARD
9 rue du Bac, 75007 Paris
ALAIN HUCHET
quai Conti, 75006 Paris (secondhand bookseller)
49 rue Daguerre, 75014 Paris
GÉRARD OBERLÉ
manoir de Pron, 58340 Montigny-sur-Canne

Recent books

GENERAL
VARIOUS AUTHORS, *Le livre du chocolat,* Flammarion, 1995
VARIOUS AUTHORS, *Chocolat, de la boisson élitaire au bâton populaire xvie-xxe siècle,* CGER, 1996
DOMINIQUE AYRAL, *Passion chocolat,* Phare international, 2000
MARIE-CHRISTINE AND DIDIER CLÉMENT, *La magie du chocolat,* Albin Michel, 1998
SOPHIE AND MICHAEL D. COE, *Généalogie du chocolat,* Abbeville, 1998
CHRISTIAN CONSTANT, *Du chocolat, discours curieux,* Ramsay, 1999
PAULE CUVELIER, GILLES BROCHARD, *Deux siècles au chocolat, la légende de Debauve et Gallais,* l'Atelier de l'Archer, 2000
HENRY AND LAURE DORCHY, *Le moule à chocolat,* Ephéméra, 1999
ANTOINE GALLAIS, *Monographie du cacao, ou manuel de l'amateur de chocolat,* 1827, Phénix, new edition 1999

SYLVIE GIRARD, JACQUES PESSIS, *Souvenirs en chocolat,* Mille et Une Nuits, 1997
NIKITA HARWICH, *Histoire du chocolat,* Desjonquères, 1992
KATHERINE KHODOROWSKY, HERVÉ ROBERT, *L'ABCdaire du chocolat,* Flammarion, 1997
KATHERINE KHODOROWSKY, HERVÉ ROBERT, *Le chocolat,* Biotop, 1998
JACQUES MERCIER, *Chocolat belge, la* Renaissance du Livre, 1997
ANNIE PERRIER-ROBERT, *Le chocolat,* Les Éditions du Chêne, 1998

RECIPE BOOKS
FRÉDÉRIC BAU, *Caprices de chocolat,* Albin Michel, 1998
PIERRE HERMÉ, *Secrets gourmands,* Larousse, 1994
YANNICK LEFORT, *La journée chocolat,* Hachette, 2000
ROBERT LINXE, MICHÈLE CARLES, *La maison du chocolat,* les Éditions du Chêne, 2000
CHRISTIAN TEUBNER, *Le chocolat,* Nathan, 1997
BLANDINE VIE-MARCADE, *Le savoir-vivre du chocolat,* Minerva, 1999

CHILDREN'S BOOKS
JEAN ALESSANDRINI, JEAN-LOUIS BESSON, *Mystère et chocolat,* Bayard Poche, 1990
FRÉDÉRIQUE BERTRAND, *Choco,* Les Éditions du Rouergue, 2000
JOHN BRANFIELD, *Sugar Mouse,* Gollancz, 1973
ROBERT CORMIER, *The Chocolate War,* Laureleaf, 1999
GEORGES COULONGES, *Une grand-mère en chocolat,* Kid Pocket, 1999
ROALD DAHL, *Charlie and the Chocolate Factory,* Knopf, 1964
IRÈNE FRAIN, *La fée chocolat,* Stock, 1995
LLUIS GARAY, *L'arbre à chocolat,* L'École des Loisirs, 1999
DIDIER HERLEM, *Mystère au chocolat,* Cascade-Rageot, 1997
SYLVIE LENÔTRE, *Les petits chefs, tout chocolat,* Hachette Jeunesse, 1993
DIANE MOTT-DAVIDSON, *Dying for Chocolate,* Crime Line, 1993
MARIE WABBES, *Le bon chocolat,* L'École des Loisirs, 1996

Guide

GUIDE DES CROQUEURS DE CHOCOLAT, Stock, 1998

Magazines

GENERAL INTEREST

LA REVUE DU CHOCOLAT, annual catalog of the Salon du Chocolat; Event International: 70 rue de la Tour, 75116 Paris, France

CHOCOLATIER, A TASTE OF THE GOOD LIFE; New York Advertising Offices: 45 West 34th Street, Suite 600, New York, N.Y. 10001, U.S.A.

CIOCCOLATTA & C. (quarterly magazine in Italian); Il Periodico Editore: 16 via Pisacane, 20129 Milan, Italy

THE INTERNATIONAL COOKBOOK REVUE (in English); Françoise de Ganay: 23 rue de Prony, 92600 Asnières, France
A review of books being published throughout the world on the theme of cooking and gastronomy.

MAGAZINES FOR PROFESSIONALS

CHOCOLAT ET CONFISERIE MAGAZINE
103 rue La Fayette, 75481 Paris Cedex 10

PLANTATIONS, RECHERCHE ET DÉVELOPPEMENT (CIRAD), PRD: 12 square Pétrarque 75116 Paris

Internet websites

Some of the websites listed are of general interest; others show the products of a specific chocolate maker and in many cases offer the opportunity to buy on the Internet.

alliance7.fr/sweets/chocolate
choco-club.com
chocoholic.com (American chocolate on line)
chocoland.com (the Salon du Chocolat's website)
chocolateshow.com (international chocolate exhibits)
chocolats.org (website for the Chambre Syndicale Nationale des Chocolatiers)
cirad.fr (tropical agronomy)
croqueurschocolat.com (website for the Croqueurs de Chocolat club)
eurochocolate.torino.it (Italian Chocolate Show)
icco.org
ifrance.com/cacao
saveurs.sympatico.ca/ency_8/cacao/cacao.htm
swisschoc.com
users.skynet.be/chocolat/fr/index.html
bonnat-chocolatier.com/fr-idx.htm
chocolat-daval.fr
chocolat-castan.com
cotedor.be
kraft-foods.de/index2.html
jeff-de-bruges.com
marquise-de-sevigne.com
mars.com
nestle.fr and chocolat.nestle.fr
roy.fr
valrhona.com

Professional organizations

CHAMBRE SYNDICALE NATIONALE DES CHOCOLATIERS
194 rue de Rivoli, 75001 Paris
The CSNC belongs to Alliance 7, which also includes other professional associations in the food industry. It gives information about the

chocolate-making profession and specific issues connected to it and is particularly active in campaigning for 5.5% V.A.T. to be levied on all goods produced by specialist chocolate makers.

CONFÉDÉRATION DES CONFISEURS ET CHOCOLATIERS DE FRANCE
103 rue La Fayette, 75010 Paris
The CCCF safeguards the continuity and high standing of the chocolate-making, confectionery, and cookie-making professions in the world of craftsmen, retailers, and smaller businesses. Each region has its own professional union of confectioners and chocolate makers.

OFFICE INTERNATIONAL DU CACAO, DU CHOCOLAT ET DE LA CONFISERIE
1 rue Defacqz, boîte 7, B 1050 Brussels, Belgium
Founded in 1930, the OICCC represents manufacturers of cocoa, chocolate, and confectionery at the world level. Its aim is to encourage scientific research and development in these industries. Europe is represented by Caobisco (the European Union association for the chocolate, cookie, biscotte, and confectionery industries).

CENTRE DE COOPÉRATION INTERNATIONAL DE RECHERCHE AGRONOMIQUE POUR LE DÉVELOPPEMENT
Registered office: 42 rue Scheffer, 75116 Paris
Research center: avenue Agropolis, BP 5035, 34032 Montpellier Cedex 1
CIRAD is a French body that specializes in applied agronomic research into hot regions of the world. Its aim is to contribute to the development of rural areas in tropical and subtropical countries. One of the twenty-eight research programs currently in progess concerns cocoa. This body has produced various publications on the subject of cocoa, and it also publishes the magazine *Plantations*.

Other organizations

L'ACADÉMIE FRANÇAISE DU CHOCOLAT ET DE LA CONFISERIE
103 rue La Fayette, 75010 Paris
Founded on January 22, 1998, the AFCC seeks to embody a moral authority in keeping with the occupations of chocolate making and confectionery, and to be the guardian

---

"Meilleur Ouvrier de France" is an award that honors excellence and quality of work, encouraging modernity by passing on know-how.
Joël Robuchon

---

of tradition and development within the context of a professional ethic. Its aim is to develop values of quality and excellence, while at the same time defending and promoting traditional chocolate and confectionery. Its forty members include renowned professionals—several of whom are Meilleurs Ouvriers de France (Best Craftsmen in France—historians, writers, doctors, and scientists, who retain their independence in the face of the commercial brands and industrial lobbies. The president of the Académie is Jean-Pierre Richard (MOF).

L'ACADÉMIE DU CHOCOLAT DE BAYONNE
Musée basque et de l'histoire de Bayonne: maison Dagourette, 37 rue des Corsaires, 64100 Bayonne, France
The ACB was founded in 1993 to contribute to the fame and reputation of Bayonne chocolate with its specific history and traditions.

Guilds

The guilds were created in France to promote the reputation of good chocolate. Each branch admits new members on the basis of the work they have done for the cause of chocolate.

CONFRÉRIE DES CHOCOLATIERS FRANÇAIS
Michel Armand, Promosuc
103 rue La Fayette, 75010 Paris

CONFRÉRIE DES GOÛTEURS DE CHOCOLAT DE FRANCHE-COMTÉ
4 Grande-Rue, 25000 Besançon

CONFRÉRIE DES MINJADORS DU CHOCOLAT FIN DU LIMOUSIN
M. Daniel Borzeix
Le Loubanel, 19260 Treignac

CONFRÉRIE DES CHOCOLATIERS CATALANS
Édouard Gomez
54 avenue du Général-de-Gaulle, 66160 Le Boulou

CONFRÉRIE DES AMATEURS DE CHOCOLAT DE LA NIÈVRE
Maurice Genepiot
28 boulevard Saint-Exupéry, 58000 Nevers

CONFRÉRIE DES ROCHERS AU CHOCOLAT DE SAINT-MIHIEL
Laurent Christ
23 rue Jeanne-d'Arc, 55300 Saint-Mihiel

CONFRÉRIE DES COUSSINS D'AMOUR
Michel Prinet
2 rue du Pin, 86200 Pouant

Professional training

Established heads of chocolate firms needing to recruit new staff for their teams are currently finding, to their great sadness, that it is very difficult to find young chocolate makers.

Teenagers do not seem to find this occupation very attractive, despite the privilege it offers of having customers who "buy for pleasure" (in the nineteenth century, confectioners were actually called "pleasure merchants"). For young people who would like to enter the chocolate business (a sector in which unemployment is unheard of), this is how they can acquire the necessary training:

CANDIDATES FOR THE CERTIFICAT D'APTITUDE PROFESSIONNELLE (CAP) can train at a Centre de Formations d'Apprentis (CFA) (Apprentice Training Center), where they need to have signed a contract with a business before they start. The course is aimed at young men and women of between sixteen and twenty-five years of age. It takes place either in one stage (two years of training for the CAP in chocolate making and confectionery) or in two stages (two years of a joint syllabus with the CAP in pâtisserie and then one year specializing in chocolate and confectionery). It is also possible to train at a lycée professionnel (vocational high school), at the École de Paris des métiers de la table (Paris School of Catering), by in-house training, or by a contract of certification.
The Brevet Technique des Métiers (BTM) is a preparation for training as a manager or foreman and can also lead to the Brevet de Maîtrise (Master's Certificate).
Le Brevet de Maîtrise (BM), awarded by the Chamber of Commerce, is a high professional qualification that is especially geared toward future heads of companies.
The much coveted title of Meilleur Ouvrier de France (MOF) is awarded on the basis of a special competition that takes place every three years and comprises tests of a theoretical, technological, practical, and artistic nature.

Sources

The works listed here are classed in chronological order of publication from the sixteenth century to the present day.

16TH CENTURY
PEDRO MARTYR DE ANGLERIA, *On the New World*, 1530
BERNARDINO DE SAHAGUN, *A General History of the Affairs of New Spain*, 1550
DIAZ DEL CASTILLO, *A True History of the Conquest of New Spain*, 1563
JÉRÔME BENZONI, *The History of the New World*, 1572
JOSÉ DE ACOSTA, *A Natural and Moral History of the West Indies*, 1590

17TH CENTURY
BARTHELEMY MARRADON, *Dialogue on Chocolate between a Doctor, an Indian, and a Man of Means*, 1618

COLMENERO DE LADESMA, *Treaty on the Nature and Quality of Chocolate*, 1635
LÉON PINELO, *The Moral Question of whether Chocolate breaks the Religious Fast*, 1636
JEAN DE LAET, *The History of the New World, or a Description of the West Indies*, 1640
HENRI STUBBE, *The Indian Nectar*, 1662
FRANCESCO MARIA BRANCACCIO, *Diatribe on Chocolate*, 1664
J. SPON, *On the Use of Coffee, Tea, and Chocolate*, 1671
PHILIPPE SYLVESTRE DUFOUR, *On the Use of Coffee, Tea, and Chocolate*, 1671
THOMAS GAGE, *New Account of Travels*, 1676
J.-P. BACHOT, F. FOUCAULT, *L'usage du chocolat est-il salubre?* 1684
PHILIPPE SYLVESTRE DUFOUR, *Traités nouveaux et curieux du café, du thé et du chocolat*, 1685
NICOLAS DE BLÉGNY, *Abrégé des traités du café, du thé et du chocolat pour la préservation et pour la guérison des maladies*, 1687
NICOLAS AUDIGER, *La maison réglée*, 1692
MARCO MAPPO, *Medical Dissertations on the Hot Drinks: Tea, Coffee, Chocolate*, 1695
F. AIGNAN, *Le prêtre médecin*, 1696
LOUIS LÉMERY, *Traité universel des drogues*, 1698
FRANÇOIS MASSIALOT, *Le cuisinier royal et bourgeois*, third edition, 1698
BONAVENTURE D'ARGONNE, *Mélanges d'histoire et de littérature*, 1699

18TH CENTURY
D. DUNCAN, *Wholesome Advice against the Abuse of Hot Liquors, particularly Coffee, Chocolate, Tea, Brandy, and Strong Waters*, 1705
L. BIET, *Le bon usage du chocolat dégraissé*, 1707
NICOLAS ANDRY, *Le régime de carême considéré par rapport à la nature du corps et des aliments*, 1710
PHILIPPE HECQUET, *Traité des dispenses de carême*, 1710
F. ARISI, *Dithyrambe sur le chocolat*, 1710
M. DE CAYLUS, *Histoire naturelle du cacao et du sucre*, 1719
THOMAS GAGE, *New Account of the Travels of Thomas Gage in New Spain*, 1720
JEAN-BAPTISTE LABAT, *Nouveau voyage aux isles d'Amérique*
MADAME DE SÉVIGNÉ, *Lettres*, 1726
MILHAU, *Dissertation sur le cacaoyer*, 1746
DENIS DIDEROT, JEAN D'ALEMBERT, *Encyclopédie ou Dictionnaire raisonné des sciences, des arts et des métiers*, 1753
LOUIS LÉMERY, *Traité des aliments*, 1755
NAVIER, *Observations sur le cacao et le chocolat*, 1772
BOISEL, PELISSART, *Observations sur le chocolat et le cacao*, 1772
DEMACHY, *L'art du distillateur liquoriste*, 1775
PIERRE JEAN-BAPTISTE LE GRAND D'AUSSY, *Histoire de la vie privée des Français*, 1782
PIERRE JOSEPH BUCHOZ, *Dissertation sur le tabac, le café, le cacao et le thé*, 1787

19TH CENTURY
ALEXANDRE BALTHAZAR GRIMOD DE LA REYNIÈRE, *L'almanach des gourmands*, 1804
PIERRE JOSEPH BUCHOZ, *Traité usuel du chocolat*, 1812
CADET DE GASSICOURT, *Dictionnaire des sciences médicales*, 1813
P. H. BOUTIGNY, *Du chocolat, de sa fabrication et des moyens de connaître sa falsification et ses propriétés alimentaires médicales*, 1825
ANTHELME BRILLAT-SAVARIN, *Physiologie du goût*, 1826
ANTOINE GALLAIS, *Monographie du cacao*, 1827
E. DELCHER, *Recherches historiques et chimiques sur le cacao et diverses préparations*, 1837
JOSEPH BARRATA, *Manuel complet, théorique et pratique du chocolatier*, 1841
A. SAINT-ARROMAN, *De l'action du café, du thé et du chocolat sur la santé et leurs influences sur l'intelligence et la morale de l'homme*, 1845
PERRON, *Du chocolat et du thé*, 1852
L. M. LOMBARD, *Le cuisinier et le médecin*, 1855
DELAFONTAINE, DESTWILLER, *Le chocolat*, 1860
A. AND E. PELLETIER, *Le thé et le chocolat dans l'alimentation publique*, 1861
ARTHUR MANGIN, *Le cacao et le chocolat*, 1862
A. DEBAY, *Les influences du chocolat, du thé et du café sur l'économie humaine*, 1864
H. FOREST, *On Cacao and its Various Species*, 1864
A. AND E. PELLETIER, *Essai historique, gastronomique et physiologique sur le chocolat*, 1865
M. F. DELAUNAY, *Le chocolat*, 1868
A. MARVAUD, *Des aliments d'épargne: thé, maté, cacao*, 1874
ÉMILE JUSTIN MENIER, *Fabrication spéciale des chocolats de qualité supérieure*, 1875
AIMÉ RIANT, *Le café, le chocolat, le thé*, 1880
E. O. LAMI, *Dictionnaire encyclopédique et biographique de l'industrie et des arts industriels*, 1900
L. BELFORT DE LA ROQUE, *Guide pratique de la fabrication du chocolat*, 1892
ALFRED FRANKLIN, *La vie privée d'autrefois*, 1893, vol. 13 "Le Café, le Thé et le Chocolat"
CARDELLI, *Nouveau manuel complet du confiseur et du chocolatier, Encyclopédie Roret*, 1896

20TH CENTURY
A. L. GIRARD, *Les sucres, le café, le thé, le chocolat*, 1907
J. FRITSCH, *Fabrication du chocolat d'après les procédés les plus récents*, 1910
EDITH BROWNE, London, C.A. Black Ltd., 1920
RAOUL LECOQ, *L'histoire du chocolat*, 1924
HENRI BLIN, *Nouveau manuel complet du confiseur et du chocolatier, Encyclopédie Roret*, 1930

A. MAURIZIO, *Histoire de l'alimentation végétale de la préhistoire à nos jours*, 1932
ALBERT BOURGAUX, *Quatre siècles d'histoire du chocolat*, 1935
DÉSIRÉ BOIS, *Vigne, café, cacao et autres plantes à boire*, 1937 (new edition, Rive Droite, 1996)
ALEXANDRE DE HUMBOLDT, *Voyage aux règions équinoxiales du Nouveau Continent*, 1945
JEAN CHAVIGNY, *La belle histoire du chocolat Poulain*, 1948 (new edition, Les Amis du Vieux Blois, 1996)
WOLF MUELLER, *Bibliography of Cocoa*, 1951
WOLF MUELLER, *Bibliography of Coffee, Cocoa, Chocolate and Tea*, 1960
FRANÇOIS LERY, *Le cacao*, PUF, 1960, Que sais-je? collection
LOUIS BURLE, *Le cacaoyer*, Maisonneuve and Larose, 1961
JEAN BRAUDEAU, *Le cacaoyer*, Maisonneuve, 1969
ANDRÉ CASTELOT, *L'histoire à table*, Plon-Perrin, 1972
HELGE RUBINSTEIN, *The Chocolate Book*, Penguin, 1982
MARTINE JOLY, *Le chocolat, une passion dévorante*, Robert Laffont, 1983
JEAN-MARIE FONTENEAU, *Le chocolat*, Dargaud, 1983
SYLVIE GIRARD, *Guide du chocolat et de ses à-côtés*, Messidor, 1984
M. ET J.-J. BERNACHON, *La passion du chocolat*, Flammarion, 1985
F. ET M. MORTON, *Chocolate, an Illustrated History*, New York, Crown Pub., 1986
H. DORCHY, *Le moule à chocolat*, Éditions de l'Amateur, 1987
SANDRA BOYNTON, *Chocolate: the Consuming Passion*, Workman, 1982 (a wild, hilarious story)
COLLECTIF DONZÈRE, *La chocolaterie d'Aiguebelle*, Mairie de Donzère, 1987
MARIAROSA SCHIAFFINO, MICHEL CLUIZEL, *La route du chocolat*, Gentleman, 1988
CHRISTIAN CONSTANT, *Le chocolat, le goût de la vie*, Nathan, 1988
ANNE HODGES, *The Chocolate Book*, Kato Pr., 1985
JACQUES MERCIER, *Le chocolat belge*, Glénat, 1989
J.-L. GOMBAUD, C. MOUTOUT, S. SMITH, *La guerre du cacao*, Calmann-Lévy, 1990
HERVÉ ROBERT, *Les vertus thérapeutiques du chocolat*, Artulen, 1990 (with a bibliography including 140 references to French and international scientific publications on the theme of "chocolate and health")
JILL NORMAN, *Le chocolat*, Robert Laffont, 1990
GUY MOSSU, *Le cacaoyer*, Maisonneuve and Larose, 1990
ÉLISE GASPARD-DAVIS, *L'homme et le chocolat*, le léopard d'or, Museum de Lyon, 1991
FRÉDÉRIQUE SALSMANN, *Chocolat Show*, Épigones, 1991 (for children)
JEAN-CLAUDE BOLOGNE, *Histoire morale et culturelle de nos boissons*, Robert Laffont, 1991
NIKITA HARWICH, *Histoire du chocolat*, Desjonquères, 1992 (work of reference with a large bibliography)

PIERO CAMPORESI, *Exotic Brew*, Blackwell, 1994
VARIOUS AUTHORS, *Nourriture d'enfance*, Autrement, "Mutations" series, no. 129, April 1992
IGNACIO DE LA MOTA, *El libro del chocolate*, Piramide, 1992
CHRISTIAN SANTOR, *Sous l'empire du cacao, étude diachronique de deux terroirs camerounais*, Orstom, 1992
JEAN-MARC TOUZARD, *L'économie coloniale du cacao en Amérique centrale*, CIRAD, 1993
COLLECTIF NOISIEL, *La chocolaterie Menier: l'inventaire*, Image du Patrimoine, Inventaire général des monuments et richesses artistiques de la France, 1994
JACQUES VIVET, *Goûter le vin; guide pratique de la dégustation*, Christian de Bartillat, 1994
LINDA K. FULLER, *Chocolate Fads, Folklore & Fantasies*, Harrington Park Press, 1994
MICHEL ORNAY, *La raison gourmande*, Grasset, 1995
OLIVIER CALON, *Le chocolat*, Du May, 1996
JEAN-MARIE PINCON, *La saga Menier*, Nestlé France, 1996
PHILIPPE BLANSBAND, *Les mangeuses de chocolat*, Lansman, 1996 (stage play)
CHRISTINE BEIGEL, *Gâteaux*, Syros, 1996
BERNARD LOISEAU, GÉRARD GILBERT, *Trucs de pâtissier*, Marabout Côté Cuisine, 1996
SERGE GUÉRIN, *Le chocolat*, Milan, 1997
PIERRE VEILLETET, *Le vin, leçon de choses*, Arlea, 1997
JEAN PONTILLON, *Cacao et chocolat*, Tech et Doc., 1998
JEAN WATIN-AUGOUARD, *Le dictionnaire des marques*, JVDS, 1997
CARLE BLOOM, *All About Chocolate*, Macmillan, New York, 1998
WILLY PASINI, *Nourriture et amour*, Payot, 1998
PASCAL COURAULT, FRANÇOIS BERTIN, *Cent ans de plaques émaillées françaises*, Ouest-France, 1998
VARIOUS AUTHORS, *Un siècle de personnages publicitaires*, Bibliothèque Forney, 1999
JOHN GLENN BRENNER, *The Emperors of Chocolate* (Hershey and Mars), Broadway Books, New York, 2000
SERGE SAFFRAN, *L'amour gourmand*, La Musardine, 2000
CHRISTINE MCFADDEN, CHRISTINE FRANCE, *Cooks Encyclopedia of Chocolate*, Barnes and Noble, 2000

Magazine consulted: **CHOCOLAT ET CONFISERIE MAGAZINE**

index

A

advertising 26, 31, 32, 33, 34, 69, 97, 98, 110
Africa 13, 41, 44, 45, 94
After Eight 80
Agrocacao 40
Amazon 7, 39
Amelonado 41, 44
Anne of Austria 13, 20
Aron (Jean-Paul) 67, 68
Asia 13, 41, 47, 83, 94
Atlan (Thierry) 95
atolle (corn porridge) 8, 19, 83
Austria 11, 78
Aztecs 8, 9, 10, 11, 19, 22, 58, 87, 94, 104, 111

B

ballotin (small box of chocolates) 74, 95
Banania 28, 29, 36, 63
Banika 31
bars of chocolate 31, 63, 82, 83, 86
    filled 75
Barry 23
Barry-Callebaut (group) 44, 59, 73, 75
beans 7, 8, 9, 11, 12, 22, 23, 32, 39, 40, 41, 42, 43, 52, 58, 59, 73, 79, 81, 83
    processing 49, 50, 51
Belgium 57, 74, 75
Bernachon (Jean-Jacques) 59
Bernachon (Maurice) 59, 64, 67
bicerin 76
Black Forest cake 64, 79
Bolivia 109
Bonnat (Félix) 59
Bonnat (Raymond) 52
Bontekoe (Cornelius) 12
bouchées (single chocolates) 31, 57, 76
Boucher (Francis) 69
Bouet (Régis) 173
Bouisset (Firmin) 26, 27, 32, 33, 97
Bounty 63
Bournville 23, 25, 79
Brazil 45, 46
Briet (Jean-Claude) 69, 97
brownies 64, 82
brown rot (disease) 40, 44
Bruges (Jeff de) 90

C

cabosse (cacao fruit/pod) 9, 24, 39, 40, 41, 42, 44, 46, 104, 105
cacao 12, 83
    cocoa, high-class 41
    cocoa, market 47
    cocoa powder 20, 23, 26, 27, 82, 174
    consumer countries 67
    depodding 42
    drying 42
    fermentation 42
    harvesting 42
    processing 37, 42, 43
    production 40, 41, 44, 45, 46, 47

Cacao Barry 59
cacao growing 39, 40, 41, 42, 43, 44, 45, 46, 47, 80
cacao tree 7, 10, 13, 25, 37, 39, 68, 109
    types 40
Cadbury 23, 25, 29, 79, 86
Cadbury (George) 23
Cadbury (John) 23, 79, 80
Caffarel (Isidore) 36, 77
Cailler (François-Louis) 71, 72
cakes and pastries 78, 79
Callebaut 59
Cameroon 41, 44
Campbell (group) 74
candy 56, 57, 98
    pill-like 63
Capiello (Leonetto) 26, 34, 97
cappuccino 76
Caribbean 40, 41
Carletti (Francesco) 11
Casanova (Giovanni Giacomo) 76, 87, 100
Cassel (Frédéric) 69
Cémoi (group) 44, 57, 100
Central America 40, 41
champurrado 83
Chaudun (Michel) 56, 69, 98
chérelles 39, 40
China 83
Choco BN 87, 89
chocolate 10, 14, 83
    and advertising 90, 94, 95, 104
    and art 97, 98, 99
    and film 95, 101, 102
    and coffee 173, 174
    and cosmetics 104
    and fashion 104, 105
    and literature 99, 100
    and music 14, 74, 89, 101, 103
    and spirits 173
    and tea 173
    and theater 101
    and the Church 16, 17
    and the medical faculty 17, 18
    and wine 173, 174
    choice 173
    coating manufacture 59, 110
    coating/plated/confectioner's chocolate 57, 59, 174
    composition 90, 107, 112, 113
    consumption 67, 108, 109, 110, 111, 112, 113
    cooking 31
    Danzig 15
    dark 29, 52, 67, 83, 107, 109, 112
    diet 113
    drink 8, 10, 11, 12, 13
    fondant 73
    filled 29
    hazelnut/filbert 23, 72
    hot 63, 76, 79, 80, 81, 82, 86, 97, 100, 172, 173, 178
    hygienic 68
    implements 19, 20, 21, 36
    keeping 173, 174

liégeoise 64
marbled 56
medicinal 11, 18, 68, 113
milk 23, 29, 54, 55, 71, 72, 78, 107, 110
organic 109, 110
origin of the word 19
powdered 82, 171
presentation 86, 95
received ideas 107, 108, 109, 110, 111
solid 10, 12, 29
spread throughout Europe 11, 12
spread to France 13, 14, 15
symbols 85, 86, 87, 90, 99
taste combinations 173, 175, 176
tasting 172, 173
Viennese 78
vocabulary 52, 53
white 56, 107, 110
chocolate cigarettes 58
chocolate cream bar 23, 79
chocolate houses 12
chocolate maker 13, 18, 23, 32, 43, 59, 79
    queen's 14
chocolate makers 11, 12, 22, 23, 49, 68, 69, 76, 77
    Chocolaterie de l'Opéra 59
    Chocolaterie du Pecq 59
    Chocolaterie du Vivarais 59
chocolate pot 19, 20, 21, 23, 36, 97
chocolate spread 74
Chocopasta 74
chocophile 110
cholesterol 108, 111, 112
chromolithographs 26, 32
Chuao 41, 46, 52
Churchman (Walter) 22, 79
Cluizel (Michel) 52, 173
coating 57, 59
cocoa butter 8, 22, 23, 44, 46, 47, 52, 56, 59, 73, 82, 104, 111, 112
cocoa drinks 63
cocoa mass 51
cocoa mass/paste 8, 43, 51, 52, 111
collections 36, 37
Colombia 40, 41
colonies 28, 29, 37, 94
Columbus (Christopher) 9, 10
cookie making 29, 79
Compagnie des chocolats and thés Pelletier & Cie (Pelletier & Co. Chocolate and Tea Company) 22
Compagnie française des chocolats et des thés (French Chocolate and Tea Company) 34, 97
competition 26, 31
conch 51, 71
    origin of the word 51
conching 23, 50, 51, 73, 75
confectionery 63
Constant, Christian 69, 99
Conticini, Philippe 64
Cortez (Hernando) 10, 19
Côte d'Or 74, 75, 100

Couzigou (Serge) 95
craft/specialist chocolate makers 31, 59, 69, 177, 178
cremino 76
Criollo 39, 40, 41, 42, 45, 47, 53
cru 52, 53, 59
Crunch 95
crushing/grinding 51
crystallized oranges (orangettes) 57
cup
    queen 20
    trembling 12, 20, 36, 97
cut test 43

D

Dairy Milk 29, 79, 80
Debauve 14, 18, 95
Debauve and Gallais 18, 68
Debauve (Sulpice) 68
Delacre (Charles) 75
depodding 50
desserts 63, 64
Diderot 20, 22
diseases 40
Dominican Republic 40
Droste (Gérard) 81, 82
Dubois (Louis) 69
Dufour (Louis) 57
Dufoux (Bernard) 69, 90
Durand (Joël) 69, 96, 97

E

Ecuador 41, 43, 46
enamel plates 34, 36
England 12, 13, 22, 23, 79
Escher (Henri) 13
European Union directive 44, 52, 111

F

Ferber (Christine) 69
Fernando Poo (Bioko) 44, 45
Ferrero 60, 76, 90
Ferrero Rocher 77
Fingers 80
foamer 9, 20, 21, 23, 83
Forastero 40, 41, 42, 44, 45, 46, 47, 53
Fourier (Charles) 23, 25
filling 57, 58, 59, 97
France 13, 14, 15, 23, 24, 25, 26, 27, 28, 40, 57, 58, 59, 67, 68, 69
Fry & Sons 23, 79
Fry (Joseph) 79

G

Gage (Thomas) 12
Gallais (Antoine) 68
Galler 74, 98
ganache 58, 64, 67
Gerard (John) 12
Gerbault (Henri) 34
Germany 20, 79
Ghana 44, 75
gianduja 76, 77, 78
GMDs 111
Godard (Sébastien) 64

Godiva 74, 75
Gold Coast 44, 75
Grenada 40
Guanaja (island) 9
Guyana 7

H
half-finished products 46, 47, 59
Henry (Rémi) 69
Hermé (Pierre) 64
Hershey 86, 104
Hershey (Milton Snavely) 29, 83
Hershey's Kisses 31, 90
Hersheyville 29, 31, 83
Hévin (Jean-Paul) 90

I
ice cream 64
imitations/counterfeits 15, 26, 32, 69
Indonesia 47, 109
industrial products 13
Italy 11, 76, 77
Ivory Coast 44

J
Jacques 75, 98
Jamaica 12, 13, 40
Japan 83
Jarriges (Jean) 69
Java 47
Jesuits 11, 16
jewelry (chocolate) 105

K
Kientzler (Julien) 64
Kinder Chocolat 77
Kinder Surprise 60, 77
Kit-Kat 63
Klaus (Jacques) 23, 97
Klaus J. Jacob (holding company) 59, 73
kneading 51
Kohler 23, 86, 95
Kohler (Charles Amédée) 23, 72
Kraft-Jacobs-Suchard (group) 72, 76, 82
Kwatta 74

L
lamination 51
Lanvin 54, 94, 95, 100
Latin America 41, 45, 94
Lardet (Pierre) 28
Le Roux 69, 99
lecithin 51, 111
Lefort (Yannick) 64, 99
Léonidas 74, 75
Lindt 23, 94, 100
Lindt (Rodolphe) 23, 73
Lindt & Sprungli 73, 77
Linnaens 39
Linxe (Robert) 67, 69, 95
Loisy, Olivier de 59
Louis XIV 13

M
M&Ms 63
machine for packaging chocolate bars 25
Madagascar 40, 45, 109
Maison du Chocolat 67, 95
Malaysia 47
malaxation 51
Marie-Antoinette 14
Mars (Frank) 31
Mars 63, 76, 82
Martinique 40
Mayas 7, 39
medicinal use 12, 13, 17, 18
Menier 18, 23, 26, 32, 33, 36, 79, 85, 86, 97
Menier (Émile Justin) 24, 25, 26, 68, 69
Menier (Jean Antoine Brutus) 24, 32, 68
metate 8, 19, 22, 76, 83
Mexico 7, 8, 10, 17, 19, 40, 41, 83
Milka 54, 72, 100
Milky Way 31, 63
mixer for cocoa beans 22
Moctezuma II 10, 19, 87, 111
mole poblano 83
Mon Chéri 77, 90, 100
molding 51, 61, 171
Mozart 14, 101
Mozart Kügel 78
Mucha (Alfonse) 34, 97
Mulhaupt (Thierry) 69
Mulot (Gérard) 69

N
Nacional 40, 41, 46
Napoleon III 15, 16
Nesquik 63
Nestlé 23, 54, 63, 69, 72, 73, 76, 95, 100
Nestlé (Henri) 23
Netherlands 11
Neuhaus (Charles) 75
Neuhaus (Frédéric) 74
Neuhaus (Jean) 74, 95
New Spain 10, 11
nibs 50, 51, 56
Nicaragua 25, 28, 68
Nigeria 44, 45
Noisiel 24, 25, 33, 68, 69
Nutella 77

O
Oaxaca 10, 19
Oceania 41
oil cake 22, 44, 46
Olmec 7
Opéra 64
Orinoco 7
Ovomaltine 63

P
palets d'or 57
Pear Hélène/poire Belle-Hélène 64
Peru 109

Perugina 76, 90
Peter (Daniel) 23, 71, 72
pharmacists 18, 24, 68
phenylethylamine 90, 112
Pius V (pope) 16
Plessis (Alphonse Louis du) 17
Pompadour (Marquise de) 14, 20
Porcelana 40
Potin (Félix) 31, 36
Poulain 23, 36, 63, 85, 97, 100
Poulain (Albert) 25, 32
Poulain (Victor Auguste) 26, 27, 32, 34, 69
powdered cocoa 22, 23, 31, 46, 52, 59, 80, 81
powders, starchy drinks 28, 36, 63
pralines 57, 74
Pralus (Auguste) 59
Pralus (François) 59
producing countries 44, 45, 46, 47
profiteroles 64, 76
Prussia 11, 12

Q
Quakers 23, 25, 80
Quetzalcóatl 7, 8, 10

R
refining 51
Richart (Michel) 69, 97
Rowntree (Joseph) 25, 79, 80

S
Sacher Torte 64, 78
Sade (Marquis de) 87, 100
Santo Domingo 109
Saint Vincent 40
Saint Lucia 40
Salon du Chocolat 83, 99, 101
Sao Tome 45
Saunion (Maison) 69
Séchaud (Jules) 29
Seneca (Federico) 90
Sérardy (Bernard) 57
Sévigné (Madame de) 14, 19, 100
slabs/bars 24, 25, 26, 32, 51, 57, 171
   filled 56
   molded 23
slavery 10, 15
Smarties 63, 80
Société Générale Suisse de Chocolats 72
Spain 9, 11, 80, 97
Sprüngli (David) 23
Sprüngli-Schifferli (Rodolphe) 73
Suchard 23, 90, 100
Suchard (Philippe) 23, 25, 72
Switzerland 13, 23, 54, 57, 71, 72, 73, 94

T
tempering 51, 61
tartuffo 77
techniques of manufacture 22, 23, 24
tejate 83

terroir 52, 53
Tezcatlipoca 7, 8
theobromine 90, 108, 112
theophylline 108, 112
Thuriès (Yves) 56, 94, 99
Tobler 23, 72
Tobler (Jean) 23, 73
Toblerone 73
Togo 109
Toltec 7, 8
torrefaction/roasting 42, 50
Treets 63
Trinitario 40, 41, 42, 44, 45, 46, 47
Trinidad 40, 41, 46, 47, 53, 102
truffles 57
Turkey 13

U
United States 82, 83

N
Valrhona 52, 54, 59, 95, 96
Van Houten 20, 36, 63
Van Houten (Coenraad Johannes) 22, 23, 81, 82
Venezuela 40, 41, 43, 46, 52
Volckamer (Johann Georg) 12

W
Weiss 56, 59, 95
Weiss (Eugène) 59
witches' broom (disease) 40, 41, 45, 46

Y
year-dated products 52
year dating 52, 53
Yucatán 7, 8, 10

index
of recipes

A
Alexandra 128
Alpine Supreme 155
Azteca Truffles 148

B
Basque Chocolate Cake 133
Bison-Grass Chocolates 132
Bitter Chocolate Fondant 124
Black Forest Cake 143
Bordeaux-style Lamprey 168
Brazilian Creams 126
Breasts of Game Birds, Cocoa-Spiced, with
Cabbage-Wrapped Thighs 170
Brioche Surprise 130

C
Classic Chocolate Recipes 115
Charlemagne's Almoner 142
Chocolate Fondant Caramels 134
Chocolate Mousse 115
Chocolate Mousse with Crystallized Orange 156
Chocolate Petits-Suisses 130
Chocolate Terrine 120
Chocolate Truffles 131, 146
Chocolate Sauce 118
Chocolate Sausage 116
Chocolate Soufflé 116
Citrus Nobilis 149
Conserve Belle-Hélène 140

D
Desert Roses 154

H
Hot Chocolate 115

I
Iced Truffles with Fresh Thyme 144

J
Jivara 152

L
Langoustines and Shrimp
Swimming Awry in Their Own Cocoa-Spiced Juices 166

M
Mendiants 136

O
Orange and Chocolate Pancakes 148
Orange Chocolate Roulade 150
Oven-Crystallized Mint Leaves 162

P
Parisian Round of Beef with Dark Chocolate Sauce 165
Potted Chocolate Creams 126
Prune Truffles 159

S
Sautéed Lamb with Chocolate 165
Savory Recipes by Prestigious Chefs 164
Shrimp in a Chocolate-Flavored
American Red Pepper and Dried Mango Tapenade 169
Soft Chocolate Cake 160
Spicy Hot Chocolate 122
Sweet Recipes by Prestigious Patissiers and Chocolate
Makers 132

T
Tarte Fridoline 138
Tasty Snack Recipes for Children 130
Truffettes Katherine 159
Turkey with Cocoa 128

W
Warszawa 158

Y
Yuletide Chocolate Decorations 131

table of recipes

Classic chocolate recipes 115

Chocolate mousse 115
Hot chocolate 115
Chocolate soufflé 116
Chocolate sausage 116
Chocolate sauce 118
Chocolate terrine 120
Spicy hot chocolate 122
Bitter chocolate fondant 124
Potted chocolate creams 126
Brazilian creams 126
Alexandra 128
Turkey with cocoa 128

Tasty snack recipes for children 130

Brioche surprise 130
Chocolate petits-suisses 130
Chocolate truffles 131
Yuletide chocolate decorations 131

Sweet recipes by prestigious patissiers
and chocolate makers 132

Bison-grass chocolates 132
Basque chocolate cake 133
Chocolate fondant caramels 134
Mendiants 136
Tarte fridoline 138
Conserve Belle-Hélène 140

Charlemagne's Almoner 142
Black Forest Cake 143
Iced truffles with fresh thyme 144
Chocolate truffles 146
Orange and chocolate pancakes 148
Azteca truffles 148
Citrus nobilis 149
Orange chocolate roulade 150
Jivara 152
Desert Roses 154
Alpine supreme 155
Chocolate mousse with crystallized orange 156
Warszawa 158
Truffettes Katherine 159
Prune truffles 159
Soft chocolate cake 160
Oven-crystallized mint leaves 162

Savory Recipes by Prestigious Chefs 164

Sautéed lamb with chocolate 165
Parisian round of beef with dark chocolate
sauce 165
Langoustines and shrimp
Swimming awry in their own cocoa-spiced juices 166
Bordeaux-style Lamprey 168
Shrimp in a chocolate flavored American red pepper
and dried mango tapenade 169
Breasts of game birds, cocoa-spiced, with
cabbage-wrapped thighs 170

contents

1 the saga of chocolate 6

Pre-Columbian America 7
The Maya civilization
The legend of feathered serpent
The Aztecs

The conquistadors and chocolate .. 9
Christopher Columbus: a missed opportunity
The good fortune of Cortez
The secret of chocolate

The spread of chocolate throughout Europe 11
An incomparable war gain

Chocolate in France 13
A royal drink
A very slow democratization

Chocolate and the Church 16
Food or drink?
When the doctors got involved

Chocolate and the medical faculty 17
The hot and the cold
The apothecaries

Implements used for chocolate ... 19
The first chocolate pots

From the cup to the saucer 20
The use of the foamer
The queen cup

The birth of the chocolate industry 22
Toward mechanization
The Van Houten revolution

The great names of chocolate 23
The Swiss pioneers
The English quakers

The French dynasties 24
Menier: the industrial visionary
Poulain: on the look out for innovations

From Banania to chocolate bars .. 28
Tins as collectibles

Chocolate and advertising 31

2 the cacao: nature's gift 38

The cacao tree 39
Cacao cultivation 39
Differing types of cacao 40
Criollo, Forastero, and Trinitario
Ordinary versus high-class cocoas

The cocoa-producing countries ... 41
From harvest to transformation .. 42
Harvesting and depodding
Fermentation
Drying
In Africa
In South America
In Asia
The marketplace in cocoa

3 chocolate every which way 48

Chocolate alchemy 49
Dark chocolate 52
Darker and darker
Pur cru (single growth)
Pure plantation (single estate)

Milk chocolate 54
Cocoa in the Swiss Alps
Cows of many colors
Grand cru milk chocolate

White chocolate 56
Filled chocolate bars 56
Chocolate candies 56
Bouchées, bûchettes, and other marvels

Filling options 57
Caramel
Cherries in brandy
Cream
Feuilleté
Fondant
Fruits and nuts
Ganache

Gianduja
Liqueurs
Honey
Nougat
Nougatine
Almond Paste
Praline

Chocolate coatings 59
Molded chocolate shapes 61
Hot chocolate 63
Chocolate bars and candies 63
Chocolate desserts 63
Mousses, creams, and pâtisseries
Chocolate ice creams

4 world taste in chocolate 66

In France 67
The chocolate hall of fame 68
Sulpice Debauve
Antoine Gallais
Jean Antoine Brutus Menier
Émile Justin Menier
Auguste Poulain
The genius of french chocolate makers 69

In Switzerland 71
The chocolate hall of fame 71
François-Louis Cailler
Philippe Suchard
Charles Amédée Kohler
Daniel Peter
Rodolphe Lindt
Jean Tobler

In Belgium 74
The chocolate hall of fame 74
Jean, Frédéric, and Jean Neuhaus

In Italy 76
The chocolate hall of fame 77
Isidore Caffarel

In Austria 78

In Germany 79

In Great Britain 79

The chocolate hall of fame 79
Joseph Fry
John Cadbury
Joseph Rowntree

In Spain 80

In the Netherlands 81

The chocolate hall of fame 82
Coenraad Johannes Van Houten

In the United States 82

The chocolate hall of fame 83
Milton Snavely Hershey

In Mexico 83

In Asia 83

Japan: tradition
China: a sweet tooth

5 chocolate, from fashionable to universal 84

A food with a wealth of symbolism 85
Chocolate as a symbol of childhood
Chocolate as a symbol of love
Chocolate as a symbol of greed

Chocolate and advertising 90
Love, affection, and chocolate
Sins of the flesh and greed
Luxury and pleasure
A far-off place
To the point of madness

The presentation of chocolate 95
Packaging with charm
Tops and fillings

Chocolate in art 97
Chocolate in classical painting
Chocolate in contemporary art
Chocolate and sculpture
Chocolate and literature

When chocolate becomes entertainment 101
Chocolate and theater
Chocolate and ballet
Chocolate at the circus
Chocolate and the cinema

Chocolate and fashion 104

6 a pleasure that does us good 106

Composition of chocolate 107

Received ideas about chocolate .. 107

The virtues of chocolate 112

7 classic chocolate recipes 114

Tasty snack recipes for children 130

Sweet recipes by prestigious pâtissiers and chocolate makers 132

Savory recipes by prestigious chefs 164

8 for true lovers of chocolate 172

Choosing chocolate 173
Single chocolates
Chocolates for Christmas
Easter chocolates
Chocolate powder

How to keep it 173
Where to keep it
How long should it be kept?

How to eat chocolate 174
The preparation
Looks are important
Touching, for sensuality
Smelling, the first step to ecstasy
Hearing, for the pleasure of imagining
Tasting, for the journey to the land of flavors

What should you drink with chocolate? 174
Chocolate and coffee
Chocolate and tea
Chocolate and wine
Chocolate and spirits

Drinks that go well with chocolate 175
Recommended wines

Some crucial tips for cooking with chocolate 176
Quality is the key
Choosing the right chocolate
Choosing the right cocoa
How to melt chocolate
Chocolate and water do not mix
Coffee and chocolate: a love story
Icing
Stencil decorations
Writing with chocolate
Dark chocolate in sauces

Drinks to complement chocolate 177

Where to find the best specialist chocolate makers 179

The best places to drink hot chocolate 180

Ice-cream makers 180

Restaurants with exciting new ideas for chocolate 180

Clubs 180

Museums 181

Events 181

Bookstores specializing in food and cuisine 181

Recent books 181

Guide 181

Magazines 181

Internet websites 182

Professional organizations 182

Other organizations 182

Guilds 182

Professional training 182

Sources 182

index 184
index of recipes 186
table of recipes 187
photographic credits 190
acknowledgments 192

photographic credits

Chapter 1

P. 6 LEAF MOTIF: frontispiece detail from *Traités nouveaux et curieux du café, du thé et du chocolat* by Philippe Sylvestre Dufour (1685), taken from *le Chocolat et ca cuisine*, published by Dargaud • chocolate: detail from photo illustration for the recipe for Soft Chocolate Cake (p. 160) © Pierre Desgrieux

P. 7 *the cacao tree*, © Artephot/Oronoz • cacao fruit, engraving taken from Dr. Aimé Riant's book *Le café, le chocolat, le thé* (1880)

P. 8 IN FILIGREE, ABOVE LEFT: Quetzelcóatl, the god of chocolate, taken from a coloring-book, *Incas, Aztecs & Mayas* • ABOVE RIGHT: Woman at the metate in terracotta, © private collection • BELOW LEFT: *The way in which the inhabitants of New Spain prepare cocoa for chocolate*, Bibliothèque Nationale de France, Paris, © Lauros-Giraudon

P. 9 ABOVE RIGHT: © private collection • IN FILIGREE: *Traités nouveaux et curieux du café, du thé et du chocolat*, by Philippe Sylvestre Dufour (1685), taken from *le Chocolat et sa cuisine*, published © by Dargaud • BELOW LEFT: *Mexican woman preparing chocolate*, Museo de America, Madrid, © Artephot/Oronoz

P. 10 IN FILIGREE: detail of a portrait engraving of Cortez, © private collection • painting by Miguel Gonzalez, *Moctezuma Offering Chocolate to Cortez* (1698), © Artephot/Oronoz

P. 11 *Still Life*, by Antonio de Pereda y Salgado, 1652, Hermitage Museum, St Petersburg, © Artephot/Oronoz

P. 12 *The Beautiful Chocolate Maker*, by J. E. Liotard (ca. 1745), Réunion des Musées Nationaux, © AKG Paris

P. 13 private collection

P. 14 ABOVE: private collection • BELOW: *The Morning Chocolate*, Pietro Longhi (1770), © Cameraphoto/AKG Paris

P. 15 *Madame du Barry (1743–1793) at her toilette, being presented by Zamor with a cup of coffee*, by Jean-Baptiste-André Gautier-Dagoty, Château de Versailles and Château de Trianon, © photo RMN/Gérard Blot

PP. 14–15 IN FILIGREE AND IN DETAIL: *Maréchal Lefebvre being made Duke of Danzig by Napoleon, after the capture of this city on May 26, 1807*, Rouffach Town Hall, © Lauros-Giraudon

P. 16 cover of a Marquise de Sévigné chocolate catalog, © private collection

P. 17 IN FILIGREE: engraving of the Debauve & Gallais store, © Debauve & Gallais collection

P. 19 ABOVE: chocolate pot, © Charlie Abad • IN FILIGREE: © private collection • BELOW: *The way in which the inhabitants of New Spain prepare cocoa for chocolate*, Bibliothèque Nationale de France, Paris, © Lauros-Giraudan

PP. 20–21 cups, chocolate pots, foamers, © Charlie Abad

P. 22 ABOVE: © private collection • BELOW: plate from the *Encyclopédie ou diction-naire raisonné des arts, des sciences et des métiers*, by Diderot and d'Alembert, © private collection

P. 23 IN FILIGREE: 19th-century engraving, Chocolate House, © private collection

P. 24 ABOVE: Poulain horse (detail), © private collection • BELOW: bar of chocolate, © Nestlé archives

P. 25 ABOVE: mill, © Nestlé archives

PP. 24–25 BACKGROUND: © private collection

P. 26 ABOVE: blotter, © private collection • BELOW: © private collection

P. 27 ABOVE RIGHT: © private collection • CENTER: poster of *Schoolboy Sitting on a Stool*, by Firmin Bouisset (1896), © Musée de Pontlevoy

P. 28 BELOW: postcard, © private collection

P. 29 BELOW: Cinebana, © private collection

PP. 28–29 Banania tins, © private collection

P. 32 ABOVE LEFT: © private collection • ABOVE RIGHT: *The Poulain Baby*, by E. Brun (1894), Musée de Pontlevoy

P. 33 ABOVE LEFT: © private collection • BELOW LEFT: © Nestlé Archives • BELOW RIGHT: design by Edia, © Nestlé Archives • BACKGROUND: poster of the little Menier girl seen face on (1897), © Nestlé Archives

P. 34 ABOVE LEFT: © private collection • BELOW LEFT: private collection

PP. 34–35 © private collection

P. 36 ABOVE LEFT: Menier chocolate vending machine, © Nestlé Archives • CENTER: chromolithograph images (left and center), © private collection • CENTER: Poulain chromolithograph image (right), © private collection • RIGHT: Royat chocolate catalog (1908), © private collection • BELOW LEFT: © Charlie Abad • BELOW RIGHT: lithographed tins of chocolate powder (left and right), © private collection • BELOW RIGHT: Banania tin (center), © private collection

P. 37 ABOVE LEFT: Révillon clock (advertisement), © private collection • ABOVE CENTER: fabric box for Marquise de Sévigné chocolates, © Hervé Robert • LEFT CENTER: Menier fan (advertisement), © Hervé Robert • CENTER: Delespaul-Havez card-board truck, © Hervé Robert • BELOW LEFT: Poulain exercise-book cover, © private collection • BELOW CENTER: album for collecting Menier illustrations (1935), © Hervé Robert • BELOW RIGHT: Guerin-Boutron clock (advertisement), © Hervé Robert

Chapter 2

P. 38 IN FILIGREE: detail of a sheet of stamps, © private collection; postcard, © private collection

P. 39 IN FILIGREE: botanical plate (1830), © private collection • IN DROPPED INITIAL: detail of an engraving taken from *Nouveau Traité physique et économique par la forme de dissertations de toutes les plantes qui croissent sur la surface du globe* (1787), by Jean-Pierre Buc'Hoz

P. 40 FROM LEFT TO RIGHT: cacao tree flowers, © Valrhona; chérelle on trunk, © Valrhona; cacao pod on Forastero tree on the Ivory Coast, © Katherine Khodorowsky; cacao-pod on Trinitario tree on Sri Lanka, © Katherine Khodorowsky; cacao pod on cacao tree, © Valrhona

P. 41 ABOVE RIGHT: early 20th-century lithographed tin, © Hervé Robert • IN FILIGREE: cacao plantation in Cameroon, © André Gamel

P. 42 picked cacao-pods, © Katherine Khodorowsky • open cacao pod, © Katherine Khodorowsky • fermentation of the seeds, © Valrhona • IN FILIGREE: Deriard label, © private collection

PP. 42–43 IN FILIGREE: detail of a Poulain exercise book cover, © private collection

P. 43 drying beans on the ground, © Valrhona • sorting of beans, © Valrhona • stocking of beans, © Valrhona • IN FILIGREE: detail of a Poulain exercise book cover, © private collection

P. 44 sheet of ten stamps issued by the producing countries (FROM LEFT TO RIGHT: Condominium of the New Hebrides, French Republic of Togo, Ghana, Dominica, Republic of Togo, United Republic of Cameroon, Mexico, Ivory Coast Republic, Dominican Republic, Samoan Islands), © private collection

PP. 44–45 IN FILIGREE: Liebig advertising chromo, © private collection

P. 46 ABOVE: drying of beans in Venezuela, © private collection

PP. 46–47 IN FILIGREE: Liebig advertising chromo, © private collection

P. 47 ABOVE LEFT: bar of Equita chocolate, © private collection • CENTER LEFT: wrapping for chocolate bar, © private collection • ABOVE RIGHT: imitation Tobler bar, © private collection • CENTER RIGHT: bar of l'Ivoirienne chocolate, © private collection

Chapter 3

P. 48 BACKGROUND: Liebig image, © private collection; Lanvin chocolate wrapping, design by Dali, © private collection

P. 49 IN DROPPED INITIAL: detail of a Suchard image, © private collection • IN FILIGREE: crusher, chromo by Guérin-Boutron, © private collection

P. 50 ABOVE LEFT: roaster at Valrhona factory, © Valrhona • ABOVE CENTER: technician, © Valrhona • BELOW LEFT: roaster and sorter, © private collection • BELOW RIGHT: winnower at the Bonnat company, used for roasting and sorting, © Bonnat

P. 51 ABOVE LEFT: cylindrical bean crusher, © Valrhona • ABOVE CENTER: conch © Valrhona • molding production line © Valrhona • BELOW LEFT: card showing the Tinchebrai chocolate factory, © private collection • BELOW RIGHT: molding and cutting, © private collection

P. 52 ABOVE: Bonnat bars, © Bonnat • BELOW LEFT: Valrhona bars, © Valrhona

P. 53 ABOVE, FROM LEFT TO RIGHT: wrapper for Beaumont bar, © private collection; wrapper for Gault et Millau bar, © private collection; wrapper for Côte d'Or bar, © private collection; wrapper for Weiss bar, © private collection; wrapper for Poulain bar, © private collection • CENTER LEFT: wrapper for Thuriès bar, © private collection • CENTER RIGHT: display box of Cluizel's Pures Origines du Monde, © Cluizel • BELOW, FROM LEFT TO RIGHT: wrapper for Hediard bar, © private collection; wrapper for Cluizel bar, © private collection; wrapper for Nestlé bar, © private collection; wrapper for Lindt bar, © private collection

P. 54 ABOVE: Suchard advertisement, © private collection • CENTER: Rolbat chocolate wrapper, © private collection • BELOW LEFT: bar of Milka chocolate, © private collection • BELOW RIGHT: bar of Côtes d'Or chocolate, © private collection

PP. 54–55 IN FILIGREE: Côte d'Or advertisement, © private collection

P. 55 ABOVE FAR LEFT: Gala Peter chocolate wrapper, © private collection • ABOVE LEFT: Huber chocolate wrapper, © private collection • Pelletier chocolate wrapper, © private collection • ABOVE RIGHT: Valrhona chocolate wrapper, © private collection • ABOVE FAR RIGHT: Nestlé chocolate wrapper, © private collection • CENTER RIGHT: Lanvin chocolate wrapper, design by Salvador Dali, © private collection • BELOW: Lolo chocolate wrapper, © private collection

P. 56 ABOVE LEFT: bar of Lindt chocolate, © private collection • BELOW LEFT: wrapper for Yves Thuriès bar, © private collection • ABOVE RIGHT: Suchard chocolate wrapper, © private collection • CENTER RIGHT: Weiss chocolate bar, Michel Chaudun's first design, © private collection • BELOW RIGHT: bar of Poulain chocolate, © private collection

P. 57 bar of Weiss chocolate, © private collection

P. 58 above and IN FILIGREE: Gitana chocolate cigarettes, © private collection • CENTER: box of chocolate cigars, © private collection • BELOW: box of Kamikaze chocolate cigars, © private collection

P. 59 ABOVE: box of Barry-Callebaut chocolate pistoles, © private collection • CENTER: distinctive Valrhona label, © Valrhona • BELOW: photo of Stéphane Bonnat, © Bonnat

P. 60 ABOVE: *Easter Eggs*, by Christian Constant, © Christian Constant • BELOW: advertisement for Marquise de Sévigné chocolates, taken from *Vogue* magazine (1931), © private collection • IN FILIGREE: chocolate moldings, © Biarritz Chocolate Museum

P. 61 Suchard image, © private collection

P. 62 Kwata advertising board, © private collection

P. 63 ABOVE LEFT: Henriet tin, © Hervé Robert • ABOVE RIGHT: Kit-Kat advertisement (Marie-Claire 1977), © private collection • BELOW: Beussent Lachelle chocolate spread, © Gérard Moreau

P. 64 photo of Pierre Hermé, © Jean-Louis Bloch-Laine • CENTER: *The Cherry on the Cake*, cake by Pierre Hermé, © Jean-Louis Bloch-Laine • BELOW: *Sesame*, cake created by Morabito. Design by Yannick Lefort (distribution by Jean Daudignac), © Alain Dubuisson

P. 65 Cover of the Prosper Montagné booklet of recipes, published by the Ministry for the Colonies, © private collection

Chapter 4

P. 66 BACKGROUND: detail of a Crefer bar, © private collection; advertisement for Schenkt, © private collection
P. 67 in dropped initial: detail of a Lanvin bar, © private collection
P. 68 ABOVE LEFT: Debauve & Gallais chocolate makers, © private collection • ABOVE RIGHT: bar of Weiss chocolate, © private collection • CENTER LEFT: Fouquet store, © Fouquet • CENTER RIGHT: Bonnat store (1884), © Bonnat • BELOW CENTER: Voisin bar, © private collection • BELOW LEFT: *Les Palets d'Or* sign, designed by Bernard Serady, © private collection • BELOW RIGHT: bar of La Marquise de Sévigné chocolate, © private collection
P. 69 IN FILIGREE: detail of a Poulain exercise book cover, © private collection • BELOW: Durand chocolates, © Franck Bel
PP. 70–71 advertisement for Kohler, © private collection
P. 71 portrait of François-Louis Caïller, © Chocosuisse, Berne • Cailler chocolate wrapper, © private collection
P. 72 ABOVE LEFT: advertisement for Suchard, © private collection • BELOW LEFT: Gala Peter chocolate wrapper, © private collection • RIGHT, FROM ABOVE TO BELOW: portrait of Philippe Suchard, © Chocosuisse, Berne; portrait of Charles-Amédée Kohler, © Chocosuisse, Berne; portrait of Daniel Peter, © Chocosuisse, Berne
P. 73 ABOVE LEFT: portraits of Rodolphe Lindt, © Chocosuisse, Berne, and Jean Tobler, © Chocosuisse, Berne • BELOW LEFT: Lindt chocolate wrapper, © private collection • RIGHT: advertisement for Toblerone, © private collection
P. 74 LEFT: Neuhaus bar, © private collection
P. 75 ABOVE, FROM LEFT TO RIGHT: bar of Dolfin chocolate, © private collection; bar of Côte d'Or chocolate, © private collection; bar of Jacques chocolate, © private collection; bar of Jeff de Bruges chocolate, © private collection • advertisement for Schenkt, © private collection
P. 76 ABOVE: Perugina box (1922), © private collection • CENTER: cacao-flavored tagliatelle, © Hervé Robert • BELOW LEFT AND RIGHT: Caffarel boxes, © private collection
P. 77 ABOVE: lithographed Vaticano tin, © private collection • CENTER: bar of Stainer chocolate, © private collection • BELOW: bar of Caffarel chocolate, © private collection
P. 78 ABOVE LEFT: bar of Demel chocolate, © private collection • ABOVE RIGHT: point-of-sale advertisement, © Hervé Robert • CENTER: front of the Sacher hotel-pâtisserie, © Hervé Robert • BELOW: Demel box, © private collection
P. 79 LEFT: box of Schmidt cocoa, © private collection • RIGHT AND IN FILIGREE: bar of Cadbury's chocolate, © private collection
P. 80 ABOVE LEFT: bar of Cadbury's chocolate, © private collection • CENTER LEFT: postcard,

© private collection • ABOVE RIGHT: bar of Blanxart chocolate, © private collection • BELOW RIGHT: bar of Crefer chocolate, © private collection
P. 81 ABOVE, FROM LEFT TO RIGHT: Van Houten lithographed tin; © Hervé Robert; Bendsdorp lithographed tin, © Hervé Robert; tin of Droste pastilles, © private collection; bar of Hemp chocolate, © private collection • BELOW: Droste cocoa tins, © private collection
P. 82 ABOVE LEFT: bar of Lulu chocolate, © private collection • CENTER: Hershey chocolate wrappers, © private collection • BELOW: bar of Ghirardelli chocolate, © private collection
P. 83 bar of Daming chocolate, © private collection

Chapter 5

P. 85 Lombard postcard, © private collection
P. 86 advertisement for Kohler, © private collection
P. 87 ABOVE: cover of Pilote magazine (1979), designed by Jean Solé, © private collection • BELOW: postcard, © private collection
PP. 88–89 advertisement board, © private collection
P. 90 ABOVE: bar of Mon Chéri chocolate, © private collection • CENTER: Jeff de Bruges card, © private collection • BELOW: Jean-Paul Hévin chocolates, © Jean-Paul Hévin
P. 91 advertisement for Frigor chocolate by Cailler, published in *L'Illustration* (1930), © private collection
P. 92 advertisement for Kohler, published in *L'Illustration* (1930), © private collection
P. 93 advertisement for Suchard, published in *L'Illustration* (1930), © private collection
P. 94 ABOVE: Nestlé advertisement, © Peter Knapp/Agence Lintas • BELOW: still from Lanvin TV commercial, © Agence Lintas
P. 95 chocolate box, designed by Sonia Rykiel, © Valrhona
P. 97 BELOW RIGHT: *Chocolate at Lunch*, by Juán de Zurburán (1620-1649), Musée des Beaux-Arts et d'archéologie de Besançon, © Lauros-Giraudon
P. 98 mask sculpted in chocolate by Michel Chaudin, © Katherine Khodorowsky • *Chocolate Flavor*, pastel by Louis J., © private collection
P. 99 study for *The Chocolate Grinder*, by Marcel Duchamp (1914), Kunstsammlung Nordrhein Westfalen, Düsseldorf, © Adagp, Paris 2001/Bridgeman-Giraudon
ABOVE: cover of *Charlie and the Chocolate Factory*, by Roald Dahl (1964), 1967 edition. Illustrations by Michel Siméon, © Gallimard, in the "Bibliothèque blanche illustrée" collection
P. 101 ABOVE RIGHT: chocolate dresses designed by Chantal Thomas, Emmanuel Laporte, and Thierry Bridron, hair by Jacques Dessange; 2000 Chocolate Parade at the Chocoland Salon du Chocolat, © Event International • BELOW: photo of *Love,*

Delight, and Chocolate, show staged in 1995 by the La Marmite à Malices company, © L.A. Khodorowsky
P. 102 ABOVE: record by the group Chocolat's (1978), © private collection • BELOW: score of the song *Le Petit Pain au Chocolat*, sung by Joe Dassin (1968), French lyrics by Pierre Delanoe, original lyrics and music by R. Del Turco & G. Bigazzi, © Sugar Music
P. 103 CENTER: CD by the group Hot Chocolate (1999), © private collection • BACKGROUND: score of *Tango du Chocolat* (1930), © private collection
P. 104 ABOVE RIGHT: "Coffee drop spasch" cookie on coffee cup, designed by Robert Stadler, © Radi Designers • CENTER: Interiors plate and coffee cup, PTS International, © PTS International • BELOW LEFT: advertisement for BC Acoustique, © Curtis & McLuhan • BELOW RIGHT: 2001 Salon du Chocolat calendar, Carla Bruni wearing macaroon jewelry by Yannick Lefort, hair by Jacques Dessange © Vanessa Lefort for Event International
P. 105 ABOVE LEFT: Longchamp scarf, © Longchamp • ABOVE RIGHT: sketch drawings by Jean Vendôme of a "chocolate" necklace and ring (December 1998), © private collection • CENTER LEFT: Chocosuisse sheet of stamps (May 2001), © Chocosuisse, Berne • CENTER RIGHT: Christiane Tixier Brooch, © Christiane Tixier • BELOW FAR LEFT: "tart and chocolate" candle, © Esteban • BELOW LEFT: Yves Rocher shower gel, © Yves Rocher • BELOW RIGHT: Choco Rock perfume by Carrefour, © Marc Santerre • BELOW FAR RIGHT: Moschino bag, © Charlie Abad

Chapter 6

P. 106 BACKGROUND: advertisements published in *Marie-Claire*, © private collection
P. 107 IN DROPPED INITIAL: detail of an advertisement for Chocolat des Pharmacies (1931), © private collection • BACKGROUND: advertisement published in *Marie-Claire*, © private collection
P. 108 advertisement for Chocolat des Pharmacies (1931), © private collection
P. 109 ABOVE: bar of Dardenne chocolate, © private collection • BELOW: lithographed tin of Laxobac chocolates, © private collection
P. 110 ABOVE LEFT: bar of Monoprix-La Forme chocolate, © private collection • CENTER LEFT: bar of Chocosoja chocolate, © private collection • RIGHT: advertisement published in *Marie-Claire* (1959), © private collection
P. 111 ABOVE, FROM LEFT TO RIGHT: bar of Carrefour Bio chocolate, © private collection; bar of Cémoi chocolate, © private collection; bar of Vivis chocolate, © private collection; bar of Le Clos de l'Arche chocolate, © private collection • BELOW: logo, © Confédération des artisans chocolatiers de France
P. 112 ABOVE: Suppléfer advertisement, © private collection • BELOW: Milka Energy chocolate bar, © private collection • IN FILIGREE: Royat advertisement, © private collection

P. 113 above IN FILIGREE: Menier advertisement, © private collection • right IN FILIGREE: © private collection • CENTER LEFT: box of No Stress chocolates, © private collection • BELOW LEFT: bar of Croix d'Or chocolate, © private collection • ABOVE RIGHT: Caro Bella chocolate substitute, © private collection • CENTER RIGHT: Cida chocolate (1950), © private collection • BELOW RIGHT: Nuxe antiaging cream, © Nuxe

Chapter 7

P. 170 IN FILIGREE: Payraud chromo, © private collection
P. 171 IN DROPPED INITIAL: logo of the Marmite à Malices club, © private collection
P. 172 IN FILIGREE: advertisement for César Impérator, © private collection; Tokay wine label, Château de Kimcsem, © private collection; Banyuls wine label, "l'Etoile," © private collection; Côte-Rôtie wine label, Guigal, © private collection; Châteauneuf-du-pape wine label, Château-la-Nerthes, © private collection

acknowledgments

The authors would like to thank those people whose determination,
patience, and confidence have enabled this book to come into being:
Laure Flavigny, Suyapa Audigier, Chloé Chauveau,
Jean-Pierre Guéno, Roselyne de Ayala,
and Stéphanie Leclair de Marco.

The authors are also deeply grateful to Claudine Girardin
(president of the Association des Gourmettes Suisses),
Anne-Gaëlle Grenet (Valrhona),
Michel Barel (CIRAD), Olivier Hulot (Touton SA France),
and Stéphane Sterne (Malongo Café France) for their invaluable
technical advice and for rereading certain passages of this book.

Editorial director: Suyapa Audigier
Graphic design and production: Guylaine & Christophe Moi
Editors: Chloé Chauveau and Marie-Claire Seewald
Jacket design and production: Guylaine & Christophe Moi
Jacket photo: Pierre Desgrieux
Illustrations for back jacket: private collection (top), photo by Jean-François Rivière (bottom),
Bibliothèque Nationale de France, Giraudon (near background), Poulain, Menier, Banania (far background),
Le Chocolat et sa cuisine, Éditions Dargaud (left inside back cover), Quetzelcóatl, coloring book (right inside back cover)
Photo engraving: Offset Publicité